THE AEF AND COALITION
WARMAKING, 1917–1918

THE AEF AND
COALITION
WARMAKING, 1917–1918

David F. Trask

University Press of Kansas

Photographs are from the U.S. Army Signal Corps Collection, National Archives.

Maps are from *American Armies and Battlefields in Europe* (Washington, D.C.: Center of Military History, United States Army, 1992) and *United States Army in the World War, 1917–1919*, vols. 4–9, *Military Operations of the American Expeditionary Forces* (Washington, D.C.: Center of Military History, United States Army, 1989–1990).

Published by the University Press of Kansas (Lawrence, Kansas 66049), which was organized by the Kansas Board of Regents and is operated and funded by Emporia State University, Fort Hays State University, Kansas State University, Pittsburg State University, the University of Kansas, and Wichita State University

Library of Congress Cataloging-in-Publication Data

Trask, David F.
    The AEF and coalition warmaking, 1917–1918 / David F. Trask.
      p.   cm. – (Modern war studies)
    Includes bibliographical references (p.) and index.
    ISBN 0-7006-0619-X (alk. paper)
    1. World War, 1914–1918–Campaigns–France. 2. United States.
    Army. American Expeditionary Forces–History. 3. Strategy.
    4. Foch, Ferdinand, 1851–1929. 5. Ludendorff, Erich, 1865–1937.
    6. Pershing, John Joseph, 1860–1948. I. Title. II. Series.
    D544.T68 1993
    940.54′214–dc20   93-7992

British Library Cataloguing in Publication Data is available.

Printed in the United States of America
10 9 8 7 6 5 4 3 2 1

CONTENTS

MAPS AND ILLUSTRATIONS

MAPS

ILLUSTRATIONS

PREFACE

This book offers a brief, up-to-date history of the operations that the American Expeditionary Forces (AEF) conducted in France during 1918. Based on a selection of representative published sources and authorities, it makes special use of the American documentary collection entitled *United States Army in the World War 1917–1919*, 17 vols. (Washington, D.C.: Government Printing Office, 1948), edited by the Historical Division, Department of the Army. The U.S. Army Center of Military History has republished this important but underused body of primary source material, which includes many French, British, and German records.

The perspective of this account differs from most American works about the AEF in that it views the campaign of 1918 from the highest level of field command, that of the two dominant soldiers, Marshal Ferdinand Foch for the Allied and Associated Powers and First Quartermaster General Erich Ludendorff for the Central Powers. These leaders dealt with the commanders of the national forces, in Foch's case most importantly with Gen. Henri Philippe Petain for France, Field-Marshal Douglas Haig for Great Britain, and Gen. John J. Pershing for the United States. This perspective is not at the level of *strategy*, which treats of the general design for the uses of national power to accomplish political purposes or goals, but at the level of what used to be called *grand tactics*, the application of military power by large organizations against enemy forces in the field to fulfill the strategic design, extending to the theater level. This work emphasizes the role of inter-Allied theater commanders in operations, which subsumes the actions of national contingents, including the AEF. However, the *policy* and *strategy* of the opposed coalitions and of the individual nations, subjects distinct from *operations*, are discussed in sufficient detail to clarify the political goals and strategic designs that influenced the campaign of 1918 at the inter-Allied and national levels. Foch, Ludendorff, and the commander-in-chief of the American Expeditionary Forces, Gen. John J. Pershing, concerned themselves primarily with field operations, although their views influenced political and strategic decisions.

Reference is made to *minor tactics*, the theory and practice of small-unit operations, only to illuminate the activities of larger formations such as corps, armies, and groups of armies. This study reflects modern revisionist examinations of minor tactics, but the emphasis throughout is on grand tactics, a much-neglected topic. The reader should consult other accounts for extensive analyses of the minor tactics, especially Paul F. Braim's recent study entitled *The Test of Battle: The American Expeditionary Forces in the Meuse-Argonne Campaign* (1987).

Most histories of the AEF reflect the views of General Pershing, whose angle of vision naturally was that of his own forces, a national contingent in Foch's mammoth inter-Allied array. This traditional outlook minimizes and sometimes distorts the actions of the coalition armies, an understandable but ultimately pernicious reflection of America's refusal to countenance entangling alliances during the long era of general peace between 1815 and 1914. Military historians have yet to recognize fully the extent to which the exterior coalition of 1917–1918 prefigured the Grand Alliance of World War II and the North Atlantic Treaty Organization. An inter-Allied perspective on the events of 1918 helps to correct this deficiency.

A consideration of the AEF's operations from the theater perspective produces an interpretation less complimentary to the Americans and their commander than most previous studies but consistent with the tendencies of recent scholarship. Historians such as Paul Braim, Allan Millett, Timothy Nenninger, Rod Paschall, James Rainey, and Donald Smythe have questioned various aspects of the regnant outlook. This book carries this trend farther.

Readers should note two conventions followed in text. Diacritical marks are eliminated, and long quotations, which are kept to a minimum, are not indented.

A number of friends and colleagues lent much-needed assistance during the preparation of this book. They include Daniel Beaver, Donald Bittner, Holger Herwig, Morris MacGregor, Allan Millett, Timothy Nenninger, John Pratt, Bernard Semmel, and Roger Trask. I alone am responsible for errors that may have crept into the text.

The staffs of the U.S. Army Center of Military History, the National Archives, and the Library of Congress, all located in Washington, D.C., were unfailingly helpful. So were the people of the University Press of Kansas, especially Michael Briggs.

This book stems directly from the recollections of my late father, Hugh A. Trask of the 112th Infantry, 28th Division, whose harrowing service in France encompassed combat, wounds, imprisonment, and influenza.

My wife, Elizabeth Brooks Trask, lent extensive support, including the burdens of travel to many battlefields in France and Belgium.

Finally I should like to dedicate this volume to several couples for whom I have exceptional regard, the fruit of friendship over many years. They are Goldalee and Michael Meyer, Marilyn and John Pratt, Maxine and Bernard Semmel, and Dorothy and Roger Trask.

David F. Trask
Washington, D.C.
January 1993

1

MOBILIZATION OF THE
AMERICAN EXPEDITIONARY FORCES

Leading histories of the American Expeditionary Forces (AEF), like those of Edward Coffman and Harvey DeWeerd written a generation ago, reflect the views of Gen. John J. Pershing as expressed in his final report of 1919 and his memoirs of 1931. According to its commander, the operations of the AEF decided the First World War. It assured victory to the Allied and Associated Powers after both belligerent coalitions had endured over four years of the most terrible sacrifices. The task was difficult because of a bumbling War Department at home and perverse interference from the Allies abroad, who opposed independent American operations, but the superior qualities of the AEF overcame all obstacles.[1]

Pershing's account did not give sufficient attention to certain developments during 1917–1918 that greatly affected the operations of the AEF. The unpreparedness of the United States ensured that its army could not fight independently at full efficiency until 1919 or 1920, two or three years after the intervention of April 1917, but an unexpected crisis during 1918 forced premature commitment of the AEF. In March, the German High Command dominated by First Quartermaster General Erich Ludendorff, deeply alarmed because of the imminent appearance of the AEF in France, launched a powerful offensive on the western front. It was designed to end the war before General Pershing could affect the outcome. The German push, which continued until the middle of July, forced Pershing to permit the employment of some of his divisions on the western front under French or British command. They served mostly as replacements for Allied divisions in quiet sectors. Some American divisions were drawn into battle. When Ferdinand Foch, the French generalissimo of the Allied and Associated Powers, stemmed the German surge and regained the initiative, he launched powerful counteroffensives. Foch's projects of July

1

and after forced Pershing to undertake operations, this time on a large scale, before the AEF was fully prepared to fight on its own in France.

How well did the Americans fight, and how much did they contribute to the victory of November 1918? Full consideration of two influences, the prolonged American mobilization and the great 1918 battle, suggests an evaluation of the AEF that differs from that of Pershing and historians who have accepted his views.

On 2 April 1917, President Woodrow Wilson reluctantly asked Congress to declare war on Germany, turning his back on a long but unsuccessful attempt to arrange a mediation of the European conflict. Earlier he had hoped both to avoid belligerency and to dominate the peace settlement. Germany's decision to wage unrestricted submarine warfare against maritime commerce on the high seas, taking effect on 1 February, banished further thought of American mediation. The president now realized that he could expect to control the postwar peacemaking only by undertaking an armed intervention on the side of the Entente Powers.

On 22 January, just before Germany announced its submarine initiative, Wilson had made a stirring appeal to the belligerents, calling publicly for negotiations to end the war. "There must be," he insisted, "not a balance of power, but a community of power; not organized rivalries, but an organized common peace." Mindful of traditional isolationist sentiment that might reject his vision of the future, he asserted: "There is no entangling alliance in a concert of power. When all unite to act in the same sense and with the same purpose all act in the common interest and are free to live their own lives under a common protection." Wilson thus committed himself to a league of nations that would provide collective security against disturbers of the peace. To prepare for the new world order, he called for a "peace without victory." It would base territorial settlements on the democratic principle of national self-determination instead of selfish national interests such as those reflected in the two sets of secret treaties that bound together the members of each contending coalition. In his second inaugural address the President noted the passing of isolationism. "We are provincials no longer. . . . The tragical events of the thirty months of vital turmoil through which we have just passed have made us citizens of the world. Our own fortunes as a nation are involved, whether we would have it so or not."[2]

Wilson reiterated these views in a memorable peroration to his war message of 2 April as he spoke of leading the American people "into the most terrible and disastrous of all wars, civilization itself seeming to be in the balance. . . . [W]e shall fight for the things which we have always carried nearest our hearts, – for democracy, for the right of those who submit to authority to have a voice in their own governments, for the rights and liberties of small nations, for a universal dominion of right by such a concert of free peoples as shall bring peace and safety to all nations and make the world itself at last free."[3]

For the moment, Wilson refused to go beyond these generalizations. To a visiting member of the British House of Commons, John Howard Whitehouse, he gave his reasons for not making more specific statements of war aims. "Having just entered the war he was not prepared at this moment to make any public suggestions to the allies. It would lay him open to the charge of desiring to dominate policy before the country had bourne [*sic*] any of the burdens of war."[4]

Wilson also told Whitehouse that "the position of America would be one of much more general helpfulness and influence if he remained . . . detached from the allies." He went to war intending to obtain the consent of both the Allies and the Central Powers to his conception of the postwar settlement. The defeat of the Central Powers would ensure their adherence, but what would ensure the agreement of the Allies? To his closest adviser, Col. Edward M. House of Texas, the president confided his intentions: "*England and France have not the same views with regard to peace that we have* by any means." How would this circumstance affect American statecraft? "When the war is over we can force them to our way of thinking because by that time they will, among other things, be financially in our hands: but we cannot force them now, and any attempt to speak for them or to our common mind would bring on disagreements which would inevitably come to the surface in public and rob the whole thing of its effect." Arthur James Balfour, the British foreign secretary, reported a similar impression of Wilson's attitude toward the secret treaties that bound the Entente Powers: they might lead to conflict between the United States and its European associates after the war. "He evidently thought in that event [the] United States being themselves unfettered might exercise powerful and valuable influence." Balfour did not complain, concluding: "Were I in his place I should have decided as he has done." Wilson's purposes were clear. Although he would fight hard to finish off Germany, he would remain somewhat detached from the Allies. He would avoid political commitments to them that might limit his freedom of action at war's end, when he expected to enjoy considerable political leverage. He would wage war in ways that would prevent both European coalitions from interfering with his peace plans.[5]

Wilson's *policy*, the body of war aims or fundamental objectives for which the nation would fight, was well defined before the United States went to war. This policy was reiterated at the moment of intervention. He had not yet defined his *strategy*, his general plan or design for the exercise of the several forms of the nation's power that would serve national goals. In particular, how would the United States make use of its military and naval strength to win the war? The War and Navy departments had done little or no war planning before April 1917 because the president feared that such activity might compromise his attempt to qualify as a disinterested arbiter. Secretary of War Newton D. Baker understood Wilson's desires. "From the time I came to Washington until we were nearly in the war . . . the President gave me the idea—although I could not quote anything he said—that to him the function of the United States was to be the peacemaker, and that the idea of intervening in the War was the last thought he had in the world."[6]

To be sure, Wilson had sponsored two extraordinarily significant pieces of national security legislation in 1916. He recognized that, if he intended to intervene effectively in world politics, he must enjoy palpable support from credible armed forces, much larger and stronger than any ever before maintained in peacetime. The Naval Law of 1916 provided for "a navy second to none," and the National Defense Act of 1916 authorized an army of much-increased size and readiness. The difficulty, of course, was that little could be done to improve the armed forces in the few short months that separated the passage of the landmark legislation in 1916 and the declaration of war in April 1917.

At the outset of American belligerency, many assumed that the United States would simply offer naval help, financial support, and war supplies. It would make only a modest contribution to land warfare, an approach consistent with its insular traditions. In the past, Great Britain had several times supported European coalitions in this manner, notably during the wars against Napoleon.

Two realities suggested this course. First, the Regular Army was very small; it numbered a mere 133,000 men scattered in the home country and overseas possessions. About 67,000 members of the National Guard were also available, fresh from service on the Mexican border where they had attempted to deal with the guerrilla leader Pancho Villa. The largest existing unit was the regiment, none of which were ready for significant combat assignments. Qualified senior officers were scarce. Of 1,081 men commissioned between 1873 and 1889, only 234 remained on active duty.[7]

Much has been written about the reform of the army between 1880 to 1917. These noteworthy improvements allowed the army to serve effectively as a constabulary for the new insular empire conquered in 1898. They did not produce large, highly professional formations that could engage the great professional armies of Eurasia on equal terms, the types of organization needed to make a significant contribution to the defeat of Germany. Gen. Peyton C. March, the army's chief of staff during the last months of the war, observed that this "very small force of about two hundred thousand men was of no practical military value as far as the fighting in France was concerned; it was scarcely enough to form a police force for emergencies within the territorial limits of the United States." An attempt to create a large American army might interfere unduly with the flow of money and goods to the Allies. The United States could make an early and influential contribution to the war by sending money, naval reinforcements, and war material to the Entente nations. It would take a long time to mobilize a huge army and put it into the war. The War College Division of the General Staff initially recommended a modest army of one and a half million. It urged that the Regular Army and the National Guard remain in the United States to train recruits.[8]

Any thought of minimizing the role of the army disappeared during the visits of special missions sent from Great Britain and France immediately after the declaration of war. Their purpose was to encourage an imposing American reinforcement. Great Britain sent the foreign secretary, Arthur James Balfour, and France dispatched a leading politician, Rene Viviani, with Marshal Joseph Joffre, no longer the French commander-in-chief. Both delegations included military and naval representatives who consulted extensively with counterparts of the American army and navy. Joffre and Gen. George T. M. Bridges, the British military representative, soon informed the War Department that the Allies were desperately in need of massive reinforcements. Bridges called for 500,000 untrained men immediately. They would train in England and serve as replacements in British divisions on the western front. Maj. Gen. Tasker H. Bliss, the assistant chief of staff of the army, noted that the Allies urged the dispatch of "small organizations, even companies, as rapidly as they can be organized," to be trained in Europe and integrated into the French and British armies. This expedient, which became known as "amalgamation," would introduce American manpower into the war quickly. Bliss definitively rejected any such course, arguing that it would produce "a greatly disproportionate loss of life" without necessarily gaining its object. "When the war is over it may be a literal fact that the American flag may not have appeared anywhere on the line because our organizations will simply be parts of battalions and regiments of the Entente armies." Bliss specified the proper course. "The time has come for the English and the French to stand fast and wait until our reinforcements can reach them in such a way as to give the final, shattering blow."[9]

Marshal Joffre, sensing that the United States would reject amalgamation, advocated realistic measures that found ready acceptance. "No great nation," he wrote later, "having a proper consciousness of its own dignity–and America perhaps less than any other–would allow its citizens to be incorporated like poor relations in the ranks of some other army and fight under a foreign flag." He settled for the early appearance of an American division in France to show the flag, which President Wilson authorized on 3 May 1917. This act would lift spirits in the Entente nations, while the United States mobilized a great army of its own for eventual deployment to Europe. Joffre had in mind a force of fifteen to twenty divisions, some three or four hundred thousand men, available for service by April 1918. He recognized a difficulty that might arise. If neither the Americans nor the Allies could find sufficient shipping to transport this army to Europe, the scheme would come to nothing.[10]

These early decisions were of the highest importance: they fixed the fundamental land strategy of the United States during the war, one that ensured a long delay before American troops could undertake extensive field operations independently. The United States would mobilize a huge army to fight on the western front under its own commanders and staffs. Its purpose was to strike the decisive blow against the German army. Soon other corollaries of this commitment became evident. The independent army would fight according to its own doctrine in its own sector of the western front with its own services of supply. Given the unpreparedness of the army, it would be 1919 and possibly even 1920 before such a force could take the field.

Surely President Wilson and his advisers gambled magnificently in determining this course. They simply assumed that the Allies would hold out until the independent American army could rescue them. This elemental decision was consistent with the president's intention to avoid political commitments that might compromise his peace plans while making an essential contribution to victory over the Central Powers.[11]

In deciding to send an American army to France, the president inadvertently took sides in a basic strategic debate. He opposed a group that included the British prime minister, David Lloyd George, which had become disillusioned with the view that only a breakthrough on the western front could decide the war. Unconcerned about the imperialist rivalries and nationalist aspirations that influenced the politics of the Mediterranean Sea, the Balkans, the Levant, and the Middle East, American leaders adopted a straightforward view. The quickest way to encompass the defeat of the Central Powers was to destroy the German army in France. Lloyd George, disillusioned by the minuscule gains from offensives on the western front and the tremendous casualties that accompanied these operations, increasingly thought of exploiting the "eastern" theaters of war. British armies were campaigning actively against the Turks in Palestine and Mesopotamia, and a large inter-Allied force based at Salonika faced a Bulgarian army in Macedonia. These fronts might conceivably offer opportunities unavailable on the stalemated western front.

President Wilson showed some interest in the "eastern strategy." On 23 May 1917, he sent Secretary of War Newton D. Baker a paper that propounded the virtues of the eastern strategy. Baker was unimpressed, arguing that the western strategy was consistent with the spirit of the nation, "first, the determination expressed by you to make the world safe for democracy, and second, the desire to bring the war to the earliest possible conclusion." The latter concern predominated. "The paramount objective ought to be the early conclusion of the war, and even if our men are not prepared to the highest point, I think we can trust the discretion of our own officers to assign them to less important tasks in the fighting until their preparation is perfected, but their mere presence on the fighting front relieves better prepared men of French and British armies for the more trying operations." Baker reflected a consensus in the American military establishment, which showed little interest in the eastern strategy.[12]

Later in 1917, after the British suffered frustrating reverses in France, Lloyd George attempted to recruit President Wilson to support of the eastern strategy. None other than the head of British intelligence in the United States, Sir William Wiseman, wrote to his friend Colonel House: "I suggest that we ought not to consider the German forces as field army but that we ought to think of Germany as a beleaguered city. This means that, instead of attacking them at their strongest, we ought to attack them at their weakest point." Soon Lloyd George wrote to Wilson. "For some time past, it has seemed to me that we ought to consider very carefully whether we cannot achieve decisive results by concentrating first against Germany's allies. . . . They are weak not only militarily but politically. They are also very anxious for peace, so that a comparatively small success might produce far-reaching results."

Lloyd George's letter produced a review of the basic strategic commitment. The War College Division of the General Staff strongly supported the earlier decision. "The Western Front is nearest to us; it can be most readily reached and with the least danger; we there fight with England and France with whom we have the greatest natural interests; and we can make our power felt on that front quicker and stronger than anywhere else; and we are there opposed by Germany, who is our only real enemy." This view prevailed in Washington, ending further consideration of a shift to an eastern strategy. Events in 1918, especially the development of a great crisis on the western front, strengthened support for concentration in France. Gen. Peyton C. March, who became the army's chief of staff in 1918 after service in France, entertained the dominant American position. "I came to duty as Chief of Staff a pronounced Western Fronter. From a military standpoint, in my judgment, the war would be won or lost on the Western Front, and I opposed at all times the slightest diversion of our troops from that objective. I preached this doctrine to the Secretary of War, and he accepted it. In addition to the military reasons, the obvious impossibility, with our limited shipping, of establishing war bases and new lines of supply to all sorts of outlying countries appealed to any clearheaded businessman."[13]

As the United States began to mobilize, the French army undertook a great offensive intended to force a decisive breakthrough. Gen. Robert Nivelle, Joffre's replacement as general-in-chief of the French army, planned a powerful operation near Reims. The German command team of Field Marshal Paul von Hindenburg and First Quartermaster General Erich Ludendorff, recognizing the vulnerability of their battered forces, sought to forestall Nivelle by withdrawing twenty-seven miles to a strongly fortified area known as the Siegfried line. This ALBERICH operation, which took place between 16 February and 5 April, cleared the evacuated region of German supplies and demolished communications, towns, and wells. It created great difficulties for opposing forces who attempted to attack across the devastation. Nivelle persisted in his attack, which began on 16 April. Lacking surprise and directed against a much-strengthened German defense, it soon failed miserably, provoking widespread disaffection and even mutiny in many French units. Afterward Nivelle attempted to blame his subordinates for his repulse, to which one of them, the unhappy Gen. Alfred Micheler, retorted: "What, you try to make me responsible for the mistake, when I never ceased to warn you? Do you know what such action is called? It is called cowardice." Gen. Henri Philippe Petain soon supplanted Nivelle. Petain's British counterpart, Field Marshal Sir Douglas Haig, launched another offensive in Flanders on 31 July, but this sanguinary operation, lasting until November, led only to terrible losses in exchange for minor gains.[14]

General Petain, imperturbable and cautious, eschewed extensive offensives throughout 1917, seeking to restore the morale of his mutinous army. On 5 May, the American ambassador in Paris, William Graves Sharp, reported that France was "sore distressed and bleeding, the exhaustion is very great—much greater than the world knows—for no other of her Allies has suffered such a drain in men and resources." The French army had endured ninety

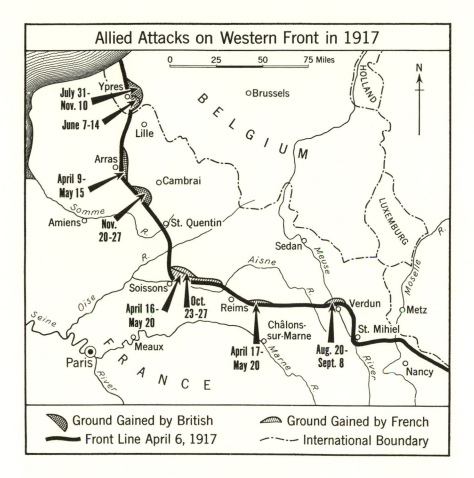

Allied Attacks on Western Front in 1917

Ground Gained by British
Front Line April 6, 1917
Ground Gained by French
International Boundary

thousand casualties in the preceding week. "The cry of France is for men—more men." Petain soon announced his views. "The equilibrium between the opposing forces . . . does not permit us, for the time being, to contemplate a breakthrough of the front followed by strategic exploitation. Therefore, what is important at the present time is to bend our efforts to wear down the opponent with a minimum of losses." To gain this goal, he called for attacks "with limited objectives which are abruptly released on a front as extensive as the number and characteristics of the various pieces of artillery available permit."[15]

Given the weakness of the Allies, Gen. Ferdinand Foch, the chief of the French general staff, emphasized the importance of the American intervention in a conversation with his British counterpart, Gen. Sir William Robertson.

Trench warfare in Champagne, 1917. German troops mow down the scattered French assault troops who reach the objective. Note the overwhelming advantage of the defense.

"In view of the Russian default and the effect it would have upon the western theatre, as well as the time it would take before the American Army could come into action, the two generals decided that military operations in France must be limited to a policy of attrition until such time as American aid, by reestablishing a superiority in our favour, would permit decisive results to be once more envisioned." While awaiting the arrival of the Americans, the French and the British would assume a defensive posture on all secondary fronts. They would reinforce their armies in France by transferring available troops from these locations to the main theater.[16]

Meanwhile Germany, of necessity standing on the defensive in France, turned to a radical maritime strategy to force victory in 1917. It staked everything on an unrestricted submarine campaign against neutral and noncombatant commerce that began on 1 February. The admirals promised success in six months; after that the Allies could not supply themselves sufficiently to continue the struggle. Ludendorff conveyed his expectations to some members of the German Reichstag in July. "We could assume with confidence that the great loss of enemy tonnage would gradually paralyse the determination of our enemies, as their living conditions at home would be seriously affected. . . . We cannot say at what moment the war industry of our opponents will break down, but it will come." Germany knew that its maritime strategy would provoke American intervention, but "great and decisive aid from the United

States will be made an extremely difficult matter on account of the shortage of tonnage." The war would be over before the Americans could affect the outcome. "We shall conquer if the nation stands firm and united behind the army." One of the quartermaster general's naval colleagues, Adm. Eduard von Capelle, expressed the German dismissal of the Americans more bluntly. He informed a committee of the Reichstag: "The example that the Americans gave us in 1898 in the Spanish-American War, where they suffered wretched fiascoes with the armies that they wanted to create, gives us a sense of calm, knowing that the American volunteer battalions will not be able to change the situation to our disadvantage."[17]

Thus, as the United States set about a furious mobilization to prepare for operations in France by 1919, Germany dug in on the western front and attempted to win the war by action at sea before a formidable American force could arrive. The exhausted Allies could do nothing except hang on until the American reinforcement could permit resumption of offensive operations.

On 8 May, Secretary of War Baker informed President Wilson that he had chosen Maj. Gen. John J. Pershing to command the American Expeditionary Forces. The most senior officer in the army was Maj. Gen. Leonard Wood, a former chief of staff, but several circumstances eliminated him from consideration. He was politically unacceptable to the administration; he suffered from a brain injury that dated from his service in Cuba after the War with Spain; and he lacked recent field service. Pershing had connections with the Republican party, but he was loyal to responsible civilian authority. A vigorous officer, he had gained valuable experience as the commander of the punitive expedition sent into Mexico to break up the bandit Pancho Villa's army.[18]

Pershing's orders gave him broad control of the American Expeditionary Forces, imposing only one significant limitation, an injunction to develop an independent army. "In general you are vested with all necessary authority to carry on the war vigorously in harmony with the spirit of these instructions and toward a victorious conclusion." Both the president and his secretary of war harked back to the experience of the Civil War in giving Pershing extensive powers. They were convinced that President Lincoln had interfered unduly with the prerogatives of field commanders, who were in the best position to make necessary decisions. Baker stated his doctrine forcefully after the war. "Our field of operations was necessarily removed a great distance from Washington. . . . it was quite impossible for us to form accurate judgments of the varying incidents in the field of operations." Because of Pershing's heavy responsibilities, "we could not do less than give him full authority and leave him untrammeled by attempts to formulate plans of action which, made at a great distance, would not be informed with knowledge of the situation which the commander at the front had when the plans reached him." Baker claimed to have said to Pershing: "I will give you only two orders—one to go to France and the other to come home. In the meantime your authority in France will be supreme."[19]

Pershing's orders, which provided that he must keep in view "the underlying idea . . . that the forces of the United States are a separate and distinct component of the combined forces, the identity of which must be preserved," faithfully reflected the early discussions with the Allied missions. Pershing supported this policy. "It was definitely understood between the Secretary of War and myself that we should proceed to organize our own units from top to bottom and build a distinctive army of our own as rapidly as possible." The general did not receive specific instructions directly from President Wilson, although he visited the White House on 25 May. Donald Smythe, Pershing's biographer, notes that Pershing found the president "cordial," but he was surprised because he "did not discuss the war or America's part in it, nor did he give instructions or outline the course he would pursue. Perhaps no field commander in history was ever given a freer hand to conduct operations."[20]

After the war, Baker explained the reasons for this independent course. The Allies and the United States shared a strong interest in defeating the Central Powers, but there might well be differences of opinion on other important matters. "It was necessary at all times to preserve the independence and identity of the American forces so that they could never be anything but an instrument of the policy of the United States." Baker left unstated the most fundamental political consideration: A victorious independent army in Europe would vastly enhance the influence of the president during postwar peace negotiations. The secretary of war also emphasized the influence of the American people. "Public opinion would not have sustained and ought not to have sustained turning over American soldiers to be lost in British and French commands." Also, the army itself would have objected. "Nor would American soldiers have been happy under any flag but their own. The whole theory of our Army differed from the theories of the French and British, just as we as a people differ from them." Finally, the independence of the American forces ensured that the Allies would sustain the size of their formations at the level of April 1917. America's army was to become "a constantly added force rather than a mere replacement."[21]

This mixture of political, nationalist, and institutional considerations explains the stubborn American opposition to amalgamation that continued even during the most critical emergencies of 1918. Among other things, it meant that

Pershing could negotiate all questions of inter-Allied military cooperation. He exercised this largely political role to the full and eventually earned broad unpopularity among Entente leaders.

Pershing arrived in France on 13 June. The 1st Division, hurriedly scraped together, followed him on 26 June, but few other troops crossed the ocean before the end of 1917. The youthful George C. Marshall, Jr., recalled the "very depressing" atmosphere in St. Nazaire when he landed there. "Every woman seemed to be in mourning, and everyone seemed to be on the verge of tears. The one thing we noticed most of all there was no enthusiasm at all over our arrival." Marshall fully recognized the unpreparedness of the 1st Division. "They were not a combat division at all, but only the raw material for one sent over for assembly in France instead of at home. Months would pass before the division could be shaped to fight and more months before it could be committed as part of an army capable of sustaining itself in the line." The commanding general set about developing plans for the American Expeditionary Forces. The home government took up the task of mobilization: acquiring necessary personnel, equipping them, and training them in organizations intended to conduct field operations. This imposing enterprise was at first helter-skelter, because the institutional structure required to conduct an efficient military buildup did not exist.[22]

The War Department had been reformed in 1903, when it received a general staff, but this change was ineffective. The general staff was small: only forty-one members were on duty when the war began, and twenty-two were assigned outside Washington. The chief of staff served mainly as an adviser to the secretary of war instead of as an executive with the authority to direct the eleven bureaus of the War Department. Bureau heads were free to operate independently; little was done to coordinate their efforts. Emergency legislation in 1917 permitted the enlargement of the general staff, but Secretary Baker at first hesitated to exert needed control of the bureau heads, either directly or through the chief of staff. Officers passing through Washington during the early months of the war noted considerable disarray. One of them, Col. Robert L. Bullard, wrote: "The great impression left is that *if we really have a great war, our War Department will quickly break down.*" Fortunately, able officers in the War College Division provided essential plans in the early stages of the mobilization.[23]

It took hard experience to identify the institutional requirements for modern total war. Even then a fundamental constraint interfered with the most needed innovation, rapid expansion and centralization of federal authority. Both President Wilson and Secretary of War Baker hoped to mobilize without making fundamental changes in the federal government. Baker preferred to bring in special advisers, the "dollar-a-year men," to deal with specific requirements instead of creating a panoply of new agencies. He retained the anticentralist and antigovernment bias of the Founding Fathers, with a commitment to individual private initiative. The statism and collectivism implicit in a great expansion of government was repellent to him. The president agreed. Robert Cuff has shown that Wilson's liberalism represented a compromise, subsuming "the idea of friendly cooperation between business and government and an ambiguity toward the role of the state." Wilson stood by his regular advisers, refusing "to displace his service secretaries as his chief advisers on military and industrial mobilization. Expert volunteers remained subordinate, although it is true that as a matter of practical administration they did perform increasingly important executive functions on a daily basis."[24]

Given the unprecedented situation and the traditional fear of big government, the institutional arrangements required to coordinate the activities of the army and American industry developed slowly during 1917. Only one such organization predated Wilson's war message. The Council of National Defense, an advisory group authorized by the Army Appropriation Act of 29 August 1916, brought together several cabinet members. They relied on representatives of the private sector for expert help. Later a General Munitions Board was founded (3 April 1917), but neither it nor the Advisory Committee of the Council of National Defense provided essential coordination of the various agencies that participated in mobilization. On 27 July 1917, the president finally acted, setting up the War Industries Board (WIB) as a subordinate entity of the Council of National Defense to referee business-government relations during the process of mobilization. Unfortunately the WIB in its early form, like its predecessors, lacked sufficient powers. It was no more effective than the general staff of the army as a supervisory and coordinating institution.[25]

However, the War Department made important progress during 1917, particularly in arranging the acquisition of necessary personnel for the wartime army and providing for their training. On 18 May 1917, Congress passed the Selective Service Act. It authorized full strength for the Regular Army and called the National Guard to federal service, but most importantly it designated conscription as the primary means of acquiring personnel. The law provided for an initial draft of five hundred thousand men and for an increment of the same number, if needed. This legislation responded to the desires of the professional military, reflecting grim experience with volunteers in earlier American wars.

General Pershing was quick to support the draft, writing to Maj. Gen. Hugh L. Scott, the chief of staff. "To those of us who really know the weakness of the volunteer system and the failure that would surely follow its continuance, it is gratifying indeed to have the administration insist upon universal selective service for the whole country and put it over accordingly." Andrew Dickson White, long the president of Cornell University and a sometime diplomat, urged the president to make use of volunteers. He suggested that he allow citizens such as Theodore Roosevelt to raise regiments. Wilson immediately objected, informing White that his professional military advisers counselled otherwise. "Any other course than that which we are pursuing in our preparations for securing an Army would be a fatal mistake, a mistake registered in dead men, in unnecessary and cruel loss of life." This view, he noted, was also that of the military missions that had recently come from France and Britain. Conscription was desirable because it assured both equity and efficiency in building the armed forces. Eventually, the selective service system produced 2,800,000 men of the 3,700,000 who served during World War I without disrupting the industrial and agricultural effort of the nation.[26]

The War Department eventually prepared forty-three divisions for service in France. The Regular Army provided eight, the 1st through 8th Divisions, and the National Guard seventeen, the 26th through 42d Divisions. Draftees filled the remaining eighteen divisions that made up the National Army, the 76th through 93d. This great task required construction of many training cantonments. Sixteen were built for the National Guard and sixteen for the National Army.[27]

Meanwhile the War Department undertook the procurement and purchasing necessary to supply the new army. In his war message, President Wilson specified that the United States would equip its forces without disrupting shipments to the Allies. Raw materials therefore flowed across the Atlantic to meet the needs of British and French industries. Ambitious plans were made to manufacture all manner of material in the United States, but much of it was never transported to Europe. It took time to gear factories for war production, and merchant shipping was used primarily to transport troops. Accordingly the Allies provided most of the material used by the AEF during 1917–1918. To obtain necessary supplies and equipment in Europe, Pershing established a General Purchasing Board and made Charles G. Dawes the general purchasing agent. Dawes directed all purchasing agents in the AEF. "Through representatives on the [General Purchasing] Board each Supply Service was kept in current touch with the resources of the European markets, which were availed of in all possible cases in preference to the transportation overseas of supplies purchased in the United States." Dawes proved remarkably adept. He purchased about ten million tons of supplies in Europe. Only seven million tons were shipped from the United States.[28]

As the home government struggled to mobilize manpower and material, General Pershing developed his plans for the organization and operations of the AEF. He exercised enormous influence on this process, much more than most theater commanders, because of the plenary authority that had been granted to him. Both Secretary Baker and General Bliss, the chief of staff during most of 1917, saw themselves as agents of the commander-in-chief. In 1919, Baker explained his relation to Pershing. "My duty to the country and its cause was to support General Pershing at every point, to give him complete freedom and discretion, and if the time ever came when I could not do that, to replace him." In 1921, Bliss told Pershing that he viewed himself as "Assistant Chief of Staff to the Chief of Staff of the AEF." This posture minimized friction between the field command and the home government, although it also created difficulties in some situations.[29]

Pershing's staff undertook the formulation of basic policy for the AEF, and it forwarded its recommendations to the War Department. Given the subservience of the secretary of war and the chief of staff, these proposals were accepted almost without question. When these desires conflicted with those of the War Department, the field commander's desires usually prevailed. Pershing left no doubt about his views on dealings with the War Department. "In the absence of any preparation for war beforehand, the principle can hardly be questioned that the commander at the front and not the staff departments in Washington should decide what he needs. . . . It remained, then, for the War Department simply and without cavil to support our efforts to the fullest extent by promptly forwarding men and supplies as requested." Anticipating unwarranted interference from the bureaus of the War Department, Pershing said: "This is going to be one American campaign where the tail does not wag the dog, and where the command actually commands." Pershing was quick to complain when he sensed "disorganization and confusion," and he usually prevailed during the first year of the American intervention. While Baker and Bliss led the War Department, the friction that might have resulted from Pershing's high-handed attitude did not occur.[30]

Pershing's invincible belief in his competence obscured an important reality, the inexperience of his staff. Gen. John Charteris, a British officer, spoke well of Pershing in a conversation with Field Marshal Haig but noted that the

Americans were where the British had been in 1914. "It will be a very difficult job for them to get a serviceable staff going even in a year's time." Pershing's biographer, Donald Smythe, notes that headquarters at Chaumont was "over-staffed and top-heavy." To see every principal staff officer for fifteen minutes each day, Pershing would have had to expend five hours. The commander took on many duties, so that he "was like a dog chasing its own tail." His chief of staff, General Harbord, believed that his superior devoted too much time to administration, slighting his "real job," command of the AEF. A reorganization in February 1918 corrected some of these problems.[31]

During the formative stages of the AEF, its staff produced three plans of overriding importance. First came the General Organization Project on 10 July 1917, which proposed a force of about a million troops for the campaign of 1918. It also called for a mobilization at home that would produce an army of three million in two years. Then came the Service of the Rear Project on 18 September, which identified the troops required to provide logistical support. Finally, on 9 October, came the Schedule of Priority of Shipments, intended to assure a rational buildup. The outcome of these documents was agreement on what became known as the Thirty-Division Program, the antici-pated size of the AEF after 1918. It would produce an army of 1,372,399 troops in thirty divisions composed of five corps, each corps to include four combat divisions, a training division, and a replacement division. The Schedule of Priority of Shipments provided for the shipment of the AEF in six phases. Six divisions, making up a corps, would be shipped in each one of the first five phases with some troops assigned to corps and army headquarters. The sixth phase would include the remaining corps and army troops. Although Pershing complained of "confusion" in the War Department and of "frightened importunities" from the Allies during 1918, he agreed that his "outlines of our requirements in men, equipment, supplies, and material gave Washington something definite to follow."[32]

Through all the early planning, Pershing remained faithful to the early strategic decisions made in Washington during the visits of the Allied missions. He wrote firmly to Secretary Baker. "We must not risk trying to fight this war by detail but must be ready by spring [of 1918] to go in and settle it before the summer is over." The secretary of war supported him, writing on 10 Sep-tember: "I want you to know that we will exercise all the patience necessary on this side and will not ask you to put your troops into action until in your own judgment both the time is opportune and the preparations thoroughly adequate." Baker especially hoped that the first American battle would be a success, bearing in mind the effect that the outcome would have on opinion both at home and elsewhere. Pershing responded on 13 November 1917. "Unless something very threatening should occur, we should not go in until we are ready. Of course, even then there will be much to learn from actual experience." He and Petain had agreed that "every effort should be made to have the first clash, if possible, a victory for the Americans. Such a result would of course raise the morale of our allies and correspondingly depress the enemy." Pershing continued to resist pressure from the British and French liaison missions assigned to his headquarters at Chaumont to amalgamate American troops into Allied formations.[33]

During 1917, Pershing devoted himself to certain special concerns that would eventually affect the operations of the AEF. Among these were the selection of general officers to hold high command in France, the size of the American division, the principles of training in the AEF, and the choice of a sector for decisive American operations.

On 28 July 1917, Pershing enunciated views on the designation of general officers for service in France to which he adhered throughout the war. His observation of the Allied armies and of conditions at the front had convinced him that "only officers in full mental and physical vigor should be sent here. Contrary course means certain inefficiency in our service and possible later humiliation to officers concerned." He was especially interested in officers with prior command experience. Pershing received strong support from the War Department. The chief of staff, General Bliss, wrote in September 1917: "If I could have done what I considered preeminently desirable, I would not as a rule have recommended [for promotion] a general officer over 45 years of age nor a colonel over 40; but that was impossible." Pershing's rejection of certain senior general officers, including Maj. Gen. Leonard Wood, caused considerable controversy at times, but competence rather than seniority or influence usually governed the appointment of general officers to commands in the AEF. Unfortunately the supply of fully qualified officers was limited, a circumstance that adversely affected the AEF in combat during 1918.[34]

Considerable debate developed over the appropriate size of the basic combat unit, which was the division. Both sides in Europe had settled on a division of fourteen thousand men, but Pershing chose a larger number, about twenty-eight thousand men. The American "square division" had four infantry regiments and two machine-gun battalions organized in two brigades with three regiments of field artillery. Several considerations influenced this decision. A square division would have more staying power than smaller European counterparts; it would generate tremendous infantry fire power at the expense of maneuver; it would help compensate for a glaring lack of trained commanders and staff officers; and finally, it would simplify efforts to absorb the obstinate National Guard. Critics of the double-sized divisions have maintained that the Allies could easily have fielded larger divisions, if they needed more staying power. Moreover, a large division expanded the responsibilities of commanders and staffs, an undesirable outcome given the short supply of American officers and their inexperience. Finally, the discrepancy between the size of the American divisions and those of the Allies caused complications in joint operations. Nevertheless, Pershing persisted in his support of the large division, and his desires decided the matter. This outcome caused difficulties at home. Training cantonments had to be expanded to accommodate the square divisions, and the National Guard divisions called to the colors were most unhappy with the wholesale changes that were required in their organizations.[35]

General Pershing gave considerable attention to the training of the divisions destined to become part of the AEF, and his training methods differed markedly from those of the Allies. Convinced that the experience of trench warfare had deprived the French and even the British of offensive spirit, he stressed what he called open warfare. "It was my opinion that victory could not be won by the costly process of attrition, but it must be won by driving the enemy out into the open and engaging him in a war of movement." Such operations must stress "individual and group initiative, resourcefulness and tactical judgment." In particular, he insisted upon training in aimed rifle fire. "My view was that the rifle and bayonet still remained the essential weapons of the infantry." He urged that training in the United States emphasize offensive open warfare. Instruction in trench warfare could take place after the divisions arrived in France. He set up a complete school system in France to minimize what he considered the perverse influence of the Allies.[36]

Pershing encountered persistent opposition to his views of training. The Allies approved of his stress on the offensive spirit, but they had come to doubt the feasibility of a breakthrough that would permit troops to maneuver extensively behind the enemy front line. Attrition, not maneuver, seemed the logical key to eventual victory, given the nature of the struggle in France. This outlook led to preoccupation with artillery, machine guns, and other means of enhancing firepower instead of the traditional small arms of the infantryman. An emphasis on combined arms operations characterized British and French training during the decisive phase of the war, a stress that developed tardily in the AEF. Some members of Pershing's staff and others in the AEF came to disagree with their leader's views on training, but the stubborn commander never wavered in his conviction that he knew better than the Allies the training requirements for service on the western front.[37]

Soon after his arrival in France, Pershing ordered inquiries about the most desirable sector of the front in which to concentrate the independent army. After the war, his G-3 (Operations) articulated the basic considerations that governed this search. The sector must be one in which the United States could "develop and employ a force numbered by the millions and . . . conditions should favor the retention of the identity of our forces." It was easy to rule out the left wing of the western front. The British army, concerned about its communications to the home islands, was concentrated in Picardy and Flanders to safeguard the channel ports. It was equally easy to rule out the central region of the front: the French army was massed there to protect Paris. This process of elimination led Pershing's staff to the right wing of the front, where the province of Lorraine immediately attracted attention. It had been a quiet sector for most of the war, and several particularly inviting objectives lay to the north and east of the front line. Among them were the iron mines of the Longwy-Briey region, the coal fields of the Saar, and above all the fortified city of Metz, a key link in rail communications from Germany to the western front. These targets fulfilled the basic requirement that the American army should attack decisive objectives and win the war for the western powers. A successful campaign in Lorraine that severed essential lines of communication would render untenable the entire German position in France. It would compel the enemy to fall back on the German borders or perhaps even the Rhine River. Other circumstances reinforced the choice of Lorraine. It was an uncongested area, offering locations for billeting and training American troops, and it was possible to develop communications with ports on the Atlantic and Mediterranean coasts to which the United States could ship men and material.[38]

As early as 26 June 1917, Pershing arranged with Petain eventually to concentrate his divisions in Lorraine, a decision that remained in place. It was immediately recognized that the initial operation must be the reduction of the St. Mihiel salient, which had been in existence since 1914–1915. This enemy bastion threatened the Verdun sector to the west and the Nancy sector to the south. Also it interrupted the important railway between Nancy and Paris, seriously restricting attempts of the Allies to maneuver troops and supply them. After the salient was reduced, presumably in 1918, it would become possible to attack eastward in 1919 toward Metz, seizing the objectives identified earlier—Metz itself, the Briey-Longwy basin, the Saar, and the lateral railway that supplied the left and center of the German line.[39]

A series of later staff reviews left intact the early decisions to concentrate in Lorraine, to conduct the initial independent operation against the St. Mihiel salient, and ultimately to launch a general attack in the direction of Metz that

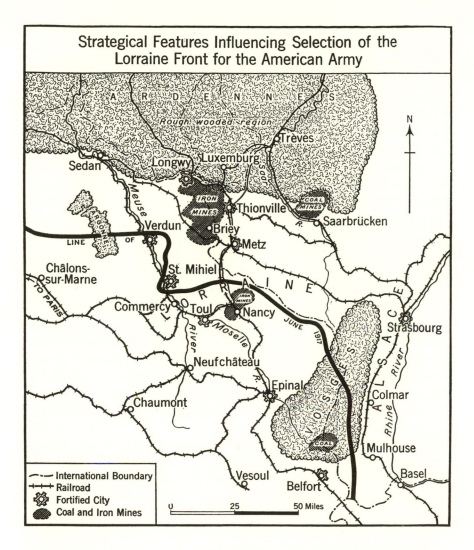

Strategical Features Influencing Selection of the Lorraine Front for the American Army

would decide the war. In November 1917, it was determined that preparations should begin in February 1918 for an attack on the St. Mihiel salient in June. Early in June Pershing noted: "The question of building up an American sector between St-Mihiel and Pont-a-Mousson has been practically decided by agreement between General Petain and myself." A few days later Colonel Fox Conner, the G-3 (Operations), reviewed the decision affirmatively and pinned down its timing. Bearing in mind that the American army would seek a decision in 1919, he wrote: "In order that we may prepare for 1919 we must put our divisions into an American sector so that we may become a homogeneous force. For reasons of morale, we must also plan to make at least a limited offensive during 1918." It seemed possible to create a purely American force under American commanders by 1 June, one that in due course could undertake the reduction of the St. Mihiel salient.[40]

Allan Millett has aptly criticized the plan to seek a decision in Lorraine. Extensive fortifications between the Ardennes and the Vosges mountains protected the area, which had been in German hands for many years. Besides, the critical railroad emphasized in Pershing's plans did not run through Metz. "Instead, it turned west at Thionville (well north of Metz) and ran northwest through Longuyon and Montmedy until it reached the Meuse River at Sedan; the line then followed the Meuse to Mezieres and turned north into German-occupied Belgium. To break this line would require an AEF offensive that advanced well past Metz." Also the resources of the area were not as critical as Pershing assumed. The Saar, for example, produced only about 10 percent of Germany's coal and iron, a significant but endurable loss. Millett concludes: "The Allies, therefore, could honestly doubt whether Pershing's great 1919 plan offered any unique prospects for victory. The basic challenge remained the same: to destroy the moral and physical ability of the German army to hold the territory west of the Rhine."[41]

The early decision to attack in Lorraine allowed Pershing from the beginning to emphasize the construction of services of the rear that could support major American operations in that region. Little-used South Atlantic harbors were available for debarkation, especially the deep-draft ports of St. Nazaire, La Pallice, and Bassens and the light-draft ports of Nantes, Pauillac, and Bordeaux. Some ships unloaded at Le Havre, Brest, and Cherbourg. In addition, the Americans used the ports of Marseilles and Toulon in the Mediterranean Sea. From these places, railroads led eastward and northward some four hundred miles to Lorraine. Certain cities were chosen as depots and command centers, especially the area embracing Tours, Borges, Orleans, Montargis, Nevers, and Chateauroux. Chaumont became Pershing's headquarters because of its proximity to the sector chosen for independent operations. The great scope of the services of the rear meant that considerable time would be needed to perfect them, another reason for the presumption that the main American effort would be delayed into 1919.[42]

Throughout 1917, both General Bliss in Washington and General Pershing in France regularly drew attention to the need for shipping to transport troops to France. Tonnage was scarce because of German submarine operations against

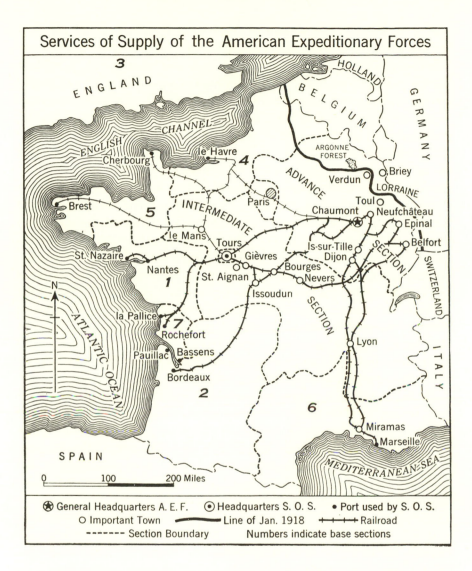

Services of Supply of the American Expeditionary Forces

maritime commerce. As early as 31 May, General Bliss accurately characterized the problem. "No military plan whatever can be made until the question of transportation is settled and then our military plan if it be a wise one must be based on the amount of such transportation." In August, Pershing urged both aggressive naval operations against the U-boats and arrangements for a "full share" of available Allied tonnage. He cabled a cogent reason for taking action: "Generally conceded that our entrance saved the Allies from defeat. Hence our position in this war very strong and should enable us largely to dictate policy to Allies in future." At the same time, General Bliss noted the intention of the United States to transport a "considerable number of troops abroad this fall and winter." It was difficult to establish a schedule because of limited tonnage. "If the Allies want us to get a strong force in France in the near future they have got to make available for our use a certain amount of tonnage which we now have not got." In September, he asked permission to negotiate shipping questions with the British, but the War Department demurred. "Our shipping must necessarily be supplied by ourselves, and the shipping board here is in direct conference with British authorities controlling their shipping." As time passed, Pershing became insistent on the maintenance of prescribed shipping timetables, especially the schedule of priorities completed on 7 October, blaming the War Department for confusion in ports. He later claimed that conditions "must have paralleled the inefficiency displayed in the management of our transport in the Spanish-American War." By December, Bliss was urging that the United States take the lead in forcing effective inter-Allied agreement on allocation of shipping, but no agreement had been reached by the beginning of 1918.[43]

Although both the government agencies at home and the AEF staff in France accomplished a great deal during 1917, considerable confusion and failure attended the mobilization, and only a few American troops reached France. Four combat divisions arrived by 31 December: the 1st (June), the 26th (October), the 42d (November), and the 2d, which had all but completed its debarkation. The 41st Division had also landed, but it served as a depot division and did not enter a training area. On 31 December 1917, a mere 176,655 American soldiers had been transported to France, far from the number required to form an independent army.[44]

Secretary of War Baker offered an optimistic appraisal of the mobilization late in 1917, but others who disparaged the necessarily chaotic process were about to cause a political tempest. In his annual report, Baker admitted that the "problems of supply are not solved; but they are in the course of solution. Sound beginnings have been made, and as the military effort of the country grows the arrangements perfected and organizations created will expand to meet it." Daniel Beaver observes that to this point Baker, "like many Americans, had been only half at war. . . . Grave fall and winter events swept away old preconceptions and confronted him with unpleasant realities." Among them were a coal shortage, inadequate shipments of foodstuffs to the Allies, a poor record of merchant ship construction, and inefficient operation of army troop transports.[45]

Critics of the machinery for the conduct of the mobilization emerged on all sides. A cogent condemnation of the War Department came from the retired chief of staff, Gen. Hugh L. Scott. In particular, he underscored the failure to establish "one and only one organ through which the Secretary commands the army—the Chief of Staff, [who] should be the medium of recommendation to the Secretary and of execution for his orders. He should have ample authority for securing the coordination of all the activities of the military establishment." Scott urged that the general staff should undertake two missions. It should support the chief of staff in his role as supervisor and coordinator and make the studies needed for "mobilization, organization, instruction, training, and movement of our armies[,] to gather intelligence, and to investigate such special projects as are referred to it." Meanwhile, others noted the weaknesses of the WIB, especially its deficient legal and political basis, which precluded its emergence as an effective director of industrial mobilization.[46]

When Congress convened early in December, it was ready to act. During the next two months, it launched no fewer than five major investigations of the mobilization, concentrating on the War Department. Senator George Earle Chamberlain (D-Ore.), chairman of the Senate Committee on Military Affairs, began hearings on 12 December. Soon he delivered a speech in New York City in which he trumpeted that "the military establishment of the United States of America has fallen down. There is no use to be optimistic about a thing that does not exist. It has almost stopped functioning, my friends. . . . I speak not as a Democrat, but as an American citizen." Theodore Roosevelt, a leading critic of the administration, was present; he rose and clapped loudly. Secretary Baker offered to resign, but the president came stoutly to his defense. "The War Department has performed a task of unparalleled magnitude and difficulty with extraordinary promptness and efficiency. . . . My association with and constant conferences with the secretary of war have taught me to regard him as one of the best officials I have ever known. The country will soon learn whether he or his critics understand the business at hand."[47]

Baker had already attempted to deflect criticism by making certain changes in the War Department. On 15 December, he set up a "war council" composed of himself, his assistant secretary, and five officers of the general staff, including the chief of staff, General Bliss. The group was to serve as an advisory panel, acting through the chief of staff to coordinate relations between the War Department and the AEF. Baker claimed that its members could "take a large supervisory view of all questions of organization and supply and give to the Government the highest value of their talents and experience." This expedient did not produce results. After a few meetings, the War Council faded away.[48]

Baker soon resorted to testimony before Senator Chamberlain's committee. On 10 January 1918, he reviewed the evolution of the institutions charged with mobilization and came to a glowing conclusion: "We can now see the entire situation. The initial rush needs are substantially supplied. The technical corps have been expanded and reorganized along industrial and efficient lines." The government had coordinated American and Allied purchasing. "By the cooperation of all interests and all people in the country the Nation is now organized, and set to its task with unanimity of spirit and confidence in its powers. More has been done than anybody dared to believe possible." Errors of judgment had occurred, but the most important goals had been achieved.[49]

Senator James W. Wadsworth (R-N.Y.) took issue with this root-and-branch rejection of vast dislocations in the mobilization. Baker's statement, he said, gave the impression that "the situation is a rosy one; that there is nothing to fear; that the rush needs . . . have been complied with; that no greater haste is necessary; that everything is fine." Wadsworth did not agree. "We have ahead of us a bigger task in the next eight months than we have had in the last eight months. It is the impression that goes out to the country with which I cannot agree." He concluded starkly: "I believe we are in for one of the greatest crises that the country has ever known."[50]

Baker's efforts to head off continuing criticism did not immediately succeed, and he was forced again to come before Chamberlain's committee in defense of his actions. Acknowledging a general impression that "the War Department has fallen down in addressing itself to the task of conducting this war," he attributed this feeling to the impatience of the American people, who wanted quick action to show that "our country is great and strong." He acknowledged past errors but stated his intention "to learn from them . . . ; not to repeat; to strengthen where there needs strengthening; to supplement where there needs supplementing." The War Department would make its "very best effort and [with] the confidence of the country back of that effort, . . . make our enemies finally feel the strength that is really American."[51]

Recognizing the futility of his rhetoric, Baker finally moved to reorganize the War Department. On 9 February 1918, he established five main divisions, including a Purchase and Supply Division to procure necessary items and a Storage and Traffic Division to provide logistical support. These two divisions were consolidated on 16 April 1918 into the Purchase, Traffic, and Storage Division. Baker also brought in a Wall Street businessman, Edward R. Stettinius, and the builder of the Panama Canal, Maj. Gen. George W. Goethals, to strengthen his administrative team. Most important, he named Peyton C. March, Pershing's chief of artillery, as chief of staff. Later he wrote: "It seemed to me that the time had come when we should have in Washington an energetic and effective administrator, who by actual experience in General Pershing's army knew the situation in France, was acquainted with General Pershing's plans, and so could more effectively direct our cooperation with the Expeditionary Force." General Bliss had been sent to France as the American Permanent Military Representative at the Supreme War Council, an inter-Allied organization created in November 1917 to provide high-level coordination and direction of the war effort. March possessed the ruthlessness and the energy needed to stimulate the War Department. His statement that "you cannot run a war on tact" summarizes his style of leadership. Baker spent much time soothing hurt feelings that stemmed from March's tactlessness. He later described the general as "arrogant, harsh, dictatorial and opinionated . . . riding roughshod over everyone." Perhaps March's influence has been overestimated. He arrived in Washington after most of the needed institutional adjustments were made, but the War Department under his whip far surpassed its previous achievements. The transformation of 1917–1918 in the War Department is a more important event in its history by far than the creation of the general staff system in 1903.[52]

While Baker strengthened the War Department, President Wilson also upgraded the powers of the War Industries Board. On 4 March 1918 he placed Bernard Baruch, another Wall Street veteran, in charge of the floundering WIB and redefined its functions, in the process enlarging them. The result was far from the unified and highly integrated system of government-business relations that some historians of the military-industrial complex have described, but it met the requirements of the wartime crisis, and it quieted criticisms of the administration.[53]

The final step toward rationalization of mobilization was the Overman Act of 20 May 1918, which gave the president discretion to consolidate federal agencies and to coordinate their activities. It was possible under this law to give General Goethals the power to control both procurement and transport, a step that broke the influence of the Quartermaster Department. Russell Weigley notes that Goethals in effect became the supply officer of the entire army, a change that for the first time created a single service of supply.[54]

A year after the declaration of war President Wilson and his associates had finally forged an organization at home that could support the American Expeditionary

Forces at a reasonable level of efficiency. Ironically, as the winter crisis worked itself out in Washington, a much greater crisis followed on the western front. Just as the War Department and Pershing's staff were poised to complete the formation of an independent army like that envisioned in the earliest days of the American intervention, earthshaking developments in Europe forced considerable modifications in the American design. Wilhelmian Germany prepared a massive offensive in France designed to end the war before the American army could decide the outcome.

2

THE EMERGENCY OF 1918

The year 1917 was one of almost unrelieved frustration for the western powers. First came the failure of the Nivelle offensive, which almost prostrated the French army. Then the exhausting British campaign in Flanders produced enormous casualty lists and minor advances. Meanwhile, German U-boats sank millions of tons of merchant shipping, placing terrible strains on the civilian populations of the Allied nations. In October, Austria almost knocked Italy out of the war when the Italian front collapsed at Caporetto. Finally, the Bolshevik revolution early in November led quickly to the end of Russian belligerency. Almost the only good news was the American intervention of April. Although the United States could provide immediate financial, economic, and naval help, the unprepared nation did not expect to influence the land warfare in France significantly until at least 1919.[1]

However, Germany found itself in a dangerous position. Its naval leaders had promised a victory at sea in 1917 while its army stood on the defensive along the western front, but this strategy went awry when the Allies managed by various measures to maintain their maritime communications. The key to antisubmarine operations was adoption of the convoy system. By the end of 1917, the Allies recognized that the submarine, while exceedingly troublesome, would not by itself force a decision. Although the French and British offensives failed, the German army suffered significant attrition. Many signs of exhaustion appeared in Austria-Hungary, Germany's main ally, raising grave questions about the durability of the central coalition. Germany had sought a quick victory in 1914 precisely because its army was more likely to win a short war than a long war. By the end of 1917, this presumption appeared increasingly plausible.[2]

Russia's collapse created a last chance for Germany. The High Command recognized that it could transfer many veteran divisions from the eastern front to France, producing temporary superiority in manpower over the Allies. Within

29

a short time, the arrival of American divisions would give the Allies a growing advantage. Although the German navy remained optimistic about its undersea operations, General Ludendorff had become skeptical. He felt "obliged to count on the new American formations beginning to arrive in the spring of 1918." He could not predict the size of the American reinforcement, but "the relative strengths would be more in our favor in the spring than in the late summer and autumn, unless we had by then gained a great victory." He did not doubt the proper course for Germany. "The condition of our allies and that of ourselves and that of the army all called for an attack that would bring about an early decision." The nominal commander-in-chief, Field Marshal Hindenburg, also recognized the American threat. "We had a new enemy, economically the most powerful in the world. . . . It was the United States of America and her advent was perilously near. Would she appear in time to snatch the victors' laurels from our brow?" His solution was the same as that of Ludendorff. "No longer threatened in the rear, we could turn to the great decision in the West and must now address ourselves to this passage at arms."[3]

During the first months of 1918, Ludendorff developed plans for a great German offensive on the western front that was given the code name *MICHAEL*. He recognized that he was taking a great gamble. On 13 February he disclosed to a conference at Hamburg that he was "more impressed than anyone by the magnitude of this military task." Victory would come only "if the organizers are relieved of everything that can possibly hamper them, the very last man is brought up for the decisive struggle, and everyone is animated by the conviction which comes from love of the Kaiser and Fatherland and confidence in the resolution of the military leaders."[4]

The western powers sensed that the German army would launch a great attack early in 1918; one reaction was to strengthen the coordination of the several national efforts. For some time, Prime Minister David Lloyd George of Great Britain had sought to arrange unity of command in France. He hoped to minimize the influence of Field Marshal Sir Douglas Haig. Sustained offensives in 1917 had produced sickening casualty lists without corresponding gains. The British leader also wanted to negate the influence of Haig's coadjutor, the chief of the Imperial General Staff, Gen. Sir William Robertson. The Italian rout at Caporetto gave Lloyd George an opportunity to gain the acceptance of an inter-Allied agency, the Supreme War Council, charged with coordinating coalition policy and strategy. Its official mission was "to watch over the general conduct of the war. It prepares recommendations for the decision of the

The German High Command in 1918: Field Marshal Paul von Hindenburg, Kaiser Wilhelm II, and First Quartermaster General Erich Ludendorff.

Governments, and keeps itself informed of their execution and reports thereon to the respective Governments." The Supreme War Council included the head of government and one other representative of each Allied power fighting on the western front. To provide expert military counsel, the Allies set up a group of Permanent Military Representatives.[5]

The Allies convened a session of the Supreme War Council in December 1917 to lay plans for improved cooperation, a direct reaction to the impending German offensive. The United States sent a delegation to Paris with Col. Edward M. House, the president's most intimate counsellor, at its head. House soon recommended that the United States endorse the Supreme War Council and that General Bliss, just completing his tour as chief of staff, become a Permanent Military Representative. True to his previous course, President Wilson refused to appoint a permanent political delegate but agreed to seat Bliss. "Please take the position," he informed House, "that we not only approve a continuance of the plan for a war council but insist on it." Opposed to arrangements that might compromise his political freedom of action, he was anxious to enhance the military efficiency of the western coalition.[6]

The Paris conference made some important decisions, of which the most significant was the creation of several additional inter-Allied organizations to coordinate various crucial efforts. Among these were the Allied Naval Council, the
Inter-Allied [Land] Transportation Council, the Allied Blockade Council, the
Allied Munitions Council, the Allied Food Council, and the Allied Council on
War Purchases and Finance. These organizations would have been helpful much
earlier in the war, but it took the approaching German offensive to generate
the political will required to bring them into existence. All made valuable contributions to the inter-Allied war effort during 1918.[7]

From the first General Bliss advocated unity of command on the western
front, although he recognized that "military jealousy and suspicion as to ultimate national aims" stood in the way. He deprecated inadequate inter-Allied
coordination, imputing the crisis in France not only to the Italian and Russian
collapses but to "the lack of military coordination, lack of unity of control
on the part of allied forces in the field." He participated actively in efforts of
the Permanent Military Representatives to create an "inter-Allied General
Reserve." This measure would enhance unity of command, one means of
preparing for the German attack. These ideas received support from the War
College Division of the General Staff. In October 1917 that body insisted that
"sole direction is obligatory in battle. . . . It is no less necessary on the general
conduct, military and political, of the war. . . . The longer the Allies put off
this unanimity of direction the more they run risks capable of compromising
the ultimate success." The War College Division believed that victory depended
on unity of command. "The multiplicity of fronts and of interest, the complications of operation [make] necessary an administrative body possessing more
extensive power than a military conference and above all a *permanent* body."[8]

General Pershing agreed with these views. He reported in January 1918 that
during a conference with Georges Clemenceau, the new French premier, and
General Robertson, he had "dwelt strongly upon the urgency of a complete
and harmonious military understanding among the allied armies on the western
front, especially as to plans of operation for the spring and summer." He was
doubtful that the Allies would decide to appoint a supreme commander or
generalissimo. "All the allies want concerted action, of course, but for the
present thorough understanding and close liaison between the high commands
appear to be the only solution."[9]

While serving with the House mission, General Bliss noted the growing
reliance of the Allies on the United States and the necessarily slow progress
of the American reinforcement. Writing to Mrs. Bliss, he noted: "It is pitiful
to see the undercurrent of feeling that the hopes of Europe have in the United

States, pitiful because it will be so long before we can really do anything, although the very crisis seems to be at hand." The status of the American divisions in France seemed to corroborate Bliss's doleful outlook. Only a few units had seen action. The 1st Division had gone into the line for training on 21 October in the Sommerviller sector east of Nancy. A German raid on 2 November caused eight casualties, and eight Americans were taken prisoner. The only other American contribution came during the battle of Cambrai (20 November–4 December 1917). Three regiments of engineers (the 11th, 12th, and 13th), supporting the British army, were drawn into the fighting. Haig characterized the latter action as "prompt and valuable assistance."[10]

At just this time Col. Fox Conner of Pershing's staff prepared a memorandum on how the AEF might respond to the Italian crisis. He declared positively: "No units of the A.E.F. are at present in proper condition to be employed in the line for other than training purposes." If a crisis forced use of the Americans, only the 1st Division could fight as a unit. Other troops would join the Allies in battalions. In other words, should the Allies encounter a great emergency, AEF units would fight under British and French flags. Conner doubted that such an emergency would arise. He proposed that the AEF maintain its "present program and resist any tendency toward the premature employment of our forces unless and until such employment is necessitated by a threatened collapse of France; a collapse appearing by actual events." For the moment, then, the threat of the German attack did not force changes in the American buildup.[11]

As Germany's intentions became more obvious, the Allies formulated their ideas about the 1918 campaign. On 18 November, General Petain presented his views to the French War Committee. He favored a waiting game, emphasizing organization of the front and positioning of reserves. Besides, he called for a supreme chief of the Allied forces to prepare plans and to control reserves. Near the end of December, he communicated his intentions to his subordinate commanders. "The Entente cannot recover superiority in manpower until the American army is capable of placing in line a certain number of large units." For the moment, "we must, under penalty of irremediable attrition, maintain a waiting attitude, with the idea firmly fixed in mind of resumings [*sic*] as soon as we can, the offensive which alone will bring us ultimate victory." The French chief of staff, General Foch, agreed that the Allies must prepare for the German offensive, but he wanted to seize the initiative at the earliest possible time. In a paper presented to the Supreme War Council on 1 January 1918, he proposed to plan powerful counterattacks. If the enemy should remain passive, he favored operations that would wear out the Germans and sustain the morale of the Allied troops. In either case, he wished "to develop these actions under the form of *a combined offensive with decisive objectives*, the moment the wearing-down process, or any other favourable circumstance arising in the general situation, offers the hope of success." On 24 January he reiterated this recommendation. "The best way to stop a powerful and sustained hostile offensive, an offensive of attrition and complete stubbornness, is to open an offensive of one's own." To support his argument, he cited the British attack on the Somme in 1916, which he believed had forced an end to the German attacks on Verdun. Like Petain, he favored inter-Allied unity of command on the western front.[12]

Seeking to constrain the fiery Foch, Petain opposed adventurism of any sort. On 8 January, he argued that "whatever our desire to resume the initiative . . . we must submit to what is patent and base our plans not upon abstract notions but upon realities." Again he noted that America "cannot make itself felt in the battle before 1919 and until then Franco-British forces will have to be husbanded with a prudence which leaves only the smallest possible part to chance." He saw "the battle of 1918 . . . as a defensive one on the Franco-British side, not through absolute choice of the command, but from necessity. Our lack of means is the cause. It is better to realize it now and to get organized accordingly." To Foch's proposal of an offensive he retorted: "If we engage them [superior enemy forces] in an offensive, we shall find ourselves stopped in the face of an enemy attack following the first."[13]

Meanwhile the Permanent Military Representatives of the Supreme War Council at Versailles drafted a Joint Note No. 12 entitled "1918 Campaign." The group saw no difficulties in protecting Great Britain from invasion. They assumed that appropriate measures would safeguard Italy. Finally, they believed that France would remain secure, if the French and British armies maintained their present strength, the American army arrived at the rate of not fewer than two divisions per month, the Allies addressed various logistical and supply problems, measures were taken to coordinate the defense, and the western front was deemed a unified theater. "The disposition of the reserves, the periodic rearrangement of the point of junction between the various Allied forces on the actual front, and all other arrangements should be dominated by this consideration [the idea of a unified theater]." The Permanent Military Representatives concluded that Germany could not force a decision in 1918, but they also decided that the Allies were in the same position because they lacked sufficient troops. An opportunity would come in 1919, "pending such change in the balance of forces as we hope to reach . . . by the steady influx of American troops, guns, aeroplanes, tanks, etc., and by the progressive exhaustion of the enemy's staying power." However, the Allies should not neglect opportunities to make decisive gains in secondary theaters during 1918.[14]

The buoyant Foch remained convinced that offensives might become feasible in 1918. In a statement to the Supreme War Council on 2 February, he concurred in the need for a defensive plan to cover the front from Nieuport to Venice. He argued that it "must be susceptible of being transformed, according to circumstances, into an offensive plan, partial or complete." The Allies should form a general reserve to support threatened areas of the front, but "these reserves must also be susceptible of being united" and employed in "a counteroffensive launched as a diversion to relieve one of the Allies from a concentrated assault directed against his lines." Earlier General Maxime Weygand, the French Permanent Military Representative, had informed Clemenceau that a general reserve by itself was not sufficient; it needed a chief. He proposed to confer tactical control of a general reserve on a general "designated for this purpose by the Supreme War Council," presumably Foch.[15]

The general reserve encountered insuperable resistance. Foch and Gen. Sir Henry Wilson, the British Permanent Military Representative, drew up a plan that envisioned the inclusion of thirty divisions in such a reserve. It would concentrate at various points behind the front, and components of this force would move to threatened locations on demand. Unfortunately for this sensible conception, both Haig and Petain opposed it, preferring to arrange mutual support themselves. Petain agreed to move the French Third Army of six divisions to the aid of the British Fifth Army, if called upon to do so. Lloyd George tried either to frighten or to cajole Haig into changing his mind. The British commander resisted. "I only had eight Divisions under my hand [as a reserve]; the position of these *may* vary from day to day, and only the C. in C. [commander-in-chief] in close touch with the situation could handle them. Versailles [headquarters of the Supreme War Council] was too distant and not in touch with the actual situation."[16]

After General Bliss arrived at Versailles, he quickly became a strong supporter of the general reserve. He informed Secretary Baker that the United States should take the lead in "bringing about absolute unity of control in this matter." Speaking to the Supreme War Council on 30 January, Bliss echoed Foch. "He was in full accord as to the necessity for a general defensive in 1918, coupled with preparations for making use of every opportunity afforded for a counteroffensive. In his opinion, the formation of a general reserve was an essential part of the general plan." In February, the Permanent Military Representatives issued Joint Note No. 14, on the "General Reserve," but Haig and Petain prevailed, and the arrangement never came to fruition. The Supreme War Council quietly abandoned the general reserve during its meeting of 14–15 March 1918. It remained to be seen whether the agreement between the French and British commanders-in-chief would suffice during the German offensive.[17]

Awareness of the approaching German attack had an especially untoward consequence from General Pershing's point of view; it revived proposals for amalgamation of American troops into European formations. When General Bliss visited Paris, he and Colonel House soon heard of the Allies' need for American troops. General Petain wished to place American divisions in quiet sectors, "relieving the French troops now there and making the latter available for an offensive elsewhere." The Americans were urged to ship two divisions per month with required service-of-the-rear troops until May 1918, when the number should increase to three divisions per month. "This would make thirty divisions [of 27,000 men], equivalent to seventy-three French divisions of 11,000 each."[18]

Pershing was quick to inform the House mission of his views. Writing to Bliss, he predicted a German offensive. "Under these adverse conditions it is possible that the Allies might hold until the American troops are strong enough to turn the balance, but it will be readily seen that the situation is liable to become grave and dangerous." He urged an American effort designed to help end the war in 1918 because conditions might become even worse in 1919. "The man-power of France and Great Britain will decrease rapidly after the beginning of next year's campaign, and the longer the war continues the greater will the demands on America become." Of greatest importance was the need to devote both American and Allied shipping to the transport of the American army.[19]

Early in December, Pershing cabled his specific recommendations to the War Department, having cleared them with Bliss, Robertson, and Foch. Germany disposed of 250 to 260 divisions to 169 of the Allies, some of the latter bound for Italy. Ludendorff could attack with a 60 percent advantage in manpower, given the Russian collapse and the Italian defeat. He asked for twenty-four divisions besides service-of-the-rear troops, insisting again on the need to curtail commercial use of shipping so that it could be used to transport troops. "The Allies are very weak and we must come to their relief this year, 1918. The year after may be too late. It is very doubtful they can hold on until 1919 unless we give them a lot of support this year." Pershing did not intend to begin decisive American operations prematurely, but he recognized the value of relieving pressure on the British and French armies by taking over quiet sectors.[20]

On 4 December, Bliss supported Pershing in an anxious cable to the War Department. "All military authorities here . . . have represented with growing urgency the grave possibilities of the military situation early in 1918." The United States must act forcefully. "All plans for the development of an independent program by the United States [must] be subordinate to the idea of the strongest possible joint effort." This latter comment might have reflected renewed pressure for amalgamation. Two days earlier, Bliss had received a pencilled note from General Robertson, the chief of Britain's Imperial General Staff. He proposed to insert American troops into the line by companies or perhaps battalions. They could be withdrawn after training and combined into divisions for use later as part of an independent American army. Robertson concluded that "the chief difficulty is American national sentiment, which we quite understand. On the other hand the system suggested is clearly one which would the most rapidly afford much needed help during, perhaps, the most critical period of the war."[21]

Not long afterward, Petain conveyed similar views on amalgamation to his liaison officer at Pershing's headquarters. The American troops in France might have to fight before completing their training. He ordered his representative "to accustom the American High Command to the idea that American regiments, indeed even American battalions, could well be called upon to serve as separate units, in the cadre of a large French unit under the orders of the French command." Foch later justified this view as a consequence of the Russian defeat and the slow arrival of American divisions. The manpower crisis dictated "the employment of American troops one month after their arrival in France, that is to say, the moment their elementary instruction was finished. The idea was to place them by regiment or even by battalion in British or French divisions."[22]

When the French desire became known to Pershing's staff, it was dismissed as unacceptable, but the episode underscored the need to put American troops by divisions into the line temporarily for training with Allied formations. This measure would strengthen French morale. Fox Conner summarized Pershing's views. He "recognized the justness of the contention of the Allies that the early appearance of our troops on the line was necessary for reasons of morale." Still, "America could not humble herself as no other nation in history had done by consenting to draft American manhood under a foreign flag." Although a German attack appeared probable early in 1918, "only the most untoward combination of circumstances could give the enemy a decisive victory, provided the Allies held firm and secured unity of action." An emergency might arise that required amalgamation, but for the moment nothing justified "either the curtailing of the instruction of our troops or the relinquishment of our plans for our own army under our own flag." Conner concluded: "The Allied cause itself demanded that we should not sacrifice the identity of our troops but that the best use be made of those forces by training and employing them in conformity with our national characteristics." The AEF would compromise only to the extent of allowing some divisions to relieve Allied units in quiet sectors as part of their training.[23]

Pershing admitted "much embarrassment" at the beginning of 1918 because the United States had not yet made a significant contribution on the western front. He placed the blame on the War Department. "Up to this time, we had been handicapped in our efforts by lack of aggressive direction of affairs at home. Whether this was due to inefficiency or failure to appreciate the urgency of the situation, the War Department General Staff, as the superior coordinating agency, must take the greater part of the blame." In these terms, Pershing shifted the responsibility for error to others, as was his wont. There was some justice in his claim, but he might have noted the extraordinary achievements of 1917 at home despite all the difficulties. He also might have observed that in any event the commitment to an independent army necessarily delayed the AEF's entry into combat.[24]

Late in December 1917, both the French and the British governments attempted to bypass Pershing by sending appeals for amalgamation directly to President Wilson. On 18 December, Baker informed Pershing of these initiatives. He also observed: "We do not desire loss of identity of our forces but regard that as secondary to the meeting of any critical situation by the most helpful use possible of the troops at your command." Thus Washington gave Pershing the power to authorize amalgamation but in the next breath informed him that "The President . . . wishes you to have full authority to use the troops at your command as you deem wise in consultation with the French and British commanders in chief." He could "act with entire freedom in making the best disposition and use of your forces possible to accomplish the main purposes in view." Soon after, when Pershing heard from the War Department about an effort by Clemenceau to urge amalgamation in Washington, he wrote firmly to the French premier. "May I not suggest to you . . . the inexpediency of communicating such matters to Washington by cable? These questions must all be settled here, eventually, on their merits, through friendly conference between General Petain and myself, and cables of this sort are very likely, I fear, to convey the impression of serious disagreement between us when such is not the case." Clemenceau proved unrepentant, informing Pershing that he would not disavow his view. "I shall exercise all the patience of which I am capable in awaiting the good news that the American commander and the French commander have finally agreed on a question which may be vital to the outcome of the war."[25]

The Anglo-French effort to force amalgamation in December 1917 led Pershing to formulate his mature rationale for an independent army. In a cable sent to Bliss on New Year's Day 1918, he summarized his views cogently. "First, troops would lose their national identity; second, they probably could not be released for service with us without disrupting the Allied divisions to which assigned, especially if engaged in active service; third, the methods of training and instruction in both Allied armies are very different from our own which would produce some confusion at the start and also when troops return for service with us." A few weeks later, Pershing mentioned another critical concern. After restating his opinion that the American army must eventually play an important role and therefore should not use itself up in a temporary emergency, he noted: "When the war ends, our position will be stronger if our army acting as such shall have played a distinct and definite part." In his final report prepared after the war, Pershing repeated this view. "Any sort of permanent amalgamation would irrevocably commit America's fortunes to the hands of the Allies."[26]

Pershing remained fully in control of American troops, an arrangement that caused increasing friction between him and European leaders. Late in December 1917, the French president, Raymond Poincare, conveyed to President Wilson a thinly veiled criticism of the American field commander for his unwillingness to accept amalgamation. Thus began overt European efforts to challenge Pershing's authority.[27]

Although the Allies failed to obtain American consent to amalgamation, their pleas produced a commitment in Washington to ship troops at an increased rate. The Americans needed tonnage, and the Allies needed troops. The British board of trade developed a scheme for transferring two hundred thousand tons of shipping from the supply of foodstuffs to the transport of American troops. Pershing must agree to incorporate these troops "by companies or battalions into the British army until they are sufficiently trained to be collected into larger units." General Robertson then proposed that the Americans ship 150 battalions without auxiliary support to serve with British divisions for a minimum of four or five months. This "150-battalion proposal" proved unacceptable because it did not provide for the transport of entire divisions, but Pershing did not want to lose the opportunity to obtain shipping. Late in January, he agreed to ship six complete American divisions in British bottoms. These men would serve temporarily with the British army while undergoing training, a period of about ten weeks. This "six-division program" was as far as Pershing would go in meeting European demands for amalgamation. He would permit American units to serve with Allied forces only briefly for training, and then only in extraordinary circumstances. He informed his fellow Allied commanders that "Amalgamation of American and Allied troops for battle could not take place except in case of absolute necessity." To Baker he conveyed his policy succinctly: "We must insist on our men being returned when called for, or at least when we get over the remainder of the organizations from which they may be taken."[28]

General Pershing hewed firmly to his stance against amalgamation during the anxious months of 1918 that preceded the expected German offensive. On 13 January he explained to Petain his desire to form an American corps in April or May. He intended to place it in the line at an appropriate location, perhaps north of Toul. General Bliss tactfully summarized the American view in a statement to the Supreme War Council on 31 January. "In order to expedite their training, some of the American troops would be attached as battalion or regimental units to the Allied forces for purposes of training." What if these European units then came under attack? The American troops would "do their duty and take part in any engagements in which they might find themselves involved, if judged capable to do so." When training was completed, the troops would be combined in "purely American divisions under their own commanders." Bliss at first was inclined to support the 150-battalion proposal, but he immediately altered his position when Pershing explained his objections to it. Despite occasional differences of opinion, Bliss regularly supported the commander of the AEF, a demonstration of loyalty that elicited fulsome praise. Pershing informed Baker that Bliss was "a most excellent choice" as a Permanent Military Representative. His relations with the former chief of staff were "most harmonious" and would remain so. "He is an able man, as square as a die, and loyal to the core. I do not think you could have found anyone to fill the place with greater credit to us all."[29]

This outcome meant that the Allies would cause difficulty, should they attempt to overrule Pershing by maneuvering at the Supreme War Council, having failed to arrange amalgamation by other means. However, on 30 January Field Marshal Haig began such an attempt with the observation that it would take more than a year for American divisions to prepare for front-line service. "He consequently did not consider the Allies could expect the American force, as a force, to be of effective support this year." Petain immediately agreed. He asserted that the AEF, if it retained its autonomy, "would be of no use to the Allies in 1918, except, perhaps along some quiet section of the front." Then he again urged amalgamation. "The entry of American troops by battalions or regiments into French and British divisions, not only for training, but also for fighting, was much the greatest assistance that the United States could give the Allies, and would furnish the solution to the crisis with regard to effectives." Amalgamation would be temporary. "The American army would get back its units afterwards and become fully autonomous." On 31 January, General Bliss gave the American reply, echoing Pershing's views. A crisis might force temporary amalgamation of troops then serving with Allied forces. He wanted it understood that "this training of American troops with British and French divisions, whether behind the lines or in actual combat on the line, is only a stepping stone in the training of the American forces, and that whenever it is proper and practicable to do so these units will be formed into American divisions under their own officers. Such a thing as permanent amalgamation of our units with British and French units would be intolerable to American sentiment."[30]

Nothing availed the Entente leadership; the United States stubbornly refused to consider amalgamation on any other than temporary terms to train or to cope with catastrophic emergencies. General Bliss put his finger on the strength of the American bargaining position when he wrote to Baker: "I doubt if anyone not present at the recent meetings of the Supreme War Council realizes the anxiety and fear that pervades the minds of political and military men here. . . . They openly state that their hope is in the man-power of the United States."[31]

The impending crisis led to a reaffirmation of the decision to concentrate all available strength in France. During the session of the Supreme War Council, Clemenceau strenuously objected to a section of Joint Note No. 12, the plan for 1918, that dealt with campaigns in the east, insisting on concentrating all available forces in France to deal with Germany. He sought only to hold in France during 1918 "till the American assistance came in full force; after that America would win the war. All he asked was, hold out on the western front this year." Lloyd George made a spirited defense of the eastern initiatives, but he did not succeed in shaking the strong commitment to the western front. The threat of the German offensive precluded any such change.[32]

In November 1917, General Pershing, recognizing the likelihood of a German offensive, reiterated his support of concentration along the western front.

He first noted the adverse psychological effect of any change in strategic emphasis. Then he observed that the troops of the Allies had been so depleted that offensive operations were conceivable only with American contributions. "It seems clear to me that the war must be won on the Western front, and that the efforts of the allies should continue as now in progress, and that every possible energy that America can exert should be put forth there, whether the role is offensive or defensive."[33]

Thus matters stood as the Allies awaited a great German offensive in March 1918. The plight of the European associates strengthened the fundamental strategic premises that American leaders had defined in May 1917. They would center their efforts on the western front, deploying an independent army and striking a decisive blow in 1919. Meanwhile, American divisions would appear on the line, primarily in quiet sectors, for training in trench warfare until it became possible to form a separate American force in Lorraine. Dispositions of the few American divisions then available in France reflected this policy. The 1st Division relieved a French division in a quiet sector north of Toul on 19 January. The 26th Division entered the French line northwest of Soissons early in February, while the 42d Division did the same thing west of Luneville later that month. On 18 March, the 2d Division took over a portion of the French lines southeast of Verdun. Other units soon became available; about 48,000 Americans arrived in January, another 49,000 in February, and 85,000 in March. This buildup heightened interest in the earliest possible creation of an autonomous American command. Maj. Gen. Hunter Liggett took an important step on 20 January, when he established the I Corps headquarters at Neufchateau.[34]

On the morning of 21 March, a sudden German attack hit the British Fifth and Third Armies on the Somme River. Soon it became evident that the Germans had gained a striking victory. They advanced many miles, the first force to do so on the western front since the earliest days of the war. The long-anticipated offensive had begun, and it immediately created a great emergency for both the British and French armies. During the crisis of 1918 two great captains joined in mortal combat, Erich Ludendorff for the Central Powers and Ferdinand Foch for the Allied and Associated Powers. This contest greatly influenced the subsequent actions of American troops in France.

3

THE GREAT GERMAN OFFENSIVE, PART I: 21 MARCH–31 MAY 1918

General Ludendorff quickly recognized both the danger and the opportunity that awaited him in 1918. The victory in Russia would allow him to create a German superiority on the western front of perhaps twenty to twenty-five divisions in the early spring, but this small advantage would disappear shortly. American troops would soon arrive in large numbers. Aware of the war weariness that afflicted the lesser Central Powers but unwilling to countenance peace overtures, he made his decision. "An offensive was necessary to keep our allies at our side and if possible to win outright before the American masses arrived. . . . The offensive was intended to make our enemies willing to make peace." Ludendorff's operations officer, Lt. Col. Georg Wetzell, expressed the political motive of the offensive more clearly in a postwar memorandum: "A thoroughgoing success on the western front was necessary in order to arrive at a [favorable] conclusion," one that would allow Germany to impose its most demanding war aims. "Only a far-reaching military success which would make it appear to the Entente powers that, even with the help of America, the continuation of the war offered no further prospects of success, would provide the possibility . . . of rendering our embittered opponents really ready to make peace. This was the political aim of the Supreme Command in 1918."[1]

Fearful of unwonted claims on German manpower in 1918, Ludendorff insisted on various political arrangements in the east designed to preserve his forces long enough to secure victory in the west. The Carthaginian peace of Brest-Litovsk was extorted from the revolutionary government of Russia, and Rumania was also forced to settle. German troops occupied the Ukraine to gain control of its wheat. After the war, Ludendorff claimed to have considered a negotiated peace, perhaps to include the return of Alsace-Lorraine to France, surrender of some portions of the province of Posen, and payment of an indemnity. He had found out that the terms of the enemy "were so severe that

43

only a defeated Germany could have acceded to them." Having gambled unsuccessfully on the submarine offensive in 1917, Germany threw the dice again
in 1918, this time on the western front, the theater of decision.[2]

Planning for the offensive began on 11 November 1917 at Mons, where Ludendorff consulted the chiefs of staff of his leading commanders—Rupprecht, crown
prince of Bavaria, and Wilhelm, crown prince of Prussia and of Germany.
Rupprecht advocated an attack on his front in Flanders between Ypres and
Lens, and Wilhelm proposed to move again in the region of Verdun. A third
possibility was an assault on the British forces entrenched between Arras and
St. Quentin. At length Ludendorff rejected the Flanders proposal because the
ground was difficult in the north and the enemy had concentrated strong forces
there. He also eliminated the Verdun proposal because it would lead the German army into hilly country and did not offer a decisive objective.

On 27 January 1918, Ludendorff decided to move in the center. There "the
attack would strike the enemy's weakest point, the ground offered no difficulties, and it was feasible at all seasons." He gave primacy to tactics in the belief
that it was foolish to move against a decisive objective "unless tactical success
is possible," a lesson he'd learned from observation of the futile Allied offensives. He had a goal in mind: a thrust near the junction of Haig's and Petain's
forces between Arras and St. Quentin toward the coast might separate most
of the British army from the French, forcing it into a small area on the channel coast. Ludendorff chose the line of least resistance in search of opportunities
to impose a decision. The isolation and defeat of the British Expeditionary
Force (BEF) would leave the French army that protected Paris with no alternative except capitulation. Foch later described Ludendorff's intentions. "By
aiming a well prepared and vigorously executed blow in the direction of Amiens,
it might be possible to separate these [British and French] armies; then, by
exploiting the initial success and widening the breach the British would be
thrown back on the sea, the French on Paris; the two principal adversaries
would thus be put out of action and the coalition broken before the American
Army could effectively intervene."[3]

Next Ludendorff designated the forces to conduct the attack. Crown Prince
Rupprecht would retain the Seventeenth and Second Armies, but the Eighteenth Army, also selected to participate, was transferred to the German crown
prince's group of armies. According to Ludendorff, this division of front-line
control was ordered with a specific purpose in mind. "I meant to exercise a
far-reaching influence on the course of the battle. That was difficult if it was

to be conducted by one [army] group only; every intervention was only too apt to become interference from above." By this device, the High Command could exercise operational control over the great offensive, wherever it might take the German army. Ludendorff moved his headquarters from Kreuznach to Spa but set up his operations branch at Avesnes. This move allowed him to travel quickly by automobile to all sectors of the front. "I intended to see a great deal for myself, and to send my staff-officers to the scenes of important events, in order to obtain impressions at first hand." In consultations with the staffs of the attacking forces, he emphasized cooperation both within and between the two army groups to ensure that critical missions were planned properly, such as cutting off the Cambrai salient and sustaining liaison.[4]

The attack, which was given the code name ST. MICHAEL," was to develop on a front of forty-three miles on the line Arras–St. Quentin–La Fere. The three German armies (Seventeenth on the right, Second in the center, and Eighteenth on the left) disposed of seventy-one divisions and almost 6,500 guns and howitzers. Crown Prince Rupprecht's group of armies on the right, including the Seventeenth and Second Armies, would make the principal attack north of the Somme River. After making a breakthrough, Rupprecht would wheel to the northwest and force the BEF to the coast. The German crown prince's Eighteenth Army was to cover Rupprecht's left flank. Ludendorff's orders for the initial attack on 21 March emphasized these missions: "The first great tactical objective of the Crown Prince Rupprecht's Army Group is to cut off the English in the Cambrai salient and reach the line Croisilles–Bapaume–Peronne. If the attack of the right wing (17th Army) proceeds favourably this army is to press on beyond Croisilles. . . . The German Crown Prince's Army Group will first gain the line of the Somme south of the Omignon stream [flowing into the Somme south of Peronne] and the Crozat Canal [west of La Fere]. By pushing on rapidly the 18th Army . . . is to secure the crossings of the Somme and the Canal."[5]

Ludendorff's plan paid considerable attention to other sectors of the western front, emphasizing deception, surprise, and preparation for possible further attacks. Rupprecht dealt with the ground between Ypres and Lens in Flanders, the German crown prince with the terrain between Reims and the Argonne Forest in Champagne, Gen. Max von Gallwitz with the Verdun area, and Albrecht, duke of Wurttemberg, with points farther south in Lorraine and beyond. These enterprises were intended to disguise the point of attack and to ensure that the German army could take immediate advantage of opportunities that might arise during the offensive. The heavy concentration of troops for the main attack on the Somme was deceptive, because communications in this region allowed the Germans to transfer troops quickly to several possible locations. One authority aptly summarizes the consequence for Haig and Petain: "So uncertain did these advantages make the place of attack that now the British commander, now the French, was convinced that he must bear the brunt of the attack."[4]

The final aspect of Ludendorff's preparation for the great offensive was the development of innovative minor tactics. Heavy emphasis was given to surprise and to close cooperation between infantry and artillery. Troops were to move at night and conceal themselves during the day, occupying attack positions only at the last moment. The artillery preparation was to be kept short but violent, emphasizing gas shells. Attacking infantry would depart from lines about two or three hundred yards from those of the enemy. The so-called storm troops would move rapidly behind rolling barrages, receiving extensive support from cannons, trench mortars, and machine guns. Taking advantage of terrain features and often attacking the enemy flanks, they were to locate weak points and infiltrate through them, leaving strong points to following troops who mopped up. Command responsibility was very much decentralized; small-unit leaders were encouraged to exercise initiative.[7]

Addressing the kaiser as his forces prepared to attack, Ludendorff summarized the meaning of the attack. He was, he said, "more than anyone impressed by the immensity of the operation." It was different from any that had gone before, such as those in Italy and Poland. "It will be an immense struggle that will begin at one point, continue at another, and take a long time." Finally he predicted success. "It is difficult, but it will be victorious." Ludendorff took great risks. Corelli Barnett aptly characterizes the decision. "*Michael* was then a desperate and final gamble. It was an attempt by purely military means to decide on the battlefield a war involving total national economic, military, social and technical power, a war that Germany was losing."[8]

On 21 March 1918, the commander of the British Fifth Army, Gen. Hubert Gough, held responsibility for 42 miles of the western front, about a third of the entire British line. He had only fourteen infantry divisions and three cavalry divisions, fewer than a fourth of the available British troops, to resist thirty-three German assault divisions of the Eighteenth and Second Armies. The British Third Army of fourteen divisions, which was lined up on a front of 28 miles, faced the German Seventeenth Army, an organization of fourteen divisions charged with the main German effort. Haig had eight divisions in reserve. His total manpower numbered 1,097,906 troops, about 10 percent

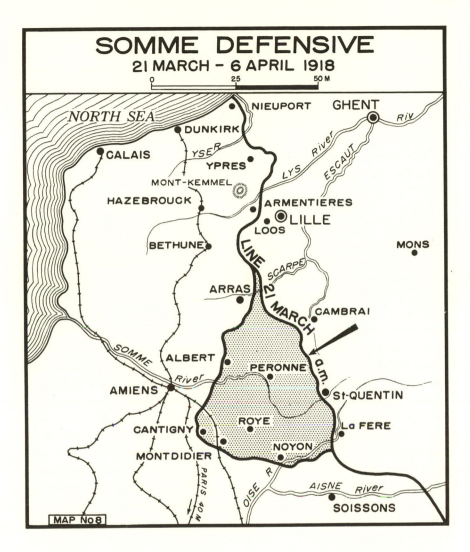

SOMME DEFENSIVE
21 MARCH – 6 APRIL 1918

0   25   50 M

NORTH SEA

NIEUPORT GHENT

DUNKIRK

CALAIS   YSER

YPRES

MONT-KEMMEL

HAZEBROUCK   ARMENTIERES

LILLE

LOOS

BETHUNE

LINE   SCARPE

ARRAS   21 MARCH   CAMBRAI

a.m.

SOMME   ALBERT   PERONNE

River   St-QUENTIN

AMIENS

CANTIGNY   ROYE   La FERE

MONTDIDIER   NOYON

PARIS 40 M   OISE R.

AISNE River

SOISSONS

MONS

LYS River

ESCAUT

RIV

MAP No 8

less than in January 1917. The Fifth Army had recently taken over several miles of front on its right flank from the French and was less prepared to defend this area than others. Haig had eight divisions in reserve. Gough's divisions covered an average front of 6,750 yards, whereas Gen. Julian Byng's Third Army to the left allotted an average of 4,700 yards to a division. Haig accepted a risk in the Fifth Army area, concentrating his troops in Flanders to protect communications to the home islands. Perhaps he also did so in the hope of resuming the failed offensive at Passchendaele.[9]

At 0440 on 21 March 1918 the German artillery began a violent artillery bombardment with over six thousand guns and a four-day supply of nine million shells, the start of a *Kaiserschlacht* (emperor battle to end the war) against the British Fifth and Third Armies. The subsequent infantry attack soon attained unprecedented success. The German force included two army groups of seventy-one divisions, moving on a front of 49 miles between Arras and La Fere. Ludendorff gained complete surprise despite general awareness that an attack was imminent. The artillery barrage orchestrated by the ingenious Col. Georg Bruchmueller, a heavy ground fog, and the skillful infiltration of the attacking divisions resulted in a first day's advance at its deepest point of 4.5 miles, an unprecedented achievement. Nineteen of the twenty-one British divisions of the Fifth and Third Armies were exhausted veterans of the failed offensive at Passchendaele in 1917. The Germans overran almost 100 square miles of Allied territory. In succeeding days the rout continued, penetrating 40 miles and covering 1,200 square miles. The British lost over 160,000 men, including 90,000 prisoners who would not fight again, and the French endured over 70,000 casualties. German losses included 160,000 casualties and over 70,000 prisoners. During the battle, Haig relieved Gough, and on 28 March Gen. Rawlinson took his place; the devastated Fifth Army became the British Fourth Army.[10]

Although Ludendorff's offensive proved successful, it developed in an unexpected way. The Eighteenth Army in the German crown prince's group of armies was supposed to support the northern attack of Rupprecht's Seventeenth and Second Armies toward Arras. However, General von Hutier's troops penetrated so deeply in the valley of the Oise River that they posed a threat to the critical communications center of Amiens. General Maurice, a shrewd observer, explained the reasons for the German success. "The Oise line had always been regarded as a quiet sector. In order to economise troops Gough had decided to hold this, apparently the least vulnerable part of his front, with a series of posts, and not to have a continuous line of defense. The dry weather, however, enabled the Germans to cross the marshes without difficulty, the fog allowed them to penetrate between the posts, often unobserved. The result of this was that the enemy were able to get behind our defenses further north and cut off the defenders." Ludendorff must now decide whether to continue his northern initiative or to accept the opportunity that the Eighteenth Army's tactical success had presented to him. On 23 March, he ordered von Hutier to thrust toward Amiens and thus divide the British and French forces. He remained interested in the northern attack to the sea on the line Peronne–Albert–Abbeville. On the same day, the kaiser in great glee awarded Hindenburg the Iron Cross with Golden Rays, last conferred on Bluecher after Waterloo.[11]

On 24 March, Haig learned that General Petain would not fully honor the arrangement to send French divisions if the Germans should attack his front. Petain had provided seven divisions immediately. The French Third Army (Humbert) and the six divisions of the French First Army (Debeney) were on the way, but he would send no more. Haig viewed this development as meaning that keeping "in touch with the British Army is no longer the basic principle of French strategy. . . . Briefly, everything depends on whether the French can and will support us *at once* with 20 divisions of good quality, north of the Somme." Later Foch described the response of Haig and Petain to the German attack on the junction of the French and British armies. It caused each commander to emphasize "preserving and maintaining his army; he therefore oriented it towards its bases, the direction best calculated to protect his own nation's interests." The result was two battles, the British fighting to safeguard the channel ports and the French seeking to protect Paris. The German kaiser, full of the initial success, declared on 26 March that if an English delegation came to sue for peace, "it must kneel before the German standard for it was a question here of a victory of the monarchy over democracy."[12]

When Petain refused to send more French troops to the British front, Haig immediately asked his government to arrange the appointment of Foch as a generalissimo. He sought by this device to obtain reinforcements from the French army. In a meeting at Doullens on 26 March, Foch received as his charge "the co-ordination of the action of the Allied Armies on the Western Front." To gain this end, he would deal with the national commanders-in-chief. Haig noted that "it was essential to success that Foch should control Petain. . . . Foch seemed sound and sensible, but Petain had a terrible look. He had the appearance of a commander who was in a funk." Haig was probably correct. Before the meeting began, Petain had said to Clemenceau: "The Germans will beat the British in the open field, after which they will beat us as well." Clemenceau, no great admirer of the new generalissimo, said to him after the conference: "Well, you have had your own way," to which Foch replied: "A nice mess! You give me a lost battle, and tell me to win it."[13]

Foch soon asked for strengthened authority so that he could exercise effective command. His explained his objection to the Doullens formula starkly in his memoirs. "The Doullens arrangement stated that he was charged with coordinating the action of the Allied armies on the western front. This implied that if there were no action there was nothing to coordinate. . . . Consequently something more was now wanted . . . the power to imply an idea of action to the Commanders-in-Chief, and to have this action carried out." Accordingly the Allied leaders, meeting at Beauvais on 3 April, gave him "all

The inter-Allied chain of command in 1918: Gen. Ferdinand Foch (top left), Field Marshal Sir Douglas Haig (top right), Gen. John J. Pershing (bottom left), and Gen. Philippe Petain (bottom right).

the powers necessary for . . . effective realization [of coordination]." He would exercise "the strategic direction of military operations." The national commanders would "exercise . . . tactical direction of the armies" and would enjoy a right of appeal to their governments, if they thought themselves endangered by instructions from Foch. On 2 May Foch's authority was extended to the Italian front, completing his command, which reached from the North Sea to the Adriatic Sea.[14]

Neither Pershing nor Bliss participated in the Doullens conference, but both were present at Beauvais, and they placed the AEF under Foch's authority. From the first, the Americans had recognized the necessity of a unified command. During the conference Pershing spoke strongly for a "single commander" to direct "all the allied armies on the western front. I stated that we had never had co-operation and would never have until we have a commander-in-chief; that no matter who the commanders-in-chief of the different armies might be, we would never have co-operation unless we have one commander-in-chief for all the allied armies on this front; that it is absolutely essential to the success of the allied cause." Bliss was no less forceful, even opposing the right of the national commanders to appeal to their governments.[15]

Meanwhile the battle continued, the German command sensing an opportunity to seize Amiens, a vital communications center. Hindenburg believed that the neutralization of Amiens would divide the British and French armies. "Tactical breakthrough would be converted into a strategical wedge, with England on one side and France on the other. It was possible that the strategic and political interests of the two countries might drift apart. . . . We will call these interests by the names of Calais and Paris. So forward against Amiens!" Ludendorff could not resist the opportunity to move against Amiens, but he did not want to give up the more northerly thrust. Accordingly, on 25 March he ordered attacks for the 28th on both sides of Arras, which were code-named MARS.[16]

This diversion from von Hutier's promising operations created an opportunity that Foch exploited immediately. On 26 March, he decided that the French and British armies must remain close to each other. The forces in position, including the shattered British Fifth Army, had to stay in place. French reinforcements would first support the British and later "constitute a mass of manoeuvre for employment under conditions to be fixed later on." Foch sought to avoid a British battle to protect the channel ports and a separate French battle to cover Paris. Instead "we would fight an Anglo-French battle to cover Amiens, the connecting link between the two armies."[17]

At length the Anglo-French defense stiffened; Ludendorff failed to gain either Arras or Amiens. On 28 March, the Germans made a mighty effort to seize

Arras, attacking on both sides of the Scarpe River, but the British lines held. General Maurice notes that the German failure to capture Vimy Ridge on this date was of signal significance. "The Germans had gained a portion only of our outpost positions, and our battle positions had everywhere resisted their assaults. This time there was no fog to help the enemy, and Haig's system of defense was completely successful. It is not too much to say that this costly repulse doomed Ludendorff's campaign to failure." Meanwhile French reinforcements helped stop the enemy 12 miles short of Amiens. On 29 March Haig wrote: "I think Foch has brought great energy to bear on the present situation, and has, instead of permitting French troops *to retire* S.W. from Amiens, insisted on some of them relieving our tired troops and covering Amiens at all costs. He and I are quite in agreement as to the general plan of operations."[18]

Attacks against Amiens on 4–5 April also were repulsed, and the offensive gradually burned itself out. The British casualties numbered 163,493 and the French about 77,000. As was so often true of major operations, the German casualties appear to have been about the same.[19]

An American authority notes that the timely insertion of French reserves and Ludendorff's mistakes were not the only reasons the Germans were denied critical objectives. Also of great importance was "the exhaustion of German soldiers and the failure of the German supply arrangements to keep pace with the rapid advance of the troops." Ludendorff in effect acknowledged his logistical problems in a message to his major subordinate commanders on 1 April. "The attack has lost its initial momentum. We must improve our rearward communications behind the attack front in order to supply the armies with ammunition." Above all, Ludendorff wished to avoid undue losses. "We must not get drawn into a battle of exhaustion. This would accord neither with the strategical nor tactical situation." He promised further offensives, but again a defending army had denied an attacking army a breakthrough. Hindenburg offered a parallel interpretation, noting Foch's successful defense of Amiens. "The French appeared, and with their massed attacks and skillful artillery saved the situation for their Allies and themselves. . . . With us human nature was urgently voicing its claims. We had to take breath. The infantry needed rest and the artillery ammunition."[20]

Foch later summarized the result of the great German attack. "The fact of vital importance was that the liaison between the two armies in the region of Hangard had been firmly maintained. . . . In [the] face of the increased strength represented by the Allies, their [the German] attacks became more and more difficult and costly, and they finally found themselves forced to stop them without having been able to achieve the strategic results aimed at." Gen. Max von Hoffmann wrote that the day Ludendorff ordered a halt to the attacks on Amiens, it was the "bounden duty [of the German Supreme Command] to tell the government that the time had come to begin peace negotiations and that there was no prospect of ending the war on the western front with a decisive victory." After that the German effort declined. Corelli Barnett writes: "The offensives that followed were always weaker than *Michael*, temporarily and locally dangerous, but never producing, as had *Michael*, a general crisis." The German historian Gerhard Ritter, who participated in the attack as an officer in the Eighteenth Army, noted the disastrous effect of the German reverse on his troops. "Once again war's end had receded into the distant future, once again hecatombs had done no more than haplessly lengthen the front. . . . Could what had not been achieved in the first great blow, struck with every resource, full surprise, and tremendous artillery barrages, now be won with far weaker forces, consisting largely of decimated and exhausted divisions?"[21]

The AEF did not join the battle. By 21 March, about 287,000 Americans had reached France, but only three divisions were in the line, none of them near the battle zone. Only one regiment, the 6th Engineers, a part of the 3d Division, entered combat. While engaged in constructing railroads west of Peronne, it was absorbed into a makeshift British force, taking part in the defensive operations that saved Amiens. Pershing proved cooperative in assigning available American divisions to quiet sectors, relieving veteran French divisions for combat, but he remained fixed in his determination to avoid concessions that would interfere materially with the formation of an independent army. Conferring with Petain on 25 March about his divisions, he emphasized his desire to form an American corps. In his diary he noted that the French general supported this measure, but "each of us agreed that it is not now the time to form this corps."[22]

Despite Pershing's desires, the emergency forced the Allies again to urge temporary amalgamation. On 27 March, the day after the Doullens conference, the Military Representatives at Versailles, including General Bliss, issued Joint Note No. 18. It stated: "It is highly desirable that the American Government should assist the Allied Armies as soon as possible by permitting in principle the temporary service of American units in Allied Army corps and divisions." These troops would not come from divisions then serving with the French. Any units temporarily assigned to Allied organizations "must eventually be returned to the American Army." The Military Representatives proposed that for the moment the United States ship only infantry and machine gun troops. The Allies interpreted this recommendation as meaning that the United States would provide 120,000 infantrymen and machine gunners per month for the next four months, a total of 480,000 troops. Haig, noting this development, commented wryly: "I hope the Yankees will not disappoint us in this. They have seldom done anything yet which they have promised." Pershing opposed this measure, but Bliss remained firmly in support. Secretary Baker, making his first visit to Europe, approved Joint Note No. 18, but on 28 March he produced an interpretation of its meaning that reflected Pershing's wishes. The commander-in-chief retained the power to control the assignment of troops serving temporarily with other armies, and Baker reiterated his general's cardinal premise. It was "the determination of this Government to have its various military forces collected, as speedily as their training and the military situation permits, into an independent American Army, acting in concert with the armies of Great Britain and France. . . . arrangements made by him for their temporary training and service will be made with that end in view." President Wilson quickly approved this statement.[23]

General Bliss soon explained to Secretary Baker his views on the use of American troops, which differed measurably from those of Pershing. He insisted that he did not "propose to make the United States a recruiting ground to fill up the ranks of the British and French armies." What he had in mind was to put divisions into the Allied armies immediately "and then form our Divisions into American Corps and American Armies serving with the British and French as the case may be, but without an independent system of supply and without an independent service-of-the-rear." Responding to the existing emergency in France, he concluded: "We will then get into the war far more quickly, far more efficiently, and with far less cost."[24]

Pershing doggedly opposed any such change of direction. He persisted in preparing a force that would eventually serve independently of the Allies with its own command, staff, and supporting services. Bliss's proposition, although appealing because it would put American troops into combat soon, ran counter to Pershing's intentions. The commander of the AEF did not interpret the emergency of March 1918 as requiring a fundamental change in his plans. On 6 April 1918, Col. Fox Conner produced a detailed memorandum for the AEF's chief of staff, General Harbord. It included a mature statement of American views on Anglo-French efforts to force amalgamation. The G-3 believed that Joint Note No. 18 in effect delivered "over 360,000 officers and soldiers to foreign commanders, down to include the regiment, but leaves us unable to evade ultimate responsibility." He then stated Pershing's central thesis. "The only hope of really winning the war lies in an American army. The formation of that army is a paramount consideration and any scheme which postpones the organization of our army, and which virtually eliminates the possibility of carrying on the training of our higher officers and staffs in conjunction with that of the troops, is fundamentally unsound." Priority shipment of combat troops would cripple the services of supply; amalgamation would commit the American reserve piecemeal, a grave operational error. Finally, he openly expressed the political consideration that underlay the AEF position. "America must have a voice in the peace councils if a peace satisfactory to her is to be formulated. She will have no such voice if her forces are used up by putting her battalions in French and British units." Pershing agreed with this analysis; he was prepared only to make some changes in the order of transporting American troops to Europe.[25]

To be sure, on 28 March Pershing went to Foch's headquarters and made a memorable gesture, offering all his troops for service in the crisis. "At this moment," he said, "there are no other questions but of fighting." He volunteered infantry, artillery, aviation, all that he had. "I have come to tell you that the American people will be proud to take part in the greatest battle of history." This statement aroused great enthusiasm, and it soon took its place in the lore of the army. Col. George Marshall, for instance, then serving with the 1st Division, wrote: "In this critical situation General Pershing rose to greatness. Surrendering the direct control of his troops, which he had so vigorously maintained in the face of repeated endeavors to prevent the formation of an American army, he released them to be scattered over four hundred miles of front. At the possible expense of the nation's prestige and even his own, he laid all his cards on the table and directed every move toward the salvage of the Allied wreck. In the midst of a profound depression he radiated determination and the will to win." Pershing's biographer, Donald Smythe, offers a less fulsome interpretation. "Practically speaking, Pershing's offer of March 28 had relatively little effect." The 1st Division moved to Picardy, but the battle ended before it entered the line. The established practice of placing American divisions in quiet sectors of the front to relieve veteran Allied divisions for combat duty continued much as before 21 March. Joint Note No. 18 had few consequences. It modified slightly the shipment of American troops in British transports as specified by the six-division plan approved in January. Combat troops would come first, but supporting echelons would soon follow.[26]

The end of the offensive on the Somme led Ludendorff almost immediately to order another attack, this one in Flanders on the line of the Lys River. He chose to undertake an early diversion in the north. Otherwise the French might strike at the southern face of the Amiens salient between Montdidier and Noyon before the Germans could organize a defense. Crown Prince Rupprecht's group of armies had already prepared an attack code-named ST. GEORGE; like that of 21 March, it was intended to divide the British and French armies. It would strike to the English channel at Gravelines. The Germans would then destroy the isolated British and Belgian forces to the north while holding off Anglo-French attacks from the south. The British line, 40 miles in length, was thinly held; fewer than two men were available per yard of front. After 21 March, Haig had weakened his defenses in Flanders to reinforce the Somme front. Gen. Herbert C. O. Plumer's Second British Army on the left or northern wing included thirteen divisions. Gen. Sir Henry Horne's First Army of sixteen divisions occupied the right or southern wing. This force faced the German Fourth Army of thirty-three divisions commanded by Gen. Sixt von Arnim on the right and the German Sixth Army of twenty-eight divisions commanded by Gen. Ferdinand Quast on the left.[27]

Hindenburg aptly described the German plan. "The fundamental idea . . . was that we should attack the great easterly bulge of the English northern wing on both sides of Armentieres, and by pressing forward in the general direction of Hazebrouck cause the whole line to collapse." Hazebrouck, like Amiens, was a critical center of communications. Ludendorff might have launched his initial attack on the Lys instead of on the Somme, but the area was impassable in March because of wet ground. Hindenburg observed later: "We thought we could not wait until . . . [April]. We had to keep the prospects of American intervention steadily before our eyes." The High Command correctly assumed that the attack on the Somme would force Haig to transfer some British troops southward, rendering the Lys sector vulnerable to a strong attack. Hindenburg concluded: "As soon as we saw that our attack to the west must come to a standstill, we decided to begin our operation on the Lys front." At the least, the move would retain the initiative and punish the British army further; at the most, it might develop into a breakthrough.[28]

The attack of 9 April, a scaled-down version of ST. GEORGE called GEORGETTE, gained the hoped-for surprise and produced remarkable early results. The German Sixth Army with seventeen divisions struck at a tired Portuguese division that held a lengthy stretch of front around Neuve Chapelle and smashed through it to a depth of 3 miles. This success thoroughly dislocated the defensive arrangements of the British First Army. The new German minor tactics succeeded as admirably on the Lys as on the Somme. On the second day of the battle, the German Fourth Army gained a success north of Armentieres

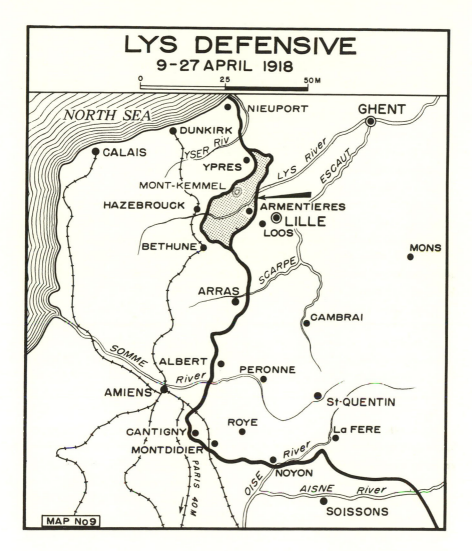

against Plumer's Second British Army. This victory led Ludendorff to throw in
reserves, again seeking to convert an operational success into a decisive breakthrough. Haig appealed to Foch for French troops, but the generalissimo was
slow to respond. He believed that the British could contain the attack, although
the defense on the Lys was in some ways more difficult than on the Somme,
because there was far less room for maneuver behind the front. Defense in depth
was impossible; the British troops had to fight in their front-line positions.[29]

By 12 April, the Germans had gained about 10 miles and were close to Hazebrouck, an advance that aroused the normally phlegmatic Haig to issue a dramatic appeal to the British army: "There is no course open to us but to fight it out. Every position must be held to the last man. There must be no retirement. With our backs to the wall and believing in the justice of our cause each one of us must fight to the end." Haig also decided to withdraw from the Flanders ridges captured at such great cost in 1917, shortening his lines and increasing the density of his defense.[30]

Fortunately for the British army, the circumstances that had denied Ludendorff a decision on the Somme exerted a similar influence on the Lys. By 16 April, Foch stated confidently: "The battle in Flanders is practically over. Haig will not need any more troops from me." Foch moved seven French divisions to the north in support of the British and the Belgians. He kept in mind always the possibility of using them to defend against an enemy thrust around Arras or to attack on the Somme. In this crisis as in that of 21 March, Foch responded as the planners of the ill-fated general reserve had intended. He maneuvered available reserves to support a threatened sector in depth. When the British defense stiffened, the German attack began to lose momentum. Ludendorff had expended valuable reserves in the earlier battle, and he was anxious to avoid another "battle of exhaustion." Besides, the logistical complications that had hampered him on the Somme also emerged in the north, and signs appeared of declining discipline. Ludendorff noted that "certain divisions had obviously failed to show any inclination to attack in the plain of the Lys." Others had lingered overlong near captured supplies, a failing that "impaired success and showed poor discipline. . . . The absence of our old peace-trained corps of officers was most severely felt. They had been the repository of the moral strength of the army." An American evaluation emphasized the enemy's failure to coordinate its operations effectively. "They had not established their supply and communications properly. German soldiers had stopped their advance to hunt for food. Certain divisions had shown a reluctance to attack on the plain of the Lys. German discipline and morale showed signs of weakening." The offensive ended on 27 April. Anglo-French casualties, around 110,000, were about equal to those of the Germans.[31]

Surely the German attack had been impressive, the British army having suffered another devastating defeat, but Ludendorff had gained none of his objectives. Trevor Wilson notes: "The Allies' rail communication remained intact; their ports continued inviolate; and no great bodies of British or Belgian troops had been isolated and overwhelmed." However, the Germans had gained positions that threatened British supply lines, especially Kemmel Hill. Control of this elevation allowed the enemy to observe British communications behind the front line. Foch recognized that the "enemy might find it to his interest to resume his advance with the intention of gaining the Channel coast at any price, and by intensifying submarine warfare in the adjoining waters, hamper communications with England and isolate the power of Great Britain." On 27 April he told Haig and the chief of the Imperial General Staff, Gen. Sir Henry Wilson, that he had not considered withdrawing toward the sea. He was struggling "to cover the channel ports and also to maintain close touch between the French and British armies." He observed that "the daily progress made by each of the two big hostile attacks had gradually diminished until, in the first of these attacks [on the Somme], the line had once more become stable. In his opinion each succeeding hostile attack would share the same fate."[32]

The AEF made a minute contribution to the defense of the Lys. Only about 500 troops in three American units–the 1st Gas Regiment (30th Engineers), the 28th Pursuit Squadron, and the 16th Engineers–joined British units and fought with them. On 12 April, Pershing again offered the 1st Division for combat service, but the German attack concluded before this unit could move to the threatened area. Preparations for an independent army precluded more than token American service in combat zones.[33]

On 20 April, while the Lys offensive was taking place, 2,800 German troops from the 78th Reserve Division raided the lines of the American 26th Division at Seicheprey, a normally quiet location on the south face of the St. Mihiel salient. This operation proved successful, the Germans gaining surprise. They inflicted casualties of 81 killed, 187 wounded, 214 gassed, and 187 missing or taken prisoner. The raiders held the trenches they occupied for twenty-four hours but abandoned them before the 26th Division could mount a counterattack. A German after-action report praised the fighting qualities of individual American soldiers, observing that none of them surrendered without resistance, but criticized their commanders. "The American leadership in the combats up to now has been found wanting. In the fighting around SEICHEPREY no influence of the command on artillery or infantry action was noticed. There was no planned employment of reserves for counterattacks or coordinated artillery fire on the points of penetration." This minor episode strengthened Allied doubts about the readiness of the AEF. Lloyd George observed wryly: "This kind of result . . . is bound to occur on an enormous scale if a large amateur United States Army is built up without the guidance of more experienced General Officers."[34]

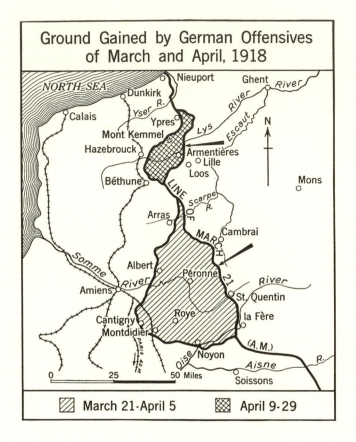

Ground Gained by German Offensives
of March and April, 1918

March 21-April 5   April 9-29

Ludendorff's failure during the first two offensives to destroy the British army and force a decision meant that Germany's advantage in manpower on the western front would soon disappear. German rifle strength at the conclusion of the Lys offensive was about 1,600,000, whereas that of the Allies was about 1,343,000. American troops were arriving in growing numbers. Nine divisions had debarked by 1 May; this number exactly doubled during May. About 85,000 men landed in March and another 119,000 in April. By 10 May American divisions occupied 55 kilometers of quiet sectors on the western front. These statistics guaranteed that Ludendorff would make further attempts to end the war before the flood of Americans overwhelmed the German army. Some delay ensued. The exhaustion that stemmed from the twin blows of March and April against the British army forced about a month's delay in further German offensives, giving the Allied troops a much-needed respite.

Meanwhile the Allies, deeply frightened by the German advance, redoubled their efforts to force some form of temporary amalgamation. Foch noted that by April the American rifle strength was a mere 70,000. "What was needed above all was that during several months the United States should send the Allies only infantry, to the exclusion of all other arms. By this means only could the British and French armies procure the 300,000 to 350,000 infantry which were needed to get through their existing crisis in effectives." Given this view, Foch received unwelcome news when Pershing talked with him on 16 April. Insisting that the president, the secretary of war, and he all favored the formation of an American army soon, the American commander claimed that its creation was "of the greatest importance in order to sustain the interest of the people of the United States in the war." He ended boldly: "As soon as two, three, or four divisions can take their part together in the war, it is my intention to assume command of them." In Pershing's view, the only unresolved question was the date for the creation of the independent force.[35]

Also on 16 April, Pershing addressed the officers of the 1st Division, which was about to enter the British sector near Cantigny, and spoke enthusiastically of the AEF. "You have behind you your own national traditions that should make you the finest soldiers in Europe to-day. We come from a young and aggressive nation." America stood for the sacred principles of human liberty; "we now return to Europe, the home of our ancestors, to help defend these same principles upon European soil." This display of chauvinism was understandable, but no amount of national tradition can substitute for experienced leadership and well-trained troops. Pershing's unwarranted presumption that the American troops were superior to others in the war helps explain his stubborn insistence on an independent army even during the greatest crisis of the war.[36]

On 19 April, Baker obtained President Wilson's approval of the arrangement that had stemmed from Joint Note No. 18 of the Permanent Military Representatives, which provided for priority shipment of the infantry and machine gun troops belonging to six divisions during May. The British ambassador in Washington, Lord Reading, interpreted the understanding as meaning that the United States would ship 120,000 combat troops per month in British transports during the next four months. When Pershing learned of this deal during a visit to London, he raised immediate objections and on 24 April, compelled an agreement that reflected his understanding of the earlier arrangement. The combat troops of six divisions would be sent in May for training with the British army. Excess shipping that became available would be used to ferry the rest of the six divisions. These troops would not fight with the British; they would become part of the independent American army. The next day at Sarcus, Pershing informed Foch of his agreement with the British. Foch assented to Pershing's insistence on forming an independent army when possible but made a chilling observation. "If we do not take steps to prevent the disaster which is threatened at present the American army may arrive in France to find the British pushed into the sea and the French back of the LOIRE, while they try in vain to organize on lost battlefields over the tombs of Allied soldiers. . . . We must look to the present needs, without considering propositions agreed to before we became engaged in the present struggle." Despite this cogent argument, Pershing refused to extend the May quota of 120,000 combat troops per month to apply also in June. From this episode Lloyd George gained the impression that President Wilson had difficulties with his generals like those of British civil authorities with Field Marshal Haig and others. "The decision of the President of the United States proved of insufficient value in face of the stubborn intransigence of the American Commander-in-Chief. He could see no further than the exaltation of his command, the jealous maintenance of his authority. It was President Wilson's first experience of just the same kind of professional egotism we had frequently experienced in dealings with our own Army heads."[37]

Throughout this period, Pershing's superiors in Washington treated the Allies with consideration, but they sustained Pershing's plenary authority to decide matters affecting the AEF. Baker wrote on 29 April to explain the discussions that had taken place in Washington. He had expressed "the present intention of our Government" but had refused to accept "a bargain from which we did not feel free to depart if the conditions in our judgment so changed as to justify a departure." He also reserved "the right to send in relatively small numbers during these four months [of] other personnel." The secretary's concluding observation must have given Pershing considerable comfort. Baker had "a very strong feeling that we ought not to make any such definite and obligatory promise as will permit representatives of the British Government to feel that they have a right to watch what we do and sit in judgment on our situation." To General Bliss, who had supported a form of temporary amalgamation, Baker wrote: "We must continue to be guided by [Pershing's] judgment of the military exigencies in France. . . . This, of course, is only just to General Pershing, upon whom the responsibility for our military operations rests, and it obviates the possibility of having to settle the same questions in two places at the same time, with discordant settlements as a result."[38]

After Clemenceau protested that the Pershing-Milner-Wilson agreement had been made without French participation, the Supreme War Council, meeting at Abbeville on 1–2 May 1918, discussed the shipment of American troops at length and came to an agreement. Foch wanted the United States to ship the same number and type of troops in June as in May. Pershing replied heatedly. "He did not suppose that the American army was to be entirely at the disposal of the French and British commands." He then reiterated his insistence upon the early formation of an independent American army. Lloyd George responded: "It would be unreasonable and impertinent . . . to treat American troops as drafts for the British army. It was to our advantage that the American army as such should take the field as soon as possible, and, speaking as the head of the British Government, he accepted that principle." He continued: "We were, however, now fighting what was probably the decisive battle of the war. If we lose this battle we shall have to provide tonnage to take what is left of the British army and the American army back to their homes." When Foch called for an extension of the May program to June, the Supreme War Council authorized Foch, Pershing, and Milner to draw up a new agreement.[39]

After spirited discussion, the council finally reached a settlement. Foch led off with a proposal to ship 120,000 American troops per month in May, June, and July. He "felt very deeply his own responsibility at a time when this great German offensive was threatening Paris on the one hand, and the channel ports on the other." He appreciated Pershing's wish to form an independent army, but his proposals would cause a delay of but a few weeks. Lloyd George then supported Foch, arguing that "if Great Britain and France had to go under, it would be an honourable defeat, because each had put the very last man into the army, whereas the United States would go under after putting in only as many men as had the Belgians. He was sure that the American nation would feel it a matter of prestige and national pride not to accept defeat after, if he might put it so, hardly putting their little finger in the struggle." In response, Pershing stressed the importance of forming the American army soon, holding that "the morale of the American troops depended on their fighting under their own flag." He also insisted that American public opinion would soon become a factor. "I called attention to the resentment that would be aroused in the United States if they [the people] should get the idea that we have no independent army in France; that already the question is being asked as to where the American army is and under what flag it is fighting." The council then accepted a proposal that endorsed the early formation of an independent American army but gave priority to shipment of infantry and machine-gun troops of six divisions in May. It provided "that any excess tonnage shall be devoted to bringing over such other troops as may be determined by the American Commander-in-Chief." This program would carry over also to June. The first six divisions to arrive would train and serve with the British; Pershing would decide the allocation of the rest. This Abbeville agreement satisfied Pershing. It "offered opportunity for greatly increasing arrival [of] American troops and as arrangement for May was already made, [it] seemed wise to accept British guarantee and extend infantry program for infantry of six divisions during June." The program for July and after remained in abeyance.[40]

Although the debate at Abbeville ended in a settlement, the Allied leadership departed with decidedly negative feelings about Pershing. Haig's reaction probably reflected those of others. "A great deal of time was wasted. . . . I thought Pershing was very obstinate, and stupid. He did not seem to realise the urgency of the situation. . . . He hankers after a *great self-contained American Army* but seeing that he has neither Commanders of Divisions, of Corps, nor of Armies, nor Staffs for same, it is ridiculous to think such an Army could function unaided in less than two years' time." Men in the ranks echoed the views of their commanders. One British soldier wrote home sarcastically on 2 May: "When is it reasonable to think that the Americans will be able to put in that immense army of three millions, fully equipped, each man, with a hair mattress, a hot-water bottle, a gramophone, and a medicine chest, which they tell us will get to Berlin and 'cook the goose' of the Kaiser?" If this force could fight in 1919, it might succeed, but was there "the slightest reason to imagine that it will come next year, or the year after, or even the year after that?"[41]

The heated discussion at Abbeville stimulated a proposal from Washington that Pershing found most irritating. On 11 May, Secretary Baker cabled the president's view. "He has been much impressed and disturbed by representation officially made to him here by French and British Ambassadors showing the steady drain upon French and British replacements and the small number of replacements now available." (The Allies had lost about 350,000 men during the Somme and Lys offensives.) Recognizing that Pershing understood the problem, he reiterated his trust in his judgment but concluded: "It has been suggested to the President that General Foch may reopen this subject with you and the President hopes you will approach any such interviews as sympathetically as possible, particularly if the suggestions as to replacements which has [sic] been presented to him is as critical as it seems." To this unwelcome proposal Pershing dispatched an uncompromising response. "While appreciating that we should give every early assistance possible to meet an emergency, I am strongly of the opinion that we must form our own divisions and corps as rapidly as possible and use them as such for the additional moral effect such an army would have." The Abbeville agreement satisfied him; it settled the matter for May and June. He did not think that Foch could consistently reopen the question until it became necessary to decide policy for the month of July. To assuage what he perceived as some concern in Washington about his intransigence, he concluded: "I wish to be understood as having every desire to meet this question in the broadest way possible and do everything to aid in this emergency, and both the President and the Secretary of War may be fully assured that I shall approach any future discussion in the spirit suggested by the Secretary of War." So matters stood as the Allies braced for new German initiatives on the western front.[42]

Meanwhile Foch did all he could to make effective use of the American divisions already in France. On 26 April, the 1st Division took over a portion of the First French Army's battle line at Cantigny. The generalissimo also arranged for the 26th, 42d, and 2d Divisions to move rapidly to the front. Three other divisions—the 32d, 3d, and 5th—were given orders to reinforce French divisions coming out of the line. These movements ensured that American units would become deeply involved in the continuation of the German offensive, but Foch still felt greatly pressed for manpower.[43]

After the 1st Division took its place in the line opposite Cantigny as a component of the X Army Corps of Gen. Eugene Debeney's First Army, it began preparations for the first purely American attack of the war. A single regiment, the 28th Infantry, made plans to seize the Cantigny plateau. This operation would improve observation of the enemy, interfere with hostile artillery fire, and improve the line slightly for future offensives. Its principal purpose was, as Allan Millett observes, "to demonstrate the skill and elan of the AEF." Pershing's obsession with the independent army meant that the AEF would avoid combat except in major emergencies until it occupied its own sector, but various considerations led to plans for a strictly limited attack on Cantigny, among them the blow to French and British morale that accompanied the German offensives, the growing concern among the Allies about the American reinforcement, and Pershing's wish to make good his claims about the quality of his troops. The general commanding the French X Corps explained the limited scope of the attack in a message to General Debeney. "The character of the operation itself (to attack by surprise, a little after daybreak, analogous to a powerful raid) has been selected at the express request of the Commanding General of the 1st Inf. Div. [Robert L. Bullard]." He expected, "counting upon the enthusiasm of the executants, . . . a complete and easy success, susceptible of having great moral effect." This optimism did not reflect recent French criticisms of the 1st Division's combat readiness, which included concern about the quality of the officers. The AEF leaders, it was argued, did not grasp the nature of the warfare in France. They depended on their experience in North American campaigns and rejected European advice, which they deemed an affront to national pride. The French also thought that the huge size of the American division posed serious logistical problems.[44] Field Orders No. 18 delineated the operation against the untested German 82d Reserve Division, which had come to France from the eastern front. Its purpose, according to Col. Hanson E. Ely, commander of the 28th Infantry, was to "cut out an awkward salient in the enemy's line at the village of CANTIGNY which salient would give the enemy an excellent jumping off place in case of an offensive on his part and give him an extensive field of observation to the west and northwest." Success would provide "excellent observation over the low ground to the east and would serve as a barrier against a hostile offensive." Three battalions were to attack after a short but violent artillery preparation that would turn into a rolling barrage. The center battalion would enjoy the support of twelve tanks. The French contributed 173 guns, including fifty large pieces, and promised to provide supporting artillery fire on the flanks of the attack. The 28th Infantry carefully rehearsed the maneuver, which was scheduled for the early morning of 28 May.[45]

Suddenly, the day before the action was to occur, a great German attack took place in Champagne against the Chemin des Dames ridge north of the Aisne River. This development would force the southward displacement of French artillery after the first day of the battle. But Bullard, with Pershing's assent, decided to proceed with the attack on Cantigny. The operation began at 0545 on 28 May.

Ely's troops gained complete surprise. The assaulting battalions drove the German defenders before them and reached their objective, a line a half mile east of Cantigny, by 0725. A German after-action report noted that the tanks, which the German defenders had not encountered previously, added to the surprise. The Americans took about 200 prisoners and suffered very few casualties in the first phase of the battle.[46]

After that the 28th Infantry encountered determined German counterattacks and extensive artillery bombardment. Some officers attributed this ferocity to the enemy's determination to spoil the American debut. One of those who planned the assault, Col. George C. Marshall, wrote: "The Germans were determined to overthrow our first success and demonstrate to the world that the American soldier was of poorer stuff than the German." Pershing shared this view, writing later: "The enemy reaction against our troops at Cantigny was extremely violent, and apparently he was determined at all costs to counteract

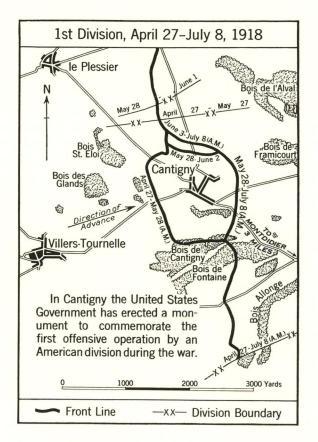

1st Division, April 27–July 8, 1918

le Plessier

N

Bois de l'Alval

June 1

May 28

April 27 May 27

XX

June 3–July 8 (A.M.)

Bois de Framicourt

May 28–June 2

Bois St. Eloi

Cantigny

Bois des Glands

May 28–July 8 (A.M.)

TO MONTDIDIER 3 MILES

Direction of Advance

Villers-Tournelle

April 27–May 28 (A.M.)

Bois de Cantigny

Bois de Fontaine

Bois Allonge

In Cantigny the United States Government has erected a monument to commemorate the first offensive operation by an American division during the war.

April 27–July 8 (A.M.)

0   1000   2000   3000 Yards

▬▬ Front Line   —xx— Division Boundary

the most excellent effect the American success had produced." Although this motive may have influenced the enemy, the German commander, General von Hutier, appears to have responded as strongly as he did because of fear that the Allies were beginning a thrust toward the critical town of Montdidier. The displacement of the French artillery to the Marne region proved serious, but two regiments from the 1st Division, the 18th Infantry and 26th Infantry, provided important reinforcements. Five German counterattacks were repulsed, but the 1st Division paid dearly in blood, suffering 941 casualties. The German 82d Reserve Division suffered much more grievously, losing almost 1,800 men. Bullard's men remained at Cantigny for seventy-three days until ordered to the area of Soissons. During this period the 1st Division suffered an additional 5,200 casualties.[47]

General Pershing made much of this little victory, but others have been less enthusiastic. In his report to the War Department, Pershing gushed: "Our staff

work was excellent and the liaison perfect. . . . The Allies are high in praise
of our troops. This action illustrates the facility with which our officers and
men learn, and emphasizes the importance of organizing our own divisions
and higher units as soon as circumstances permit. It is my firm conviction that
our troops are the best in Europe and our staffs are the equals of any." This
message concealed too much, especially the effective German reaction and the
large number of American casualties. Colonel Marshall's observation was much
more appropriate: "Cantigny was but a small incident." Millett observes that
the operation did not test Pershing's views on open warfare, the most significant
difference between American doctrine and that of the Allies. Smythe cogently
summarizes the meaning of Cantigny. "It is perhaps the saddest commentary
on America's war capabilities that, one year and two months after commencing
hostilities, at a time when the European powers were maneuvering and lock-
ing in battle divisions, corps, armies, and army groups, the greatest American
combat effort was to capture an obscure village using one regiment, slightly
reinforced. When one recalls that a regiment is only one-fourth of a division,
truly the mountainous AEF labored mightily and brought forth a mouse."
The limited character of the attack reflected Pershing's larger purpose; the
employment of an independent army precluded extensive American operations.
In any event, the battle then developing along the Marne River quickly overshadowed the little action to the north. Ludendorff's third major attack drew
many American soldiers into combat for the first time.[48]

4

THE GREAT GERMAN OFFENSIVE, PART II: 27 MAY–17 JULY 1918

The German High Command persisted in its ambition to conclude the war by driving the British left wing in Flanders into the sea, but it was essential before resuming operations in that region to pull Allied reserves elsewhere. This consideration was the motive for the assault on the Chemin des Dames ridge between Soissons and Reims that began on 27 May. It was intended to reach the line Soissons–Reims south of the Aisne River, from which attacks could be launched on both flanks to secure Compiegne and Reims. A move toward Paris would surely attract French reinforcements to the area. Cyril Falls summarizes Ludendorff's intentions succinctly. To draw French reserves southward, "he would launch a great diversionary offensive, give them a terrible mauling, draw their reserves south, and then, when possible, fall upon the British yet again." Difficult terrain put a premium on surprise.[1]

As it happened, the Allies had but four French divisions and three exhausted British divisions in the center attack zone, with only nine other divisions in reserve. These defenders would have to stop forty-one attacking divisions under the German Crown Prince. The American intelligence service had predicted the point of attack, but the local commander at the Chemin des Dames, Gen. Denis Auguste Duchene, ignored the warning and committed a cardinal tactical error. He eschewed an elastic defense, packing his troops into an exposed forward position, making it easy for the expert German artilleryman Colonel Bruchmueller to organize a devastating bombardment. Ludendorff's plan called for secondary attacks from both flanks of his main effort, creating a front of about 34 miles. As in the past, Ludendorff was unsure of what might happen. "How far the attack would take us could not be foretold. I hoped it would lead to such an expenditure of force on the part of the enemy as would enable us to resume the attack in Flanders."[2]

The attack, code-named *BLUECHER*, gained complete surprise; the German Seventh Army (von Boehn) in the center (fifteen divisions) rolled quickly over the Chemin des Dames and the Aisne River, reaching the Vesle River at Fismes on the first day. This advance of 10 miles was only the beginning. Success led Ludendorff to exploit the opening, again allowing favorable tactical developments to guide his decisions. In five days, the Germans advanced 30 miles to Chateau-Thierry on the Marne River, only 56 miles by road from Paris, capturing over 50,000 prisoners and 600 guns. They also cut the Paris-Nancy railroad, an important link to the more easterly sectors of the western front. Soissons fell, but Reims remained in French hands. An exodus from Paris took place; perhaps a million people left the city.[3]

Foch was as surprised as Petain and the local commanders, but he quickly reinforced the threatened area. He recognized the mistake that Duchene had made on the Aisne front. "For a commander who wishes to keep his freedom of action on the far side of a river or on its banks, it is an indispensable precaution that its bridges are guarded by a carefully organized system of defense, so that they may be always at his disposal. This precaution was lost sight of on the Aisne as it had been on the Somme." In any event, Foch quickly moved five American divisions then training with the British to quiet sectors of the French front. This measure released experienced French divisions for combat service on the Marne. Haig also sent three divisions to an area west of Amiens for possible use. As in previous offensives, the defense stiffened, particularly on the shoulders of the salient. The German divisions soon outran both their artillery and their supplies and fell victim to exhaustion. Hindenburg observed that "the fighting had carried us much farther than had originally been intended. Again unexpected successes had filled us with fresh hopes and given us fresh objectives. That we had not completely attained those objectives was due to the gradual exhaustion of the troops we employed." Remembering the limited purpose of the attack on the Chemin des Dames, the High Command called a halt by 4 June. Hindenburg concluded: "It was not in keeping with our general intentions that we should employ more divisions in the operation in the region of the Marne. Our gaze was still directed steadfastly at Flanders."[4]

An American unit made a timely contribution to the containment of the German attack. On 31 May, the 3d Division under Maj. Gen. Joseph Dickman took up positions on the south bank of the Marne at Chateau-Thierry as part of the XXXVIII Corps in the French Sixth Army. These troops blew up the main bridge spanning the river and repulsed all German efforts to cross. Legend insists that the American action stopped the Germans. In truth, the German attack had almost run its course, but the action was of great psychological importance, announcing the American presence to the beleaguered Allies in clear terms.[5]

There was no denying the brilliance of Ludendorff's success on the Aisne, but the attack put his troops in a difficult position. The advance of 30 miles had extended the former front of 59 miles to 94 miles, and the narrow salient was subject to artillery fire at important points. It was most difficult to supply the troops who held it. An American commentary noted: "The supply situation of the Germans was awkward. There was only one narrow-gauge railway leading from Soissons into the new area, and it was dangerously close to the front lines. The transportation system was unfavorable; for the keys to it were the railway and road centers of Soissons and Reims, one of which was in close range of the Allies and the other in their possession." Besides, no important objective was in view. As on the Somme and the Lys, Ludendorff pursued local success too far, sacrificing valuable reserves without gaining important objectives.[6]

There followed, on the line of the Aisne, a month of local attacks in which the American 2d Division played a leading part. Ordered into the line on 4 June as part of the French Sixth Army, it attacked Belleau Wood two days later. The Fourth Marine Brigade captured the small village of Bouresches but encountered strong resistance in Belleau Wood itself, especially from well-placed machine-gun nests. The Marines' casualties on 6 June, a thousand officers and men, exceeded the total losses in the previous history of the corps. Further attacks in the next few days proved fruitless. Maj. Gen. John A. Lejeune, a Marine officer of exceptional ability, reported on these assaults, which were made without artillery preparation. "Each time little progress was made and it became apparent that the reckless courage of the foot soldier with his rifle and bayonet could not overcome machine guns well-protected in rocky nests." When the wood was finally cleared of its defenders on 25 June, artillery made a crucial contribution. The French commanding general, Degoutte, in gratitude, renamed the wood the Bois de la Brigade de Marine. Lejeune concluded: "Again, was decisively shown the great importance of artillery to infantry. Infantry alone without materiel, makes little or no progress. If the enemy combines personnel and materiel, we must do the same or lose the game." When units of the 2d Division attacked the village of Vaux on 1 July, a twelve-hour artillery preparation preceded the assault, which gained its objective without serious loss. Total casualties in the 2d Division for the period 6–26 June were 170 officers and 8,793 men, of whom over a thousand were killed in action. The Fourth Marine Brigade alone lost 112 officers and 4,598 men.[7]

German evaluations of the 2d Division's operations in June, like those of the Cantigny attack, praised the troops but emphasized the failings of command

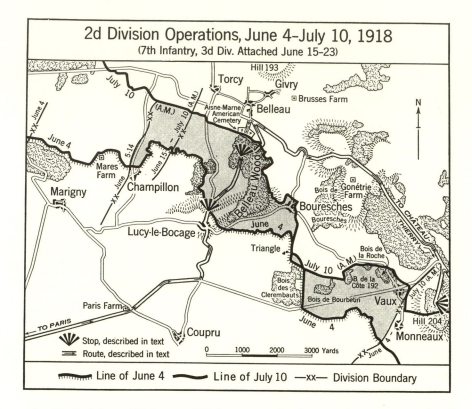

2d Division Operations, June 4–July 10, 1918
(7th Infantry, 3d Div. Attached June 15–23)

and staff. One German officer observed on 12 June: "The American soldier is courageous, strong, and clever. He is at his best in guerilla warfare. The manner in which large units attack is not up-to-date and leadership is poor. Neither the command [n]or the troops are afraid of suffering losses when desirable terrain is to be gained." Another report rated the division as "very good"; it lacked only "the necessary training" to make it "a very worthy opponent." This latter refrain appeared in still another report on 2 July 1918. "The leadership . . . is not yet up to the mark. When in action as larger independent units, the Americans will not be able to dispense with French guidance for the time being." Ludendorff reflected this evaluation in his comment on the actions around Chateau-Thierry. "Americans who had been a long time in France had bravely attacked our thinly held fronts, but they were unskilfully [*sic*] led, attacked in dense masses, and failed. . . . Our tactics had proved sound in every way, our losses, compared with those of the enemy and the large number of prisoners, though in themselves distressing, had been very light."[8]

American evaluations have generally paralleled those of the Germans. The Historical Section of the Army War College saw the struggle as one of attrition, in which "American courage combatted German doggedness and skill. . . . Though artillery played its part, the bayonet, the hand grenade, and the machine gun determined the outcome." Tangible gains were "inconsequential" compared with the heavy losses. "Beyond any material result, however, was the psychological effect upon the armies and the people of both sides, created by the dramatic intervention of the American division at this time and place." Donald Smythe offers a similar if mordant interpretation. Nineteen days of sacrifice had produced little – "a woods named Belleau and two villages named Bouresches and Vaux. In all history, nothing important had happened in these places, nor has anything since. . . . The importance of Belleau Wood was not strategical, or even tactical, but psychological." The issue was, as Gen. Hans von Boehn, commander of the German troops in the area, put it, "not a question of the possession of this or that village or woods, insignificant in itself; it is a question whether the Anglo-American claim that the American Army is equal or even the superior of the German Army is to be made good."[9]

On 9 June, Ludendorff again returned to the offensive. Plan Gneisenau specified an attack in the Montdidier-Noyon sector west of the Marne salient. Ludendorff's immediate purpose was to improve his imperfect position, although again his larger intention was to draw reserves south. He still planned to deliver a decisive blow in Flanders. General von Hutier, commanding the German Eighteenth Army, would attack on the line Montdidier-Noyon, seeking to capture Compiegne and thus open rail communications to Maubeuge. General von Boehn, commanding the German Seventh Army, would attack on the west face of the Marne salient south of Soissons. His purpose was to gain control of the rail line between Soissons and Montdidier. Success would build a bridge between the Amiens salient created in March and the new Marne salient, strengthening the German position considerably and renewing the threat to Paris.[10]

On this occasion, Ludendorff failed to gain surprise, so important in his earlier thrusts, and the results were meager. Von Hutier began the offensive on 9 June with thirteen divisions on a twenty-mile front. Von Boehn moved on the next day with three divisions on a front of six miles, but the Germans had to relocate artillery hurriedly, thus revealing their intentions. The French Third Army was ready, having established an elastic defense with seven divisions in line west of the Oise River and ten others in reserve. Both the primary and secondary attacks gained little ground against the defenders, which included the American 1st Division, still at Cantigny. Successful French counterattacks on 11 June forced Ludendorff to order suspension of the drive, which ended on 13 June. Ludendorff wrote of this battle: "The action of the Eighteenth Army had not altered the strategical situation . . . nor had it provided any fresh tactical data." Besides, Foch did not move reserves in great numbers to the area. He recognized that "the enemy in Flanders [was] still so strong that the German army could not attack there yet."[11]

The check between Montdidier and Noyon greatly alarmed the German High Command. Several weeks must elapse before it could make another attack, and American troops were arriving in great numbers. By July, Ludendorff recognized that the United States must have about twenty divisions in France, "more than I believed possible. . . . not only had our March superiority in the number of divisions been cancelled, but even the difference in gross numbers was now to our disadvantage, for an American division consists of twelve strong battalions." While these inexperienced troops would have difficulties, they "could release English and French divisions on quiet fronts. . . . This was of the greatest importance and helps to explain the influence exerted by the American contingent on the issue of the conflict. It was for this reason that America became the deciding factor in the war."[12]

Although the American reinforcement rapidly reduced the German superiority on the western front, the Allied leaders continued to press Pershing for troops. The AEF commander maintained his belief that these transfers would compromise the formation of an independent command.

The Supreme War Council gathered again on 1–2 June, this time at Versailles, where sharp exchanges occurred when Pershing showed reluctance to continue the shipment of combat troops only. During a private meeting, Lloyd George proposed to send a letter to President Wilson conveying Foch's views. Pershing countered with a telegram from Washington that requested a decision on troop shipments from Foch, Haig, and Pershing–a means of bypassing the council. Lloyd George complained that it was difficult to make inter-Allied decisions because the United States did not have a political representative on the Supreme War Council. He still wanted to raise the question. When Pershing objected, Foch bluntly asked the American whether he was prepared to allow the enemy to push the French back to the Loire because of his views on the shipment of American troops. When Pershing responded affirmatively, the generalissimo threatened to refer matters to the president. Pershing then said angrily: "Refer it to the President and be damned. I know what the President will do. He will simply refer it back to me for recommendation and I will make to him the same recommendation as I have made here today." These exchanges revealed that irritation with Pershing remained alive and well among the leaders of the Entente. The French briefly contemplated a request to President Wilson that he remove the general but did not take action.[13]

Despite the heated discussion at Versailles, Pershing, Milner, and Foch reached a compromise. They agreed to give priority of shipment to 170,000 combat troops in June and 130,000 in July. Since as many as 250,000 troops could be transported per month, the remaining 190,000 would be support troops. Pershing had disconcerted the gathering by reporting that only about 263,000 trained combat troops were then available in the United States. This revelation explains the reason for the final sentence in the Pershing-Milner-Foch agreement. "We recognize that the combatant troops to be despatched in July may have to include troops which have had insufficient training but we consider that the present emergency is such as to justify a temporary departure by the United States from sound principles of training especially as a similar course is being followed by France and Great Britain." Haig confided his exasperation at Pershing in an irritable entry in his diary. "[Gen. Sir Henry] Wilson told me that in a conversation he and Foch had just had with Pershing, they discovered that the Americans had already nearly exhausted their supply of trained men. For two or three months recruits had not been enlisted. Really the ignorance of the Americans is appalling." No doubt Haig was especially disappointed because his civilian superior, Lloyd George, failed to obtain control of the American troops then attached to the BEF.[14]

Lloyd George, Clemenceau, and Vittorio Orlando, the Italian premier, seeking to bypass Pershing, dispatched a letter to President Wilson that expressed their view of the crisis in manpower. They urged continuing priority shipment of American combat troops, noting that Foch had only 162 divisions in hand to contend with the 200 under the German High Command. The generalissimo, they added, believed that the United States must eventually supply 100 divisions. To attain this objective at the earliest possible moment, the United States would have to draft at least 300,000 men per month. Pershing reported his response to this message. "I told them that America was fully alive to the necessity of doing everything possible and would do so. I can only add that our program should be laid out systematically and broadly and men called out as fast as they can be handled." He reiterated his wish to ship entire divisions after July with necessary auxiliary troops, an approach consistent with his plan to conduct independent operations. After the war he characterized his view at this time. "On the one hand, there was a critical situation which must be met by immediate action, while, on the other hand, any priority accorded a particular arm necessarily postponed the formation of a distinctive American fighting force and the means to supply it. Such a force was, in my opinion, absolutely necessary to win the war."[15]

On 3 June, Foch arranged the transfer of several American divisions then training with the BEF to the French front. The extension of the lines caused by the German offensives dictated this movement. Two divisions went to the Aisne-Marne sector and three to quiet sectors in Lorraine and the Vosges Mountains. This arrangement appealed to Pershing because it brought the units closer to the projected American sector in the east. Anticipating British complaints, he informed the War Department of the understanding that American divisions would enter the battle when there was a manifest need. "Any claim on the part of the British that the troops training with them were being taken unnecessarily or in violation of the understanding is untenable." Foch, he continued, was the commander-in-chief; his orders must be obeyed or "the theory of a supreme command fails."[16]

During this period, Pershing also made known his decision not to send any more divisions to the BEF for training, an aspect of his determination to form an independent American command when possible. To Haig he justified his action in familiar accents. "At the request of General Foch I have planned to send all [American] divisions embarked during the present month to our own divisional areas." He was concerned because of "the fact that American units are so widely dispersed. I feel that the matter of assembling the larger American units is becoming more and more urgent as my forces increase."[17]

This course dismayed his European military colleagues. Gen. Sir Henry Wilson, the chief of the Imperial General Staff, wrote in considerable dudgeon to Foch, arguing that Pershing had violated "a plain and clear arrangement with President Wilson." He believed that six American divisions should always serve on the British front for training. Those who completed training would then revert to Pershing's command; others arriving in France would take their place. "General Pershing would receive trained divisions much more rapidly and we would have the constant support and assurance that such a magnificent body of troops would always give us." He concluded plaintively: "Please think this over. I know that the Prime Minister [Lloyd George] is much distressed by this affair." Haig's pique was again confided to his diary. "Pershing by his obstinacy has carried the day and . . . he will *concentrate* all his American Divisions somewhere! . . . The question of providing efficient Divisional Commanders will be a difficult one for the Americans to solve." General Petain complained to Clemenceau about press reports that American divisions would soon gain some respite as American units replaced them. "This conception appears to me very dangerous, threatening, if it gains circulation, to give false ideas concerning the American cooperation by exaggerating the latter." A long time would pass "before American forces can seriously turn the scales in our favor."[18]

Foch now attempted to negotiate a satisfactory arrangement with Pershing. On 17 June, he suggested that his aide, Gen. Maxime Weygand, and Col. Fox Conner, the AEF's G-3, should draw up a plan for presentation to the Supreme War Council that would arrange the shipment of American troops. The generalissimo wanted to attach twenty American regiments from four divisions then training with the BEF to twenty French divisions. Pershing replied that he already had a study under way to decide how to place three million men in France by 1 April 1919. Foch then noted the healthy effect of the American presence on French and British troops, an indirect justification of his desire to associate American divisions with Allied divisions. To this remark Pershing replied that "all soldiers like to be with their own people"; he wanted to bring all his troops into "one American fighting army." Foch accepted this view in principle, suggesting that, when formed, an independent force might undertake an offensive in September or perhaps in the spring of 1919. Pershing thought that his army could fight in September. Foch responded: "While agreeing perfectly with this idea, . . . he [Foch] should like him [Pershing] to consider turning over some of the divisions going into the American training sector a few of the best advanced regiments to serve in the most fatigued French divisions. . . . the effect of young, vigorous American soldiers on the wornout [sic] French divisions would be most advantageous; . . . the Americans might in the meantime learn something and . . . they would certainly have a strong tendency to put the tired French divisions on their feet." These units would return to Pershing by the first days of August. His plan, he concluded, was "first, building up the British army in manpower and second building up the morale of the French army, and [third] in August the assembling of the American army."[19]

Pershing soon rejected Foch's proposal; he remained convinced of the need to separate his troops from the Allied armies. Besides his emphasis on training for open warfare, which the Allies thought useless, he was convinced that the poor morale of the French and the British armies adversely affected his units. He told Secretary Baker: "The fact is our officers and men are far and away superior to the tired Europeans." When a French official, Andre Tardieu, ventured criticism of American commanders and staff, Pershing responded forcefully. "We had now been patronized as long as we would stand for it, and I wished to hear no more of that sort of nonsense."[20]

On 10 July, Pershing met Foch at Bombon and obtained a commitment to
form the American First Army soon. The American commander was most concerned with the selection of a sector for his independent force, urging the Toul-
Nancy area. Foch replied archly: he was going to be "still more American than
the Americans." He thought it possible to form an army of thirteen divisions by
the end of July, but it was necessary to maintain the Allied divisions at their
present number. To meet this requirement, Foch wanted to put American
divisions lacking artillery into quiet sectors or in training areas. From these
positions they could support French troops on the front line. Pershing agreed to
this proposal. Foch objected to the Toul-Nancy location, inclining toward the
front near Chateau-Thierry, but the final decision was not made at Bombon.[21]

These discussions with Foch led Pershing to formulate a comprehensive manpower plan for the coming twelve months that became known as the
100-division program. On 19 June, he informed General March that the Allies
could resume the offensive during the fall and continue it in the spring of 1919.
The United States should prepare a strong force to assure a decision in 1919. He
gave as reasons for making this commitment the war-weariness of the Allies—
"I do not believe they will hold out beyond another year"—and the utility
of striking the Germans while they were at their weakest "before they can
recuperate by conscription in Russia, as now seems possible." On the same
day, he presented these views in a cable to General March and Secretary Baker.
He called upon them to place an army of sixty-six divisions, about 3,000,000
men, in France by 30 June 1919. On 25 June, only six days later, Pershing
cabled another proposal that called for eighty divisions by April and a hundred by July, a result of a recent conference with General Foch.[22]

On 23 July, March forwarded the War Department's reaction through General
Bliss. It was possible to place eighty divisions in France by 30 June 1919, a
force approximately equal to the 162 Allied divisions then located on the
western front. Limited capabilities precluded a larger number. Pershing persisted in his advocacy of a hundred divisions, arguing on 17 August: "It is my
fixed opinion after careful study that this is the very least American force that
will insure our victory in 1919." When Secretary Baker came to Europe in September, he discovered that Pershing had planned on the assumption that the
AEF would have a hundred divisions in July 1919. This confusion stemmed from
facile assumption that eighty combat divisions meant also an additional eighteen
depot divisions, one for every five combat divisions. The total force would
number about 5,000,000 men. General March soon clarified the plan: "80 divisions does not mean 80 combat divisions, but 80 divisions including combat
and base divisions." Pershing would receive only about 4,260,000 troops.[23]

The adoption of the eighty-division program was the last major development in the long and tangled process of determining the size of the AEF. After the middle of July, the quickening pace of military operations overshadowed staff discussions of this question. American planning had assumed completion of the mobilization in 1919, the earliest date contemplated for full-scale employment of an independent American army. Pershing's dogged persistence in this plan placed limits on the combat exposure of American divisions until the German offensives ended in July and about two months beyond.

Pershing's defense of his plans for an independent army engendered growing criticism from both civilian and military leaders in Europe. This development eventually aroused concern in Washington, leading to proposed changes in the commander-in-chief's authority. Colonel House, who maintained close communication with French and British leaders, concluded that something should be done to curb the American commander-in-chief. On 3 June 1918, he suggested to Wilson that Pershing "should confine his activities to the molding [of] our army into an efficient fighting machine and directing it against the enemy." He should "be relieved of all questions of policy except where his opinion is asked," eschewing direct contacts with the prime ministers and foreign secretaries of the Allies. "He should be in touch with Foch and Foch should be in touch with these." After some hesitation, Secretary Baker inclined to a comparable view. On 6 July, he wrote tactfully to Pershing, observing that "the American people think of you as their fighting general, and I want them to have that idea more and more brought home to them." He had in mind two measures. One was to send Gen. George W. Goethals, the builder of the Panama Canal then serving in the War Department, to head the Services of Supply. This arrangement "would place General Goethals rather in a coordinate than a subordinate relationship to you, but of course it would transfer all of the supply responsibilities from you, to him and you could then forget about docks, railroads, storage houses, and all the other vast industrial undertakings to which up to now you have given a good deal of your time and, as you know, we all think with superb success." His other suggestion was to transfer Pershing's political responsibilities to General Bliss, the American Military Representative at the Supreme War Council. "As the President deals in matters of military diplomacy with General Bliss, it would seem that he could with profit relieve you of some part of the conferences and consultations which in the early days you were obliged to have with the British War Office and the French War Office, thus simplifying the presentation of InterAllied [*sic*] questions to the President."[24]

The day after Pershing received this bombshell, he rushed a cable to the War Department, giving vent to strongly negative reactions. He began by observing that his staff and the Services of Supply had assumed responsibility for many functions that he had earlier exercised himself. "When it becomes necessary for me to be constantly at the front I shall retain control through the general staff." Then he objected to the appointment of Goethals. The supply system was "intimately interwoven with our whole organization. The whole must remain absolutely under one head. Any division of responsibility or coordinate control in any sense would be fatal." A single command fixed responsibility and avoided conflicting authority. He cited this idea as the one that had led to the appointment of General Foch as supreme commander. "I very earnestly urge upon you Mr. Secretary that no variation from this principle be permitted." Pershing quickly made General Harbord, his former chief of staff then commanding the 2d Division, the head of the Services of Supply, a means of stifling growing criticism of that organization. Nothing more was heard from Washington about Goethals because Pershing offered a sound objection to coordinate command and his superiors in Washington wished to preserve his command prerogatives. Smythe notes: "Rarely has an overseas commander received greater support from his superiors."[25]

Pershing acquiesced in the shift of his political responsibilities to General Bliss, lacking a compelling argument to make against this step and enjoying good relations with the former chief of staff. He informed March that Bliss had "excellent judgment, and is very highly regarded by the allied official world." General March had written separately to Pershing about his work load, observing that his political responsibilities had developed because President Wilson had refused to send a diplomatic representative to the Supreme War Council. Altered circumstances suggested an early change. "It seems inevitable that a subdivision of your work must be made in the near future, which will take off your shoulders the burden of personal conferences with Prime Ministers and other diplomatic representatives of the powers engaged, and release you to straight military duty, which, of course, is what you were sent there for." Pershing replied that the chief of staff had exaggerated his political role, and besides, no one could represent the president except perhaps Colonel House. He did not believe it necessary to send anyone to France for this purpose. General Bliss could discharge necessary functions at the Supreme War Council, of which one would be further negotiations about the shipment of American troops. On 24 June, Bliss received word from General March that President Wilson would no longer consider proposals on this subject emanating from any single nation. "Such recommendations must come from the military representatives at Versailles representing all the nations." By implication, this arrangement had already transferred the burden of these dealings to General Bliss.[26]

General March, who energetically asserted his authority as chief of staff, increasingly irritated Pershing. Late in July he complained directly to the secretary of war. March had assumed "the attitude of Commanding General of all the armies rather than that of Chief of Staff speaking for his Chief." He also noted: "As to this Goethals matter, while you wrote about it, I understand General March wanted to order it out of hand." A few weeks later Pershing proposed that someone "who has actually gone through this organization here from beginning to end" should replace March. Nothing came of this initiative, but it showed Pershing's continuing preoccupation with the maintenance of his extensive prerogatives.[27]

Meanwhile Ludendorff had prepared a fifth major strike on the western front, fully aware that daily his position became more dangerous because of the flow of American troops to France. Hindenburg concurred: "It was of great importance to us that our new operation should begin soon. Thanks to the arrival of American reinforcements, time was working not for us but against us." As in the past, Ludendorff intended to seek a decision in Flanders, but the reserves available to Haig in that area were still imposing in numbers. "Again and again our thoughts returned to the idea of an offensive in Flanders," but the strength of the British positions forced postponement. To draw British divisions from the north, he settled on an offensive elsewhere. Ludendorff decided to hit the eastern side of the Marne salient in Champagne, striking both east and west of Reims. Besides helping to displace some British reserves positioned to counter Rupprecht's attack in Flanders, which was scheduled to begin ten days later, it would improve German communications between the Aisne and Marne salients. Success in Champagne and in Flanders would set the stage for the final German offensive, which would feature attacks on Paris and Amiens.[28]

The German crown prince, designated to undertake the offensive, decided upon a speedy converging attack to pinch off territory south of Reims and force the capture of that city. His instructions concluded: "Rapid execution . . . is of fundamental importance for the success. The first two days of the attack and the first night are decisive." West of Reims, von Boehn's Seventh Army would cross the Marne at Chateau-Thierry and move up the river valley toward Epernay. Farther east, von Mudra's First Army and Karl von Einem's Third

Army would attack in the direction of Chalons-sur-Marne. These latter two columns would join south of Reims, cutting off that city and forcing its surrender before the Allies could bring up reserves. The Germans expected an Allied counterattack on the west face of the Marne salient. The Ninth Army and the right wing of the Seventh Army were ordered to contain any move of this nature.[29]

After the war, Ludendorff remembered having said to an aide: "If my blow at Rheims succeeds now, we have won the war." He learned later that Foch had commented at this time: "If the German attack at Rheims succeeds we have lost the war." Kaiser Wilhelm himself came to the front of the German First Army to observe the assault. The German High Command had reached the crossroads of the war. Defeat would force it to resume a defensive posture all along the western front, a gloomy prospect given the growing manpower of the Allies. For Foch, the repulse of the German attack would open offensive possibilities that had been denied to him earlier. He had been the exponent *par exemplar* of the attack throughout his tenure as generalissimo.[30]

Essential to German success in earlier offensives had been the ability to gain surprise, but because the French developed excellent intelligence, Ludendorff failed to gain this advantage in Champagne. On 5 July, sufficient information was available to permit a remarkably accurate estimate of the German objectives. By 11 July, the French could predict the direction, front, and day of the attack. On 14 July, captured German prisoners revealed that operations would begin with a bombardment at midnight and an infantry assault several hours later. Meanwhile Foch positioned French and British divisions from Flanders between the Oise and Marne rivers, from which they could move efficiently to any threatened point.[31]

On 5 July Petain prescribed arrangements to contain the impending attack, emphasizing elastic defense. Only a few troops would defend the first position, an outpost line. The main defense would take place along a second position against tired advancing troops that had moved beyond their artillery support. These dispositions reflected Foch's analysis of German methods in 1918. "Their characteristics were surprise, violence, rapidity of execution, manoeuvring to widen the initial breach, and an effort from the start to penetrate deeply into the adversary's defensive system." The antidotes to these tactics were good intelligence, provisions for defense in depth, and immediate counterattacks, especially against the flanks of the enemy penetration.[32]

On 15 July, Ludendorff attacked with twenty-four divisions of the German Seventh and First Armies on line and seventeen in reserve. The Seventh Army moved from the eastern side of the Marne salient, driving toward Epernay and eastward to a planned junction with the First Army, which struck east of Reims toward Chalons-sur-Marne. Reims would then fall, permitting use of its rail communications to support German forces in the Marne salient.

Even before the German infantry moved out, the operation began to fall apart. Just before midnight, French artillery fire fell on suspected areas of concentration and river crossings, catching many German troops in the open and destroying bridges. When the First Army's attack got off, the Germans discovered that Gen. Henri Gouraud's French Fourth Army had arranged a "false front" defense. When the assault echelons moved through the thinly held first position, artillery fire devastated them. Tired units were unable to penetrate the strongly held second position. When German artillery was brought up to support the attack, it too came under heavy bombardment. The German crown prince's war diary described the result. "This first day of battle has again shown that decisive, apt leadership can readily evade any superior attack by [adopting] a 'mobile' defense. The leader must decide when to fall back in time to positions in the rear, and how to create a deep foreground, and to abandon some terrain to the enemy, as thereby he will force the enemy to bring up a superior attack artillery, whose fire will fall harmlessly on abandoned trenches; subsequently requiring the enemy to [effect] a new artillery concentration . . . thus procuring sufficient time for his troops to organize resistance in a new defensive system." The astute General Maurice succinctly summarized the outcome. "Throughout the three and a half years of trench warfare on the Western Front no attack made on such a scale had met with so little success."[33]

The German Seventh Army's attack west of Reims against the French Fifth and Sixth Armies made more progress, but it fell far short of its objective. The American 38th Infantry, a regiment of the 3d Division, gained its nickname "Rock of the Marne" because of stubborn resistance on the right of the Allied line. Several other American divisions—the 26th, 28th, and 42d, and a black regiment, the 369th Infantry of the 93d Division—participated in this "Second Battle of the Marne." The Americans fought under their divisional commanders with French corps and army commanders and staffs, serving well as temporarily amalgamated troops despite Pershing's predictions to the contrary. The Germans established a bridgehead across the Marne at Dormans about 4 miles in depth, but this gain only implicated them more deeply in an indefensible position.[34]

After failing to gain appreciably on the second day of the battle, Ludendorff had to call a halt. The offensive ended on 17 July. Hindenburg reported the outcome sadly. "We seemed to have very little left of all we had striven for.

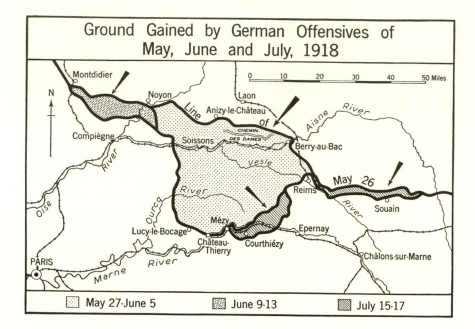

Ground Gained by German Offensives of May, June and July, 1918

Legend: May 27-June 5 | June 9-13 | July 15-17

The operation had apparently failed and, so far as the French front was concerned, nothing definite has been gained." He retained hope that the German army could recoup in Flanders, but no further German offensives took place after the debacle of 15–17 July.[35]

Ludendorff discerned in this reverse the beginning of decisive defeat. "The attempt to make the nations of the Entente inclined to peace before the arrival of the American reinforcements by means of German victories had failed. The energy of the army had not sufficed to deal the enemy a decisive blow before the Americans were on the spot in considerable force. It was quite clear to me that our general situation had thus become very serious." His five offensives had greatly depleted his reserves. In March, he had a total of 207 divisions with 82 in reserve. By July his reserves had shrunk to 66 highly questionable watered-down divisions, while American troops poured into France at the rate of over 250,000 per month. Although he had occupied ten times the amount of ground that the Allies had seized in 1917, taking 225,000 prisoners and 2,500 guns, his gains fell short of decisive objectives.[36]

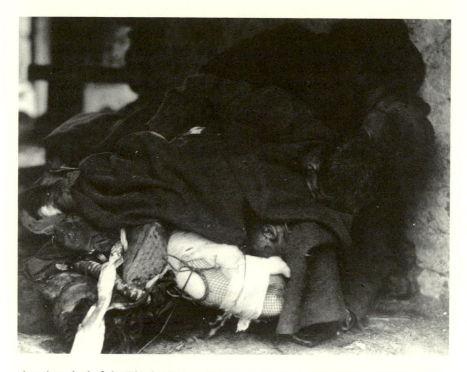

American dead of the Third Division, killed in action on 14 July 1918 at Coirboin.

Foch now sensed an opening, and he seized the initiative immediately. His counteroffensives of 1918 began on 18 July in the very sector where three days previously the Germans had hoped to win a signal victory. Earlier Petain had said: "If we can hold on until the end of June our situation will be excellent. In July we can resume the offensive; after that victory will be ours." On this occasion, he proved himself a sound prophet.[37]

5

THE LIMITED ALLIED COUNTEROFFENSIVES: 18 JULY–26 SEPTEMBER 1918

General Foch inaugurated preparations for his counteroffensives as early as 20 May 1918, when he ordered planning for two attacks. One would come between the Somme and Oise rivers to restore communications around Amiens, and a second would follow on the Lys River to free Ypres and the coal fields around Bethune. The continuing series of German offensives delayed these operations but finally created an opportunity to attack the salient between the Aisne and the Marne rivers. This target had a base of about 37 miles and a depth of about 28 miles.

Foch sensed that in the Aisne-Marne sector "this deep but comparatively narrow pocket, . . . the railways constituted the only suitable lines of supply for his [Ludendorff's] troops, and these all passed through Soissons." If the Allies succeeded in interdicting these lines, Ludendorff could no longer consider an attack toward Paris from around Chateau-Thierry. Therefore, on 14 June Foch directed Petain to plan "an offensive operation having as its purpose the capture by us of the plateaus dominating SOISSONS on the west, with a view to preventing the enemy from using this place, which is of considerable importance to him." Gen. Charles Mangin, commanding the French Tenth Army, assumed responsibility for the operation, and on 20 June he produced an initial plan.[1]

This project rapidly broadened as the French received information about Ludendorff's plan to attack Reims. Foch decided to move against both flanks of the Marne salient. He sent Mangin's Tenth Army, supported by Degoutte's Sixth Army, from the western flank astride the Ourq River eastward toward Fere-en-Tardenois. Gen. Henri Berthelot's Fifth Army was moved westward from the eastern flank between Reims and the Marne toward Arcis-le-Ponsart with Mitry's Ninth Army on his left. The coming operation would collapse the salient and, among other things, free the Paris-Chalons railroad that ran through the Marne valley. Petain issued orders for this converging attack on 12 July. The Tenth and Sixth Armies included thirteen French divisions and four American divisions in the first line and seven French divisions in the second line. The Fifth Army would have nine divisions on its front. On 13 July, Petain set the attack for 18 July. McEntee neatly summarizes the idea of this offensive. "It was to constitute a counter-thrust in the Fere-en-Tardenois area and a defense against the German attack on either side of Reims. This meant a double role for the Allies."[2]

Foch concentrated all available troops between the Oise River and the Argonne forest, a force that ultimately totaled thirty-eight infantry divisions and six cavalry divisions. This aggregation was enough to defend around Reims and to attack near Soissons. He also could rely on expanding reserves. "The American army, which already counted twenty-seven divisions in France, was continually receiving reinforcements." Because the Germans lacked replacements, the Allies would soon regain a majority in rifle strength on the western front. Foch concluded: "By the middle of July it could be seen that the time was fast approaching when the opposing forces would be sensibly equal. If the enemy did not attack, the hour had come for us to take the offensive; if he did attack, to accompany our parry with a powerful counter stroke."[3]

After the last German attack began on 15 July, General Petain attempted to cancel the counteroffensive scheduled three days later, but Foch learned of this attempt and scotched it. Petain had ordered Gen. Marie-Emile Fayolle, commanding the Group of Armies of the Reserve, to "suspend the Mangin operation in order to enable me to send your reserves into the battle south of the Marne." When Foch heard of this step, he telephoned Petain. "It must be understood that until there are new developments that you will communicate to me, there can be no question at all of slowing up and less so of stopping the Mangin preparations." Foch later explained his reasoning. The German attack would have three days in which to develop, but "once this delay was ended, we could attack him in flank, from the Aisne to the Marne, on a front of twenty-five miles, in a new direction and on fresh ground, unexpectedly and in force; in a word, under conditions calculated not only to neutralize his advantages, but even to render them disastrous. To effect this, we had only to inexorably maintain our plan and execute it in accordance with our previous intention of seizing the initiative and pronouncing an offensive between the Aisne and the Marne."[4]

Emerging suddenly from the dense forest of Villers-Cotteret, the French Tenth and Sixth Armies attacked the west face of the Marne salient at 0435 on 18 July,

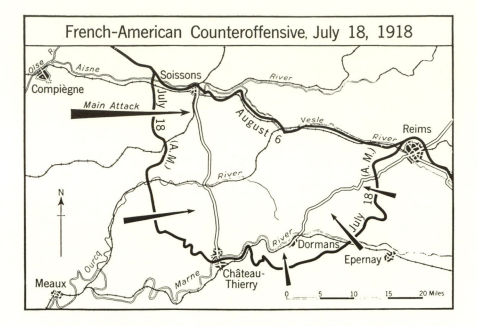

French-American Counteroffensive, July 18, 1918

gaining complete surprise, and quickly smashed through the German lines. Mangin omitted a preparatory bombardment, settling for a rolling barrage ahead of the attacking troops. The spearhead of the Tenth Army, the XX French Corps commanded by General Berdoulat, included two of the most experienced American units, the 1st Division (Summerall) and 2d Division (Harbord), with the French 1st Moroccan Division, of which the French Foreign Legion was a part. Pershing had arranged for General Bullard, the III Corps commander, to lead the American divisions in this movement, but Bullard recognized that his headquarters was not yet ready to function. General Liggett participated in the Aisne-Marne offensive as a corps commander. His I Corps (the American 26th Division and the French 167th Division) formed part of the French Sixth Army, which attacked from the vicinity of Chateau-Thierry. The French Tenth and Sixth Armies captured 10,000 prisoners and several hundred guns on the first day. Later they interdicted the rail communications from Soissons to Chateau-Thierry that sustained the German Seventh Army. Ludendorff had sent much of the German artillery northward for the projected attack in Flanders. Recognizing too late his error, he cancelled this movement on the afternoon of 18 July and returned to the Marne area. He soon ordered suspension of the operation in Flanders. The reverse at Soissons also meant the death

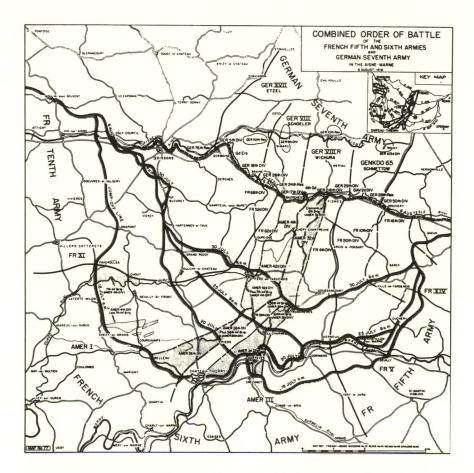

of the end-the-war offensives aimed at Amiens and Paris. The German chancellor, Count Georg von Hertling, summarized the circumstances starkly. "We expected grave events in Paris for the end of July. That was on the 15th. On the 18th even the most optimistic among us understood that all was lost. The history of the world was played out in three days."[5]

In his war diary, the German crown prince forthrightly admitted two miscalculations. He had underestimated the size of the enemy build-up, and he had assumed that the offensive against Reims would force Foch to weaken his attack. This latter assumption would have been proven correct, if Petain had been allowed to cancel Mangin's thrust. In other words, the German crown prince did not believe that Foch had sufficient resources to accept the dual responsibility of defending Reims and attacking the Tardenois region. The combination of efficient Allied defensive operations near Reims and enough full-strength divisions to attack southwest of Soissons was too much for the German defenders. Finally, the German crown prince emphasized the crucial impact of the enemy's armor. "The tanks, employed in numbers never known before and much better developed technically, rolled ahead of the infantry in long, connected lines. . . . the infantry opposing these fire-spitting, rapidly moving machines felt themselves deserted and lost their nerve." German tactical adjustments soon neutralized the tanks, preventing the Allies from cutting off large numbers of German troops, but Foch's initiative forced the Germans to abandon further offensive measures. Ludendorff immediately pointed out the correct response to an attack such as that of 18 July. "An attack must be recognized quickly, and swiftly followed by the alerting of all weapons and firing without delay, especially by the artillery, against important targets. Where the enemy could attack by surprise as on July 18 and effect a broad and deep penetration, this must have been lacking."[6]

Mangin's success forced the German High Command to order a phased withdrawal from the Marne salient northward to the line of the Vesle River. Hindenburg recognized the adverse consequences for the morale of his troops, but he had no alternative. The German army must "retire step by step, save our precious war material from the clutches of the enemy, and withdraw in good order to a new line of defence which nature offered us in the Aisne-Vesle sector." Hurried and sometimes costly reinforcement of the battered front-line units slowed the French Tenth and Sixth Armies sufficiently to permit a German retirement to the line of the Ourq River between 20 July and 29 July. During the last phase of the Aisne-Marne offensive (30 July–6 August), the Germans retreated to the Vesle, a maneuver dubbed the BLUECHER movement. To scrape together sufficient reserves of infantry, the German High Command had to disband about ten divisions, palpable evidence of extensive attrition. Having pinched out the Marne salient, Foch chose for the moment to pause on the line of the Vesle. Recognizing that he faced a strong defensive position, he wanted to avoid wasting precious resources in fruitless attacks. Besides, he was committed to important operations elsewhere.[7]

As the attack of 18 July 1918 began, twenty-five American divisions in France backed by over 1,000,000 support troops were scattered across the western front. They engaged in varied activities. Three (the 27th, 30th, and 33d) were serving with the British army while training for action. Seven (the 37th, 78th, 80th, 89th, 90th, 91st, and 92d) were training behind the French lines in areas identified for this purpose. Two others (the 41st and 83d) were designated as depot divisions. The 42d division was assigned to the French Fourth Army

German machine gunners firing at American troops near Fismettes on the Vesle River in July 1918. The Allies encountered positions of this type at every turn. Artillery and machine-gun fire imposed heavy casualties on all elements of Foch's inter-Allied army.

in Champagne, and the 92d Division was assigned by regiments to French divisions in the Argonne forest. Farther east beyond St. Mihiel, another American division (the 82d) served in sector with French forces. Four others (the 5th, 32d, 35th, and 77th) were brigaded with the French in quiet sectors located in Alsace. As noted above, the units transferred to the French armies for operations against the Marne salient were the 1st and 2d Divisions, serving as part of the French Tenth Army in its XX Corps. Four divisions were assigned to the French Sixth Army for the same attack (the 3d, 4th, 26th, and elements of the 28th).[8]

The AEF made a measurable contribution to the Aisne-Marne counteroffensive. About 270,000 troops of eight divisions participated in the movement to the Vesle, a total that far exceeded the number (about 140,000) who fought during the five German attacks from 21 March to 15 July. On 5 August, two American corps headquarters, the I Corps (Liggett) and the III Corps (Bullard) commanded the entire front of the French Sixth Army. Double-sized American divisions made up close to 25 percent of the Allied troops who took part. This reinforcement had a salutary effect on the morale of the Allied forces.

Hindenburg commented ruefully on the result: "The steady arrival of American reinforcements must be particularly valuable for the enemy. Even if these reinforcements were not yet quite up to the level of modern requirements in a purely military sense, mere numerical superiority had a far greater effect at this stage when our units had suffered so heavily."[9]

The eight American divisions that made contributions to the Aisne-Marne offensive were temporarily amalgamated into the French Tenth, Sixth, and Ninth Armies. They suffered terrible losses. The 1st and 2d Divisions in the XX Corps of the Tenth Army took about 11,000 casualties during the initial attack southwest of Soissons. A participating regiment, the 26th Infantry, lost all but 200 men; the highest ranking officer who survived was a captain. The 26th Division served in the Sixth Army as part of the American I Corps until the 42d Division relieved it on 25 July. These two divisions suffered almost 11,000 casualties. The 3d Division, part of the Ninth Army, absorbed almost 8,000 casualties. The 4th, 28th, and 32d Divisions also participated in the offensive, the 4th with the Sixth Army in the initial attack and the other two in the pursuit of the German army from the Ourq to the Vesle between 28 July and 2 August. Maj. Gen. Hunter Liggett, commanding the American I Corps, which included the French 167th Division and the American 26th, noted the significance of his command's activities after it entered the line on 4 July. "It was the first time since our Civil War that an American Army Corps had functioned in action, and the first time that an American command had foreign troops under its control since our War of Independence." He recognized that "success in action would go far to remove all objections to the formation of higher units under American command and staff."[10]

General Pershing later insisted that his divisions assured the success of the attack on the Marne salient. "Due to the magnificent dash and power displayed on the field of Soissons by our First and Second Divisions the tide of war was definitely turned in favor of the Allies. . . . The force of American arms had been brought to bear in time to enable the last offensive of the enemy to be crushed." This boastful claim exaggerated the useful but limited American role in operations, although the bulge in manpower that stemmed from the presence of the American army in France made a critical contribution to the victory. Pershing's statement also obscured various operational failings. On 31 July a French officer noted: "Aside from their limited combat experience, the combat value of the Americans suffers from faulty and too brief training." They lacked expertise in important areas: marksmanship, protection against gas attack, and the use of hand grenades. Besides, "little was noticeable of the influence of the command, of systematic employment of reserves for counterattack or of coordinated action of infantry and artillery." A recent evaluation argues that at Soissons the Americans "advanced in steady lines across open wheat fields as German machine-gunners shot them down. . . . Formations were too dense; little use was made of fire and maneuver; infantry cooperation with the supporting French tanks was poor; and artillery support was equally lacking." Observers both friendly and hostile unanimously praised the valor of the Americans. Just as regularly they cited the professional errors that the inexperienced troops, commanders, and staffs committed at this early stage of their service on the western front.[11]

On 24 July, barely a week after the attack on the Marne salient, Foch called Petain, Haig, and Pershing to Bombon to discuss the next phase of the campaign. The generalissimo recognized that after four months of defensive operations "imposed upon us by the enemy's numerical superiority, a victorious counter offensive had once more placed in our hands the initiative of operations and the power to direct the progress of the events in this long, vast war." He now sought to mount "a series of well ordered actions," employing "all the Allied resources as rapidly as possible, so as to prevent the enemy from recovering before we could effect his definite destruction." The limited operations he had in mind were designed to accomplish several purposes: (1) to augment the "moral ascendancy" gained on 18 July; (2) to sustain pressure on Ludendorff so that he could not organize a stable defense; (3) to impose attrition on the enemy's irreplaceable troops; (4) to recover valuable economic resources; and (5) to capture important lateral communications, especially rail lines, needed to maneuver Allied forces effectively to all points on the western front. Foch did not propose by these limited, coordinated attacks to force a decision upon the enemy; he viewed them as preliminary to a general assault. Nevertheless Cyril Falls reports him as musing at about this time: "What am I risking, after all? I asked myself. You can prepare for the worst and another year of fighting, but there is no crime in hoping for the best—decisive victory within a few months."[12]

Foch recognized that a breakthrough along conventional lines was all but impossible; he stressed unremitting pressure designed to cause irreversible attrition and eventual collapse. When one of the principal Allied leaders asked him about his intentions should Ludendorff attack, he answered by "striking out three rapid blows, with his right, with his left and again with his right, following these by launching out a vigorous kick." General Maurice describes Foch's purpose. "He determined not to be drawn into a protracted struggle, not to attempt the great break through until the enemy's reserves were exhausted, and he proposed to exhaust these reserves by a series of limited punches. Hence the three short, sharp blows, followed by the big kick." Foch himself stressed the necessity to coordinate the separate thrusts: "Although we wished to at-tack at the outset on only one point, our successive initiatives ought to be prepared as a part of one and the same series, so that each of them could, without delay, take advantage of the moral ascendancy gained by the previous one and the disorder brought about in the enemy's dispositions." It was im-portant also to fix the direction of the attacks "to arrive finally at one single resultant. This would notably increase the effect of our operations taken as a whole." In adopting this course, Foch avoided Ludendorff's tendency to pur-sue tactical successes too far and to neglect the coordination of offensive strikes.[13]

Foch had in mind four limited enterprises, all aimed at enemy salients. The first was the attack on the Marne salient already in progress, which would free the Paris-Chalons railway. The second was an attack on the Amiens salient in Picardy to free the Paris-Amiens railway. A third was an attack along the Lys River in Flanders to recapture a mining region in that area and to eliminate pressure on Dunkirk and Calais. The fourth was an attack on the St. Mihiel salient in Lorraine to free the Paris-Avricourt railway. This operation was as-signed to the American First Army. At last, Pershing would command a predominantly American force. These operations, Foch insisted, "must suc-ceed each other at brief intervals, so as to embarrass the enemy in the utiliza-tion of his reserves and not allow him sufficient time to fill up his units." The principal tactical emphasis was on surprise: "Recent operations show that this is a condition indispensable to success."[14]

The national commanders-in-chief agreed to Foch's plan, although each cited difficulties. Haig claimed that his forces were still recovering from the devastating losses of March and April. Petain emphasized the general weakness of the French army after four years of fighting. Pershing said: "The American Army asks nothing better than to fight, but it has not yet been formed." Foch recognized the truth of these observations but argued that "a proper combina-tion of our forces would make the contemplated programme practicable, especially as we could carry it out at a pace which I would fix as circumstances arose—my idea being to hasten or slow it up according to the success obtained as we went along."[15]

General Rawlinson, the commander of the British Fourth Army, had already begun to make plans for an attack east of Amiens to relieve the Paris-Amiens

Gen. (later Marshal) Ferdinand Foch (left) and Gen. John J. Pershing in June 1918.

railroad from German bombardments. His preparations reflected the principles of attack first tried at Cambrai in November 1917 and improved upon at Hamel on 4 July. In the latter instance, the Australian Gen. John Monash undertook to clear an enemy salient between Villers-Bretonneux and the Somme River. His plan stressed surprise and close cooperation between armor, artillery, aircraft, and infantry—a fully realized application of combined arms doctrine. Tanks with infantry led the attack, closely following a moving artillery barrage.

Meanwhile aircraft attacked enemy antitank weapons and dropped ammunition to advancing infantry. This blow overcame German machine guns and forced defending infantry into dugouts, which were easily dealt with. Monash summarized his views cogently. "The true role of infantry was not to expend itself upon heroic physical effort, nor to wither away under merciless machine gun fire, nor to impale itself on hostile bayonets, nor to tear itself to pieces in hostile entanglements." Instead ground troops should "advance under the maximum possible array of mechanical resources, in the form of guns, machine guns, tanks, mortars and aeroplanes." Infantry would move with light loads and without serious fighting responsibilities at this stage. They were "to march, resolutely, regardless of the din and tumult of battle, to the appointed goal; and there to hold and defend the territory gained; and to gather, in the form of prisoners, guns and stores, the fruits of victory." Four companies of the American 33d Division took part in the success at Hamel. When General Pershing learned that these units were to attack, he attempted unsuccessfully to withdraw them. This episode hardened Pershing's opposition to American combat service under European commanders.[16]

Plans for the Amiens offensive applied Monash's principles on a large scale. Foch strengthened the attack by arranging for Debeney's French First Army to advance to the south of Rawlinson's much-augmented command. The BEF—now reconstructed, refreshed, and retrained—was poised to resume the offensive on 8 August.[17]

At 0400 on 8 August, two thousand guns opened on the German lines, and the 456 tanks and infantry of the British Fourth Army moved forward immediately on a front of over 12 miles. The assault echelons gained total surprise against the German Second Army (von der Marwitz), which had but six skeletal divisions on line, averaging about 3,000 effectives each. Tanks administered a shock comparable to Bruchmueller's bombardments in the earlier German assaults. On the first day, Rawlinson's Australian and Canadian Corps advanced over 6 miles, inflicting over 27,000 casualties and taking over 13,000 prisoners and 300 guns. His cost was only 9,000 casualties. Simultaneously, the French First Army struck south toward Roye and Lassigny against the German Eighteenth Army (von Hutier). On Rawlinson's left the British Third Army (Byng) and First Army (Horne) also gained ground. The attack continued until 12 August, when the British reached the devastated battlefields of 1916, about 12 miles in advance of the position occupied on 8 August. Foch wanted to continue the attack, but Haig objected successfully, arguing that further operations would produce heavy losses without commensurate gains.[18]

The techniques of Hamel succeeded remarkably at Amiens. Limited mobility had returned to the battlefield because of effective cooperation between infantry, armor, artillery, and aircraft, but this innovative use of combined arms did not presage a decisive breakthrough. Two British authorities summarize the reasons: "The infantryman still walked at three miles per hour and the tank at much the same average pace. The roads through the old fighting zones were still too appalling to permit vehicles to carry significant numbers of troops to open country beyond." Foch "abandoned the grand tactics of the breakthrough for those that sought a progressive loosening of the front." An American authority agrees: operational success in 1918 stemmed from "sustained attrition and demoralization" rather than "decisive penetration and exploitation." The key to victory was unrelenting pressure rather than envelopment. On 22 August, Haig issued an order calling for "the most resolute offensive. . . . Risks which a month ago would have been criminal to incur ought now to be incurred as a duty. It is no longer necessary to advance in regular lines and step by step. . . . Reinforcements must be directed on points where our troops are gaining ground, not where they are checked." Foch applauded this statement, writing to Haig on 26 August: "It is this persistent widening and intensifying of the offensive—this pushing vigorously forward on carefully chosen objectives without over-preoccupation as to alignment or close liaison—that will give us the best results with the smallest losses, as you have so perfectly comprehended."[19]

The British victory at Amiens threw the German High Command into confusion. After the Allied success of 18 July, Ludendorff recognized that his army was in great difficulty, having failed to impose a decision before the arrival of massive American reinforcements. As he withdrew forces to the line of the Vesle River, he contemplated various possible Allied thrusts, but he assumed that these would "take the form of only isolated local attacks." He thought that his troops could contain these thrusts and mount limited counterstrokes. "Even in extremely critical situations we had hitherto always succeeded in discovering a strategical remedy, and I had no reason to suppose we would not do so again." He recognized that Germany must now seek a political settlement, but he believed that his army was strong enough to force an acceptable peace. Then came the attack of 8 August, which Ludendorff dramatically characterized as "the black day of the German army in the history of this war." He now recognized the consequences of exhausting his reserves while the Allies received many American divisions. All thought of the offensive disappeared; "our only course . . . was to hold on" while seeking an early end to the war.[20]

For the moment, the High Command weighed the possibility of retiring immediately to the strong fortifications that guarded lateral communications

along the western front. These were known as the Hindenburg line. Gen.
Friedrich von Lossberg, a specialist on defense, urged such a course, but Ludendorff decided to stretch out this movement. He did not wish to leave communications sufficiently intact to simplify Foch's advance, and he also hoped
to extricate essential material. Foch recognized his antagonist's motives, saying early in September that "the man could still get away if he did not worry
about his baggage." In any event, the future of the Central Powers depended
on Ludendorff's ability to foil Foch's coordinated attacks, wherever he made
his stand.[21]

The German generals speedily recognized that the Allies had adopted new
operational doctrine, much of it derived from observation of Ludendorff's attacks from March to July, and they tried to adjust. To avoid surprise, the German crown prince emphasized the need for a deep outpost zone in front of
the main line of resistance with skillful use of machine guns. "As heretofore,
the defense will be conducted from positions organized in depth; it will be
elastic and in the spirit of the offensive. Organization of the position, which
must be pushed more than before, will conform to this requirement." He also
stressed combat intelligence: "The thorough and uninterrupted observation
of the enemy with all the means of reconnaissance must be insisted upon. The
best picture of the situation can be obtained through prisoners." These were
sound instructions. They served the Germans well during the last months of
the war, but no amount of properly applied doctrine could counter the
precipitous decline in German rifle strength by comparison with that of the
Allies after July 1918. The American buildup created this situation. On 20
August, a German officer spoke to a member of the kaiser's retinue "in very
grave terms" about the American presence. The United States already had thirty
divisions of 40,000 men each; they were "fighting with great dash, whereas
our troops are tired."[22]

On 13–14 August 1918, a series of exchanges at Spa between the German
High Command and leaders of the civil government laid bare the extent of
the German predicament. On 13 August, Ludendorff communicated his views
to the German chancellor, Hertling, and the new foreign minister, Admiral
Paul von Hintze. "It was no longer possible by an offensive to force the enemy
to sue for peace. Defense alone could hardly achieve this object, and so the
termination of the war would have to be brought about by diplomacy." On
the next day, Hintze adopted Ludendorff's point of view in a meeting with
Emperor Wilhelm, who instructed him to begin peace negotiations, possibly
through the Queen of the Netherlands. It was understood that this initiative
must await a favorable turn in the battle. No such circumstance ever developed;

Germany thus squandered an opportunity to mitigate the severe terms that the Allies might seek to impose. Ludendorff was largely responsible for this course. He failed to clarify fully for the civil leadership the extent of the military peril. During the remaining months of the war, the German people, their government, and their army fought with ever declining prospects of victory, while the Allies attacked with ever growing expectations of success.[23]

The defeat at Amiens forced Ludendorff gradually to shorten his lines, the only device available to compensate for losses of manpower. Foch had arranged to launch his third limited counteroffensive in the Ypres-Lys area, but before this attack could occur the German army withdrew from the salient in Flanders. On 26 August, Ludendorff ordered the German Fourth and Sixth Armies to retreat to the line Wytschaete–front of Armentieres–west of La Bassee. The German commander summarized the reasons for this decision starkly: "to shorten the front [and] . . . effect economy of force by relying upon prepared positions and thereby create reserves." The advance of the British Second Army, which was completed by 4 September, finished the occupation of the evacuated area. Two American divisions, the 27th (Maj. Gen. John F. O'Ryan) and the 30th (Maj. Gen. Edward M. Lewis), participated in this operation, fighting in the Dickenbush area. Meanwhile further attacks on 21 August at Bapaume by the British Third Army (Byng) and later on 2 September by the Canadian Corps against an extension of the Hindenburg line known as the Drocourt-Queant switch line pushed the Germans back to the Canal du Nord.[24]

On 18 August, the French began the Oise-Aisne offensive; like the British operations it pressed the Germans slowly toward the Hindenburg fortifications. The American III Corps (the 28th, 32d, and 77th Divisions) under General Bullard, which was assigned to the French Sixth Army (Degoutte), made extensive contributions to this bitter fighting. The Allies broke through the German defenses along the Vesle River and reached the Aisne River. On 30 August, the 32d Division gained the distinction of capturing Juvigny. These advances brought the Allies almost to the positions they had occupied before 21 March 1918. The reaction of the German Seventh Army to the Allied attacks in the Oise-Aisne sector typified that of Ludendorff's other forces. "The mission of the Seventh Army will be to continue to fight a defensive battle. This mission is more beset with trials than our majestic offensives, but nevertheless it must be assumed with all our energy and must be executed in such a manner that we not only ward off the enemy but inflict such losses upon him that his strength is broken and we come out victors."[25]

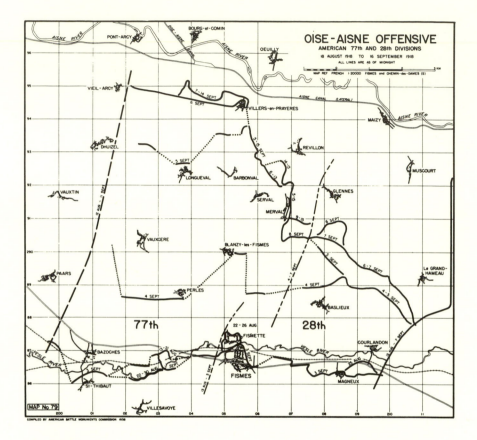

There remained only the American reduction of the St. Mihiel salient to complete Foch's series of limited counteroffensives, an assignment that finally forced the creation of the American First Army. On 9 August, Foch asked Pershing to leave four divisions with the French on the Vesle. Discussions with Petain fixed that number at three, the units of the III Corps (Bullard) then serving with the French during the Oise-Aisne offensive. These divisions returned to American control early in September. The American First Army was officially formed on 10 August, and its headquarters was established at Neufchateau. Pershing formally assumed command on 30 August at Ligny-en-Barrois, but in the meantime he moved to recover control of three of the five American divisions then serving with the BEF. Pershing informed Foch that he wanted to score "a striking success" in his initial operation at St. Mihiel. "It is not only the effect which an American success would have on the enemy but the effect on the Allied morale and especially on that of the American people, leading as it will to redoubled efforts, which causes me to be especially anxious to assemble the greatest possible number of my troops for this operation." Haig had no alternative but to concur in this request but privately expressed dismay. "What will history say regarding this action of the Americans leaving the British zone of operations when *the decisive battle* of the war is at its height, and the decision still in doubt!" Two days later he maintained that retention of the American divisions would have assured "immediate and decisive results" because of the "tired and demoralised state of the Germans on this front." The result was that three American divisions then in the British zone – the 33d, 78th, and 80th – were returned to Pershing. The 27th and 30th Divisions remained with Haig. Foch ensured that these latter organizations would be available for both training and operations. As noted above, they participated in the Flanders campaign at the beginning of September.[26]

The American First Army of fourteen divisions formed to attack the St. Mihiel salient was woefully short of artillery, tanks, and aviation, a consequence of the priority given to the shipment of infantry and machine gunners. Pershing therefore obtained French help in these categories. Among other units, Foch allotted ninety-nine batteries of French 75s, fifty batteries of heavy howitzers, and twenty-one squadrons of aircraft. He also provided artillery staffs for two of the three American corps because the Americans had only one such organization. Pershing never came close to completing his design for a completely independent army. He depended heavily on the Allies for support in deficient categories until the end of the war. The American G-3, General Conner, attributed the American shortages to the decision to give priority of shipment to infantry and machine-gun troops, making it necessary "to arrange with the French for a great part of the corps and army artillery, aviation, and other services. . . . The French High Command always responded most generously to our requests and we conducted all our attacks with a dominating force of artillery and of aviation." The American Battle Monuments Commission emphasized Pershing's reliance on European supplies. "Except for four 14-inch naval guns on railway mounts, the American First Army throughout its entire service on the front did not fire an American-made cannon or shell, and . . . no American-made tank was ever available in Europe for use in battle."[27]

The initial objective of the First Army, the St. Mihiel salient, had fallen to German troops on 24 September 1914, and French efforts to regain it were turned aside in 1915. During 1916, it was used as a base for the German attacks at Verdun. After that it became a quiet sector; both sides trained and rested troops there. Located between the Moselle River to the east and the Meuse River to the west, it covered the Briey iron mines and the important communications center of Metz. It also threatened surrounding French territory, including the regions between Bar-le-Duc and Nancy and between Bar-le-Duc and Verdun. If the Allies wished to undertake operations west of the Meuse or east of the Moselle, they must eliminate the salient. Shaped like a triangle with its apex at St. Mihiel and its base anchored on the towns of Haudiomont and Pont-a-Mousson 25 miles apart, it had a depth of 16 miles. To the northeast of the base stretched the Woevre plain. The heights of the Meuse to the northwest afforded excellent observation, as did the hills of Loupmont and Montsec east of St. Mihiel. The countryside was low-lying, marshy, and subject to flooding. Roads were few and unpaved.[28]

The German troops in the salient, part of Composite Army C commanded by General Fuchs, manned extensive defenses. At the base of the salient lay the Michel Stellung, which was composed of two lines, the first well fortified, the second less so. Two fortified positions guarded the salient itself, the outer Wilhelm position and the inner Schroeter position 5 miles to the rear. The American Battle Monuments Commission described these defenses as "a veritable field fortress" that included "elaborate systems of trenches, barbed-wire entanglements, concrete shelters and machine-gun emplacements." Three German divisions known as the Combres Group guarded the west face of the salient. Elsewhere the I Bavarian Corps provided troops for the Mihiel Group (two divisions) near the nose of the salient and the Gorz Group (two divisions) on the south face. Another organization, the 255th Division of the German Nineteenth Army, entered the area on the day of the battle, taking position on the left flank of the German defenses. These units were low rated and under strength, containing a mere 23,000 combat troops. Seven other divisions formed a reserve.[29]

General Pershing's original plan for the attack on the St. Mihiel salient, which became known as the August Plan, reflected staff work that reached back to the early days of the AEF. The reduction of the salient was to precede a thrust through the Michel Stellung toward Metz. The Americans intended to gain control of important economic zones and most importantly the railroad that supplied the German armies to the west. This scheme reflected the early American decision to field an independent army and to strike a final, decisive blow that would win the war. The First Army was formed with the August Plan in mind. On 16 August, First Army headquarters produced a mature order for the reduction of the St. Mihiel salient. It specified as the minimum objective the reopening of the Paris-Avricourt railroad near Commercy that connected Nancy to the west. Two attacks by as many as fourteen divisions would envelop the salient, forcing the defenders to evacuate it. The principal effort would be directed against the south face through Thiaucourt and the other attack would strike the west face through Fresnes. Pershing would conduct further operations to the east, depending on "the degree of surprise realized during the first day's operations." Foch identified the Paris-Avricourt railway as the principal objective, but he also expected other results "such as hitting the enemy as hard a blow as possible, obtaining the maximum benefits to be expected from a major operation, conquering an advantageous base for subsequent operations."[30]

At this juncture, a sudden switch in Foch's plans forced a fundamental change in American operations. Haig, emboldened by success, urged Foch to turn when possible from local attacks to a general offensive against the huge salient that Germany had pushed into France and Belgium. He proposed to attack the west face of this salient in the direction of Cambrai, first breaching the Hindenburg line and then interdicting the railroad that supplied the Germans at a point near Maubeuge. Pershing should attack the south face from positions west of the Meuse River toward Mezieres, another town on the railroad that supplied the Germans. Loss of the railroad between Maubeuge and Mezieres would force Ludendorff into a general withdrawal, perhaps as far as the German border. This supply line was needed to sustain the troops defending the Hindenburg fortifications. To interfere with Ludendorff's ability to concentrate forces against the BEF, the American army would directly support Haig's operations. These ideas appealed strongly to Foch, who had begun to consider a general attack. He soon began preparations for the vast double envelopment that Haig had envisioned, a strike against the shoulders of the German line. Petain proved supportive; the two main attacks would take place to the left and the right of his main forces, promising to simplify the tasks of the French army.[31]

Foch must now deal with Pershing, who for many months had planned to follow the reduction of the St. Mihiel salient with a push eastward toward Metz. "I was led to reduce the Woevre operation [St. Mihiel] to a far smaller scope than I had in mind when I wrote my instructions of August 17th; and in addition I was led to ask General Pershing to undertake a new offensive." On 30 August, Foch revealed his desires to Pershing. He proposed to attach four to six American divisions to the French Second Army; this combined force would attack north between the Meuse River and the Argonne forest. West of the Argonne, an American army of eight to ten divisions would join the French Fourth Army astride the Aisne for a second northward attack. These operations would limit the American force assigned for the attack on the St. Mihiel salient to eight or nine divisions, and the shift of the First Army westward would preclude an eastward move toward Metz.[32]

These unexpected and unwelcome proposals greatly agitated General Pershing, who sought to reverse them. He first argued that a limited attack on the St. Mihiel salient would take as many divisions as would the preliminary phases of a move toward Metz. Especially disturbed because Foch's plan would split his forces and again delay independent American operations, he suggested that his army might follow St. Mihiel with a concentration west of the Meuse for an attack toward Mezieres. Foch thought this suggestion worthy of consideration, but he noted the difficulties that would arise because of the time constraints. Pershing must attack St. Mihiel by 10 September and the other objective by 15–20 September. To Pershing's views about the number of divisions required for the attack on the salient, Foch responded: "The Germans would fall back from St-Mihiel at the first sign; . . . we would only be playing into their hands if they could engage a large number of our troops for a certain length of time; . . . he did not look for much resistance." Pershing then returned to his concerns about splitting his forces. "He did not want to appear difficult, but . . . the American people and the American government expect that the American Army will act as such and shall not be dispersed here and there along the Western Front. Each time that we are on the point of accomplishing this organization, some proposition is presented to break it up." This statement was too much for Foch who asked: "Do you wish to take part in the battle?" Pershing responded: "Most assuredly, but as an American Army." After further discussion of American operations west of the Meuse, possibly on both sides of the Argonne forest, the meeting broke up.[33]

Pershing then set about blocking Foch's new design. On 31 August, he dispatched a memorandum that systematized the arguments he had advanced on the previous day, and he added some thoughts. Among them was the observation that the American buildup since 1917 had been designed to support an attack eastward into the Woevre. He thought it necessary either to abandon the attack on the salient or to postpone the operations west of the Meuse. Then he offered a suggestion that must have annoyed Foch exceedingly. He wanted to conduct the reduction of the salient but then "withdraw as many divisions as practicable and reconstitute and train them with a view to their employment in attack either in the region of Belfort or Luneville." After that he would consolidate his forces and prepare his army for an attack in the winter. During January–February 1919, he would take over the front from St. Mihiel to Switzerland. He added that if Foch persisted in his plan to move toward Mezieres from west of the Meuse, he would agree to attack either east or west of the Argonne forest with an independent command.[34]

Foch then moved to settle matters, calling Pershing to a meeting at Bombon on 2 September, to which he also invited Petain, a supporter of his plan. The day before this gathering, he responded to Pershing's message of 31 August with a note that repeated his intentions. He still called for a preliminary operation at St. Mihiel but also for the attack west of the Meuse, the nature of which he wished to discuss at Bombon. If necessary, he proposed to abandon the reduction of the salient. When Foch met Pershing and Petain at Bombon, they reached a compromise. Foch bowed to Pershing's insistence on conducting an independent American operation. In return Pershing agreed to follow the St. Mihiel action with an attack between the Meuse and the Argonne in association with the French Fourth Army, which would operate to the west of the Argonne. Pershing later explained his choice of the Meuse-Argonne sector instead of one farther west. "In my opinion, no other Allied troops had the morale or the offensive spirit to overcome successfully the difficulties to be met in the Meuse-Argonne sector and our plans and installations had been prepared for an expansion of operations in that direction." Pershing decided to attack the St. Mihiel salient on 10 September with eight to ten divisions, halting on the line Vigneulles–Thiaucourt–Regneville. He would then move to the Meuse-Argonne sector for an attack by twelve to fourteen divisions between 20 and 25 September. Other American divisions would join this attack when available, including those recuperating from the St. Mihiel operation. The French Fourth Army would support this attack on the left; both the French and American armies would come under the command of General Petain.[35]

The decision to move on both the St. Mihiel salient and the Meuse-Argonne sector entailed considerable risk. American divisions, perforce still inexperienced, must transfer speedily from the salient to a strongly fortified sector defended by determined enemy forces. Donald Smythe, Pershing's biographer, believes that this enterprise was "really too large an undertaking." Basil Liddell Hart, a British authority, notes that "each attack interfered with the other. And the consequences were compound not simple." The AEF, about to wage war for the first time in large numbers, suffered for the rest of the war from Pershing's insistence on making the attack against the St. Mihiel salient. This decision precluded use of the best American divisions during the early stages of operations west of the Meuse. Pershing offered one powerful rationale for his course, the need to eliminate a threat to the rear of the Meuse-Argonne sector, but his need for a quick, easy victory to justify his faith in his troops and his policy of forming an independent army were of equal or greater importance. It is also conceivable that he hoped eventually to resuscitate the eastward attack that he had contemplated since 1917. Personal and national ambitions were not easily submerged during World War I, even during the most difficult times. Such considerations constantly influenced the Allies; the Americans were not immune from the same proclivity, especially the stubborn, self-righteous Pershing.[36]

First Army headquarters now produced a revised design for the attack on the St. Mihiel salient that became known as the September Plan. The new scheme retained the principal features of the August Plan, a primary assault on the south face of the salient and a secondary attack against the west face. Added were holding attacks and raids against the nose of the salient. Maj. Gen. Joseph Dickman's IV Corps (89th, 42d, and 1st Divisions) was assigned the principal attack against the south face of the salient. It would move between Limey and Marvoisin toward Vigneulles. To his right, Maj. Gen. Hunter Liggett's I Corps (82d, 90th, 5th, and 2d Divisions) was to make a supporting attack. The V Corps under Maj. Gen. George H. Cameron (26th, part of the 4th, and the French 15th Colonial Divisions) was given the mission of striking eastward across the heights of the Meuse south of Les Epargues toward Vigneulles. Then it was to link with Dickman's troops, cutting off the defending German units. At the nose of the salient, the French II Colonial Corps was assigned the task of supporting the attacks on its left and right flanks. Three divisions constituted the reserve (the 35th, 80th, and 91st Divisions). Use of the most experienced American organizations (the 1st, 2d, 4th, 26th, and 42d Divisions) against St. Mihiel meant that Pershing must rely during the initial phases of the Meuse-Argonne offensive on inexperienced troops. Some 550,000 American and 110,000 French troops of all branches were to attack 23,000 German and Austrian combat troops in the salient, the effective strength of seven divisions usually on line. French artillery swelled the total of artillery weapons to over three thousand guns, and Allied help brought together almost fifteen hundred aircraft, the largest concentration ever made to that date. One authority notes that the assemblage "made an army nearly four times as large as Grant's Army of the Potomac at its maximum strength, three times Napoleon's Grand Army at Leipzig, nearly twice the German army at Sedan in 1870, and much larger than either the Japanese or Russian armies at Mukden, the largest on record before 1914."[37]

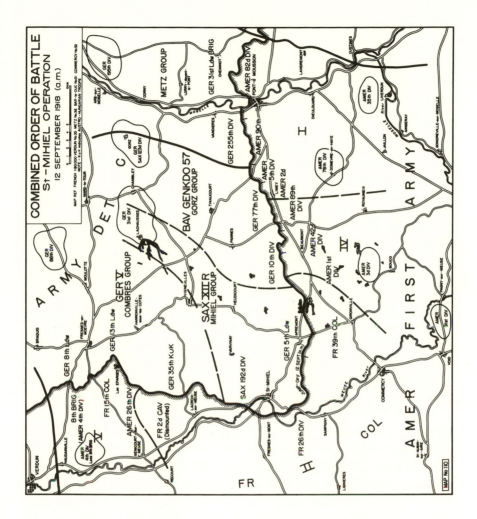

COMBINED ORDER OF BATTLE
St-MIHIEL OPERATION
12 SEPTEMBER 1918 (a.m.)

MAP REF: FRENCH 1:80,000 VERDUN No.35, METZ No.36, BAR-le-DUC No.51, COMMERCY No.52
NOTE — 4 & 5 INDICATE AUSTRO-HUNGARIAN TROOPS

MAP No.110

To mislead the German defenders, the First Army undertook a deception known as the "Belfort ruse." The headquarters of the VI Corps was ordered to Belfort; its mission was to convince the enemy that the American attack would take place in that area toward Mulhausen. Long after the war, Col. Arthur L. Conger gave details of this operation, which included efforts to plant documents. After intentionally failing to put away some official information, he remembered: "I left my room for five minutes to walk around the corridor of the principal hotel in Belfort and upon my return found it [a copy of a document] gone as I hoped it would be."[38]

The Belfort ruse may have created some confusion, but the German Composite Army C realized that the Americans were preparing an attack on the salient. This circumstance stimulated the German High Command to order a retreat. Hindenburg called the salient "a tactical abortion." He thought it "possibly . . . a matter of reproach to us that we had not evacuated this position long before, certainly as soon as our attack on Verdun was broken off." On 1 September, a German intelligence group noted rumors of impending attacks in several locations and expressed surprise at the relative inactivity of Pershing's divisions. It seemed possible that the Americans were "held back in order to undertake an attack independently in the near future, under American command," but the point of attack was not specified. Ludendorff recognized that an attack on the salient was likely. The Army Group commander, Gen. Max von Gallwitz, gave instructions to Composite Army C to withdraw to the Michel position if faced with an enemy attack. The local commander, Fuchs, wanted to resist, but Ludendorff demurred. "The forces for repulsing a broad attack . . . are not at present available. The attack is therefore not to be met in the present forward combat zone, but in this case, avoiding it by a withdrawal into the Michel [position] is contemplated, though only in the event of an enveloping attack." On 8 September, Ludendorff ordered Gallwitz to hasten his withdrawal from the St. Mihiel salient, but the army group commander did not do so. This hesitation stemmed from the wish of Composite Army C to deal with the American buildup by making a spoiling attack. Much as Foch had predicted, Ludendorff would have none of this scheme. Composite Army C began the withdrawal, which was called the Loki movement, on 11 September, taking out heavy material but no troops at this stage.[39]

As Composite Army C reluctantly prepared to evacuate the salient, American intelligence began to receive intimations from enemy deserters and prisoners that the Germans, aware of the impending attack, planned to withdraw. The daily "Summary of Intelligence" for the period 7–11 September 1918 listed various reports to this effect. On 8 September, for example, a deserter from the 35th Austro-Hungarian Division reported that his unit was to withdraw if attacked. "In confirmation of this the deserter states that no new work is under way, and that in the past week some heavy guns and ammunition for heavy guns have been sent to the rear. He personally saw shells of 150 caliber being sent to the rear on a narrow gauge line." On 9 September, an Alsatian deserter reported that "the enemy is removing material from the sector, as if a withdrawal was imminent." As usual, prisoner interrogations were confusing. On 11 September, a Rumanian prisoner reported that two big guns had been removed from his sector, but he knew nothing about a planned withdrawal. Pershing's intelligence officers noted that radio traffic in the salient was normal. They concluded that the enemy troops were still in position, although they might be evacuating heavy equipment and supplies. Thus the reports of the German withdrawal did not lead to last-minute changes in American plans. Pershing recognized that the enemy might have prepared to withdraw from the region. He knew that they had information about the impending attack, which he thought might lead them to reinforce their positions. He decided to include his most experienced divisions with raw units. "Anything short of complete success would undoubtedly be seized upon to our disadvantage by those of the Allies who opposed the policy of forming an American Army."[40]

The complexity inherent in organizing over half a million troops delayed the attack until 12 September. It began at 0100 with an intense artillery bombardment from three thousand guns that lasted until 0500, when I and IV Corps moved against the south face of the salient. Two hundred and sixty-seven light tanks commanded by Lt. Col. George C. Patton, Jr., accompanied them. At 0800 V Corps attacked the west face. Meanwhile the French II Colonial Corps began its holding attacks at the nose of the salient between the American IV Corps to its right and the V Corps to its left. Although the enemy knew that an attack was in the offing, it was not expected for several days. Tactical surprise benefited the Americans; they advanced in all areas without undue difficulty, taking advantage of air cover provided by nearly fourteen hundred airplanes, many of them French and English, under the command of Col. William E. Mitchell. The chief of staff of IV Corps soon reported that the enemy was "apparently disorganized and . . . retreating as rapidly as possible before our troops. He has offered but little resistance." His greatest problem was the road net. "Great difficulty [was] experienced, on account of the bad condition of roads, in bringing up ammunition and rations." The chief of staff of

An ammunition wagon mired in mud blocking an American column as it moves against the St. Mihiel salient in September 1918. Commanders experienced great difficulty in providing adequate supplies and communications.

I Corps made much the same observation. By nightfall, the American columns driving toward Vigneulles were only 10 miles apart.[41]

At noon on 12 September, General Fuchs recognized that his forces were in danger of being cut off, and he took immediate action. Initially the Mihiel Group was ordered to retreat to the Schroeter position, but it was soon decided to continue the movement to the Michel position without making an interim stand. By 0400 on 13 September, Fuchs completed the Loki movement. Shortly after that, just after daylight, elements of the 1st Division of IV Corps and the 26th Division of V Corps met near Hattonchatel and Vigneulles. Fortunately for the Germans, Pershing had given his corps commanders very little freedom of action. When he sensed the opportunity to effect an early junction, he was unable to get orders to his front-line commanders in time to hasten the movement to Vigneulles, a delay that allowed thousands of Germans to escape capture.[42]

By the afternoon of 13 September, the American forces had reached all objectives specified in their orders and had begun to consolidate their gains. The First Army had gained its main goals, seizure of the Paris-Avricourt railway and removal of threats to Allied positions adjacent to the salient. Pershing reported the capture of nearly 16,000 prisoners, 443 guns, 752 machine guns, and large amounts of material. The First Army had suffered only 7,000 casualties, although the daily rate of 3,500 casualties per day was high. About

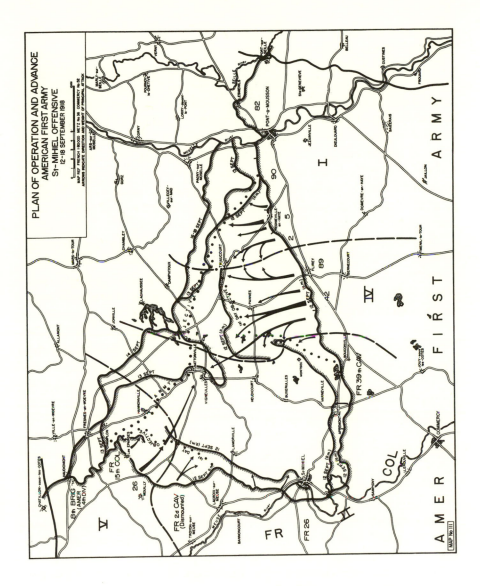

PLAN OF OPERATION AND ADVANCE
AMERICAN FIRST ARMY
St-MIHIEL OFFENSIVE
12-18 SEPTEMBER 1918

MAP No III

3,000 more casualties occurred during the period of consolidation after 13 September. Further operations were designed merely to improve defensive positions. All activity ceased by 16 September. Ludendorff and von Gallwitz thought that the First Army might continue its attack, but the Americans immediately began the exceedingly difficult task of moving the First Army to the Meuse-Argonne sector. Hindenburg, stung by the German reverse, reacted angrily to von Gallwitz's request for reinforcements. "I am not willing to admit that one American division is worth 2 German. Whenever commanders and troops have been determined to hold their position and the artillery has been well organized, even weak German divisions have repulsed the mass attacks of American divisions and inflicted especially heavy casualties on the enemy."[43]

Some of Pershing's commanders wanted to continue the drive, breaking through the Michel position and moving on to Metz despite the commitment to transfer to the Meuse-Argonne sector. Col. George Marshall opposed further attacks because of Foch's orders. Nevertheless he concluded: "There is no doubt in my mind that we could have reached the outskirts of Metz by the late afternoon of the 13th, and quite possibly have captured the city on the 14th, as the enemy was incapable of bringing up reserves in sufficient number and formation to offer an adequate resistance." Brig. Gen. Douglas MacArthur, a member of the 42d Division, also thought that it would have been easy to capture Metz.[44]

Others recognized the difficulties that would have arisen. Contrary to Marshall's information, German reserves were available to defend the powerful fortress of Metz. Continuation of the First Army's movement presumed an ability to move men, materials, and especially artillery forward at an efficient pace. General Liggett offered an authoritative rebuttal of Marshall and MacArthur. "The possibility of taking Metz and the rest of it, had the battle been fought on the original plan, existed, in my opinion, only on the supposition that our army was a well-oiled, fully coordinated machine, which it was not as yet." Had the attack continued, he thought that the First Army "would have had an excellent chance of spending the greater part of the winter mired in the mud of the Woevre, flanked both to the east [by the Metz fortifications] and the west [by artillery positions in the heights of the Meuse]." He defended Foch's plan, which precluded any exploitation of the gains made on 12–13 September. "Marshal Foch was exceedingly wise to limit us to the immediate task of flattening out the salient and protecting our rear for another attack to the westward." A British authority, Basil Liddell Hart, made another observation of considerable significance. To interdict the railway supplying German armies farther west, the First Army would have had to move beyond Metz. "It is well to remember that Pershing would at least have to reach the Longuyon-Thionville stretch of lateral highway, a further twenty miles beyond the Michel line, and to have gone far enough beyond it to intercept the line running back from Longuyon through Luxembourg. It would have demanded a penetration deeper and quicker than any yet made by the Allies on the western front. With an untried army surely this was a remote hope. . . . It is more than likely that the eventual result would have justified Liggett's opinion and Napoleon's maxim: 'With a new army it is possible to carry a formidable position, but not to carry out a plan or design.' "[45]

Pershing later praised his victory unreservedly. Besides the territory gained and the material captured, he saw it as vindication of his insistence on forming an independent army. His triumph depressed the morale of the enemy and gave his troops "explicit confidence in their superiority and raised their morale to the highest pitch." He also claimed doctrinal vindication. "For the first time wire entanglements ceased to be regarded as impassable barriers and open-warfare training, which had been so urgently insisted upon, proved to be the correct doctrine."[46]

Many authorities have disagreed with this rosy interpretation. Composite Army C had planned to withdraw and did so when it recognized the extent of the American attack. A victory it was, but some have held that in effect the Americans simply relieved the Germans in their trenches, hardly an imposing feat of arms. The operation did not prove the soundness of training in open warfare. Surely the assault of the First Army both accelerated and confused the Loki movement. If the Germans had resisted, they would have been unable to cope with the huge mass of the First Army, but they might well have inflicted terrible damage before accepting defeat. Besides, the easy victory concealed a multitude of American miscarriages during the attack, the consequences of forming the First Army before its units were fully prepared for combat. Donald Smythe has catalogued various deficiencies: the artillery and infantry were often uncoordinated; "discipline was lax. . . . Pilfering of prisoners was almost universal"; commanders failed to replace damaged telephone communications with "a horse relay system"; commanders located themselves too far from the front lines to maintain control; orders were unnecessarily long and confusing; traffic control broke down completely. Smythe concludes: "Far from being impressed by the American effort, many felt that it revealed serious deficiencies which boded ill for the future." No one, however, questioned the valor of the American army. Cruttwell emphasized its fighting qualities. It "had shown the greatest boldness and dash," but these very attributes contributed to "carelessness about liaison, overstepping of boundaries, overrunning the barrage. As further events were to show, in an army of self-confident individualists, these defects could not easily be eradicated."[47]

The German commanders offered various excuses for their defeat. Von Gallwitz complained of the vulnerable character of the position, and Fuchs emphasized the small number of troops available for the defense. The difficulties of the Americans did not escape observation. One German observer noted clumsy movements and inadequate commanders: "The enemy was helpless when confronted by a new situation and unable to exploit the success. . . . The entire lack of military skill was also evident in the pursuit. No advantage was taken of favorable opportunities for attacks on flanks and envelopments." These deficiencies allowed Army Group C "to break contact with the enemy in one night and occupy positions within a short distance and be again ready for combat."[48]

In any event, the success at St. Mihiel completed Foch's series of four limited counteroffensives. Without exception, the generalissimo gained his purposes. Each attack improved lateral communications and complicated those of the enemy. Each improved morale among the victors and depressed the German ranks. Of great significance for the immediate future was the terrible attrition imposed on Ludendorff's forces. The Germans could not replace their losses, whereas American reinforcements more than compensated for casualties inflicted upon Foch's armies. Finally, these reverses prevented the German government from gaining an opportunity to inaugurate peace negotiations that might lessen the adverse consequences of defeat.

Even as the Americans prepared their attack at St. Mihiel and the French and British armies advanced toward the Hindenburg line of fortifications, Foch busily prepared for a turn to a general offensive. This motive had led him to veto an extension of the American attack eastward out of the St. Mihiel salient. This huge series of coordinated attacks, eventually scheduled to begin on 26 September 1918, provided the supreme test of the operational premises that had produced the stirring victories of 18 July–16 September.

6

FOCH'S GENERAL COUNTEROFFENSIVE, PART I: 26 SEPTEMBER–23 OCTOBER 1918

After the Allied victories during the period 8 August–16 September 1918, Ludendorff's shaken armies fell back grudgingly to the Hindenburg line. These defenses protected their lateral communications. General headquarters moved from Avesnes to Spa. The number of German divisions declined from 207 late in May to 185 by the third week in September, and German infantry battalions were reduced from four to three companies. Twenty-two divisions had to be cannibalized, and the continuing arrival of new American divisions constantly increased Foch's superiority in rifle strength. Ludendorff observed telltale signs of declining German morale. "Shirking at the front became more prevalent, especially among men returning from home leave. Overstaying of leave increased, and the fighting-line was more thinly manned." The first quartermaster general could only plead for determined resistance to impending attacks. On 15 September, reacting to an Austrian bid for peace negotiations, he stated: "The German army . . . must prove to the enemy that we are not to be conquered. As we fight we must wait and see whether the enemy's intentions are honorable, in case he is ready to engage in peace negotiations this time, or whether he will again reject peace with us, or we are to purchase this peace on terms which will destroy the future of our people." Foch feared that Ludendorff might order a retreat to the line Antwerp–Brussels–Namur–the Meuse–the Chiers–Metz–Strasbourg, shortening his front and concentrating his remaining manpower. Unremitting pressure prevented any such movement.[1]

Foch realized that he should now attack the Hindenburg line in front of the British troops on the line Cambrai–St. Quentin–La Fere–St. Gobain, but he recognized that he also must engage the enemy elsewhere. If he advanced only in Picardy, he "ran the risk of seeing all the enemy reserves massed to meet the onslaught of our armies, and, aided by a powerful system of fortification, in a position to frustrate our efforts." He must therefore launch a series

The Hindenburg line southwest of Bellicourt on the St. Quentin canal, scene of the British breakthrough in September 1918, showing wire entanglements and trenches. These fortifications protected critical rail lines needed to sustain the German defense.

of coordinated attacks that would immobilize the enemy forces elsewhere than in Picardy and "by their convergent directions, make them harmonize their efforts with those produced by our already successful enterprises. In short, extend the front of our offensive while keeping it always headed in the same general direction." The employment of the American army on the right and the Belgian army on the left would create this extension. Foch's grand conception entailed the destruction of the great salient, sometimes called the Laon bulge, that the German army had driven into France and Belgium. Powerful attacks on the west and south faces of the salient would force a retreat at least to the line Antwerp–the Meuse.[2]

On 3 September, following his discussions with General Pershing about the future operations of the American First Army, Foch issued the initial directive for his huge enterprise. The British army would attack eastward in the general

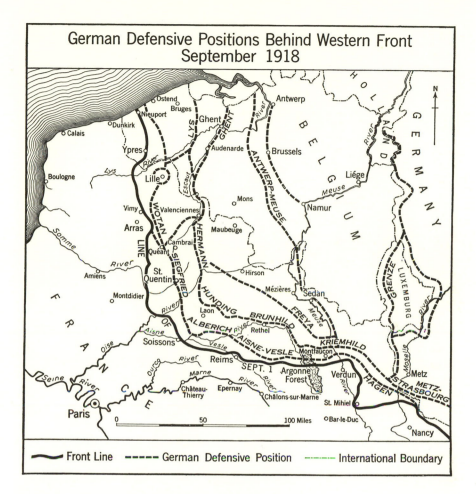

German Defensive Positions Behind Western Front
September 1918

direction of Cambrai–St. Quentin. The French armies in the center would drive
the enemy beyond the Aisne and the Ailette. On the right, the Americans
would strike northward between the Meuse and the Argonne in the general
direction of Mezieres. They would coordinate their operations with those of
the French Fourth Army (Gouraud) on the left. The American First Army's
attack would reach the line Dun-sur-Meuse–Grandpre–Challerange–Sommepy
and then would move on to the line Stenay–Le Chesne–Attigny, from which
it would threaten Mezieres. The basic objective was to interdict the railway
behind the Hindenburg line that ran from Lille in the north through Aulnoye,
Avesnes, Hirson, Mezieres, Sedan, and Metz to Strasbourg. The British would
drive to the Maubeuge-Aulnoye area and the Franco-American force to the

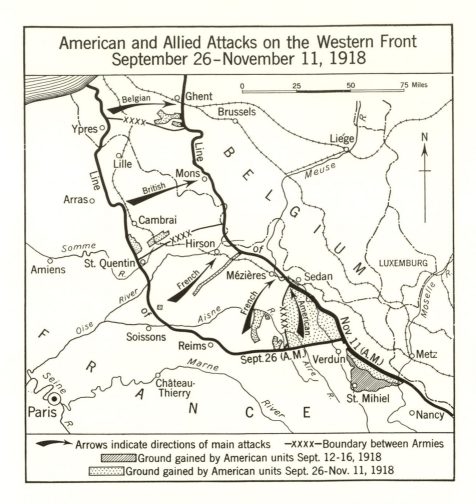

American and Allied Attacks on the Western Front
September 26–November 11, 1918

Mezieres-Sedan area. These operations would deprive the Germans of an essential rail connection and force a broad retreat.[3]

The plan for the general counteroffensive also included an inter-Allied attack in Flanders toward Ghent from the positions gained early in September. This movement was part of Foch's effort to keep Ludendorff occupied along the entire western front so that he could not reinforce the most threatened areas. A thrust north of the Lys River would clear the Belgian coast and threaten German communications north of the Ardennes region. On 11 September, Foch formed the Flanders Group of Armies to undertake this attack. King Albert of Belgium commanded this group with the help of the French General

Jean Degoutte. It included the Belgian Army, the British Second Army (Plumer), the French Cavalry Corps, and the French VII and XXXIV Corps. Just to the south, the British Fifth Army (Birdwood) would move against Lille.[4]

Foch soon fixed the schedule for the three coordinated thrusts that made up the general offensive:

September 26: Franco-American attack toward the Mezieres-Sedan area between the Meuse and Suippe rivers on a front of 44 miles, the American First Army (fifteen double-sized divisions) and the French Fourth Army (twenty-two divisions), the two forces joining at the west side of the Argonne forest.

September 27: British attack in the general direction of Cambrai between Peronne and Lens by the First Army (twelve divisions) and Third Army (fifteen divisions).

September 28: Belgian-French-British attack by the Flanders Group of Armies toward Ghent between the English Channel and the Lys River (British Second Army [ten divisions], Belgian Army [twelve divisions], French Sixth Army [six divisions]).

September 29: Franco-British attack toward Busigny between Peronne and La Fere by the British Fourth Army (seventeen divisions, including two American divisions) and the French Tenth Army (fourteen divisions).

Two hundred miles separated the Flanders Group of Armies in the north and the American First Army in the south. The numbers of troops engaged far exceeded the total of those who took part in the preliminary battles during August–September 1918. Britain's official history noted the distinctive feature of this plan. During previous Allied offensives the enemy had managed to reinforce threatened locations. "Now he was attacked everywhere at once, was forced to disperse his reserves, and, although the Allied margin of superiority was not very great, he was, in the result, nowhere strong enough to hold his ground."[5]

On 25 September, just preceding the opening of the offensive, and on 27 September, just afterward, Foch drew the attention of the national commanders-in-chief to certain essential considerations. He was concerned above all with engaging the enemy and maintaining unremitting pressure. His commanders were enjoined to exploit all ruptures of the line of resistance and to avoid any halts in exploitation. These injunctions applied particularly to the French Fourth Army and the American First Army. "Under the conditions now existing, the main thing is to develop before anything the shock power of the Allied armies." Foch hoped to prevent the enemy from organizing a defense.

"If we do not give him time enough to pull himself together, we shall be confronted everywhere with nothing but disorganized units, mixed up together,
or, in any event, improvisations hastily made." These instructions were designed
to prevent the German army from effectively reconstituting defensible positions after the initial engagement.[6]

The terrain features of the Meuse-Argonne sector posed exceptionally difficult
obstacles for the American First Army. To its right ran the Meuse, an unford-
able river, and on its right bank rose the heights of the Meuse. These hills
overlooked a region to the west that included several ridges, of which the most
imposing was the hill of Montfaucon, 342 meters high. To the north, the
wooded heights of Romagne and Cunel provided excellent observation of the
surrounding territory. On the First Army's left, the Argonne forest allowed
the German defenders to observe the territory to the east and provided cover
for troops within it. A small stream, the Aire River, flowed northward parallel
to the forest, emptying into the Aisne River at Grandpre. The region constituted a double defile with a hogback down the middle that passed through
Montfaucon and the Romagne-Cunel heights. The attacker must move up the
defiles on both sides of the hogback. Only two inadequate roads gave access
to the battlefield. It is hard to imagine a more difficult position to attack.[7]

The German defenders constructed four distinct sets of fortifications, taking
advantage of east-west ridges. The southernmost of these, the first defensive
position, followed the line Regneville–Bethincourt–Boureuilles–Vienne-le-
Chateau. Five kilometers north of this position lay the Giselher Stellung. Six
kilometers farther came the most formidable barrier, the Kriemhilde Stellung,
running through the wooded heights of Cunel and Romagne. It was an
eastward extension of the main Hindenburg fortifications running through the
Aisne valley known as the Hunding-Brunhilde Stellung. The fourth line, the
Freya Stellung, was much less well developed. It bestrode the Barricourt heights,
another strong wooded position. Various intermediate lines and switch positions further strengthened the defense. Throughout the region well-sited
machine-gun nests, pill boxes, barbed wire entanglements, and artillery batteries added to the natural strength of the Meuse-Argonne defenses.[8]

These fortifications were deemed so formidable that the German Group of
Armies Gallwitz (nineteen divisions) allocated only the German Fifth Army
of five divisions to their defense. The First Army staff calculated that German
command could reinforce the area at the rate of four divisions on the first day,
two on the second, and nine on the third. German reserves were concentrated

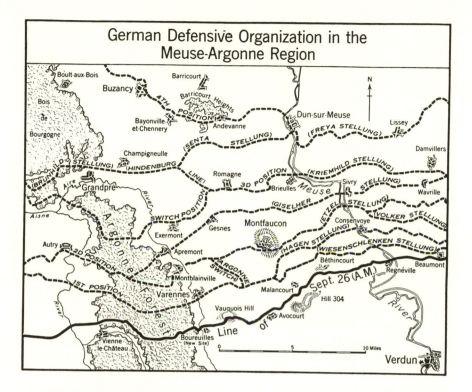

German Defensive Organization in the Meuse-Argonne Region

around Metz, probably to guard against an attack eastward from the St. Mihiel salient. The defending divisions were generally of poor quality, including Saxon and Austrian organizations of dubious dedication. These units were seriously depleted, at a third of their normal complement. However, the German command was sufficiently competent and the region so favorable for defense that an attacking force could expect stubborn resistance.[9]

Pershing had only ten days to concentrate his forces. He had to relocate three corps headquarters, fifteen divisions, and corps and army troops. Seven divisions came from the St. Mihiel area, three from the Vosges Mountains, three from the Soissons area, one from a training area in the Haute-Marne, and one from near Bar-le-Duc. This circumstance led to unfamiliar command relationships. For example, General Liggett's I Corps for the Meuse-Argonne attack included the 28th and 77th Divisions from the Vesle River sector near Soissons, the 92d Division from the Vosges Mountains, and the 35th Division from the vicinity of Nancy. None of these divisions had been under Liggett's command during the reduction of the St. Mihiel salient. Col. George C. Marshall, who coordinated the movement, made use of trains, motor transport, and marching columns, all moving at night to conceal the concentration from the enemy. Somehow about 200,000 French troops were moved out of the Meuse-Argonne sector and about 600,000 Americans into it. Despite continuous confusion and monumental traffic jams, the movement was completed by 26 September. Many French troops—the II Colonial Corps, the XVII Corps, and the 5th Cavalry Division, seven divisions in all—were assigned to the First Army. They were placed just to the east of the Meuse River with some American troops.[10]

The gap of only ten days between the conclusion of the St. Mihiel attack and the beginning of the Meuse-Argonne offensive meant that Pershing must employ untested troops during the initial phases of the second operation. Experienced divisions were unavailable, notably the 1st, 2d, 26th, and 42d. Only four of the nine divisions designated for the attack on 26 September had seen action. Four of these lacked their organic artillery, entering the battle without an opportunity to familiarize themselves with the guns assigned to them. Some units had neither completed their training nor served in quiet sectors of the front. The only veteran outfit was the 33d Division.[11]

General Pershing's objective was somewhat altered just before D-day. Mezieres had been designated as the American objective in early discussions, but by 16 September, the French Fourth Army, operating between the Argonne forest and the Suippe River, had inherited this task. Gen. Henri Gouraud's troops were to gain the line Rethel–Attigny on the Aisne "with subsequent direction toward Mezieres." The American First Army was to move first to the line Dun-sur-Meuse–Grandpre, linking with the French north of the Argonne forest. It would then advance to the line Stenay–Le Chesne, aiming at Buzancy and Stonne. These operations would support the French task of clearing the line of the Aisne River preparatory to the French capture of Mezieres, which would interdict Ludendorff's lateral rail communications. However, the principal effort on the right wing of Foch's converging offensive must come from the First Army. Pershing apparently construed his objective as the section of the railroad between Carignan and Sedan southeast of Mezieres, although Foch did not specifically assign it to him. Characteristically, he insisted that "the sector assigned to the American Army was opposite the most sensitive part of the German front then being attacked."[12]

The First Army's plan of attack, Field Order No. 20 issued on 20–21 September, aimed at a rapid, deep penetration of the German defenses, seeking to overrun them before the enemy could bring up reinforcements. Three corps on line were to advance in two days through the main battle line, the

Giselher Stellung, and the Kriemhilde Stellung. This surge of about 10 miles would reach the line Dun-sur-Meuse–Grandpre. After completing this great effort, another bound of about 8 to 12 miles would put the First Army on the line Stenay–Le Chesne. Then Pershing's forces to the east of the Meuse, largely French, would seize the heights of the Meuse, securing his right flank. Finally, the Americans would move on the Sedan-Carignan railroad.[13]

The critical aspect of the plan was the initial assault on a front of twenty miles intended to penetrate the Kriemhilde Stellung in two days. The V Corps (91st, 79th, and 37th Divisions), commanded by Maj. Gen. George H. Cameron, was to capture Montfaucon Hill on the first day. The I Corps (77th, 28th, and 35th Divisions), commanded by Gen. Liggett, would advance on the left down the valley of the Aire River. Maj. Gen. Robert L. Bullard's III Corps (4th, 80th, and 33d Divisions) would move forward to the east of Montfaucon Hill. These drives would create deep salients on each side of the elevation, outflanking it and assuring its fall. Then the Americans would pierce the Kriemhilde Stellung. The advance of the I Corps east of the Argonne and that of the French Fourth Army west of the Argonne would outflank that formidable wooded barrier and force its defenders to withdraw. The artillery of I Corps would suppress enemy fire from the Argonne, and that of III Corps would neutralize enemy artillery firing from the heights of the Meuse. Some artillery support also would come from the troops on line just east of the Meuse, the French XVII Corps and the American IV Corps. Besides almost 2,800 guns, the Americans had at their disposal 182 small tanks, 142 of them manned by Americans under the command of Col. George S. Patton, Jr., and attached to the I Corps, and 821 airplanes, of which Americans manned 604.[14]

Pershing's plan was extraordinarily demanding, but various considerations led him to adopt it. He counted heavily on surprise. Besides, he expected to enjoy an enormous preponderance of manpower during the first days of the battle. He would send nine double-strength divisions close to full complement against only five weak German divisions at no more than one-third strength. Of great importance also was his faith in his men, so often proclaimed during the controversies over the formation of an independent force. "It was thought reasonable to count on the vigor and the aggressive spirit of our troops to make up for their inexperience." The difficulty with this plan, as Allan Millett has observed, was the inability of the American artillery to reach the Kriemhilde Stellung. The inexperienced American staff could not yet move artillery forward quickly. It was hoped that aircraft and tanks could provide sufficient support to ensure success.[15]

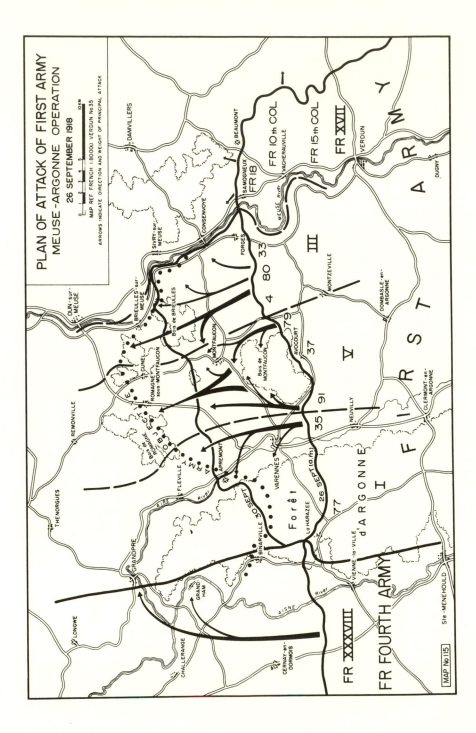

PLAN OF ATTACK OF FIRST ARMY
MEUSE-ARGONNE OPERATION
26 SEPTEMBER 1918

MAP REF FRENCH 1:80.000 VERDUN No 35
ARROWS INDICATE DIRECTION AND WEIGHT OF PRINCIPAL ATTACK

MAP No 115

At 0230 on 26 September, a tremendous barrage from 2,775 artillery pieces, most of them French, opened on the German front line between the Meuse and the Argonne, and at 0530 the three American corps began their advance behind a rolling barrage. To the left, the French Fourth Army also attacked, the two armies advancing on a front of 44 miles between the Meuse and the Suippe. The First Army had made strenuous efforts to gain surprise, and initially the attack went well; the first German line was quickly overrun. Soon after that, progress began to slow. The inexperienced 79th Division, given the task of seizing Montfaucon Hill, encountered strong resistance. German defenders made their principal stand on the second line of defense, the Giselher Stellung, which ran through the hill. Despite desperate efforts, the V Corps did not capture Montfaucon until midday on 27 September. The 4th Division to the right in the V Corps had an opportunity to seize the hill but adhered to rigid boundary assignments and did not do so. By this time, the first German reinforcements were arriving. Instead of quickly bursting through the German third line of defenses, the First Army did not pass beyond the Giselher Stellung.[16]

General Bullard, commanding the III Corps next to the Meuse River, recalled the complications that developed during the first four days of the battle. "The resistance of the enemy was steadily stiffening. Wherever his machine guns were encountered—and they were encountered after the passage of the first line—the progress was exceedingly difficult. Indeed, his first defence seemed to be almost wholly machine guns." After that a new challenge presented itself. "We began to catch a heavy artillery fire from the high ground on the right bank of the Meuse. It was becoming exceedingly annoying, the more so as we advanced." Only local gains were recorded after the initial attack. Pershing's growing anxiety was reflected in a directive transmitted to the corps commanders. He ordered them to locate their division and brigade commanders "as far up toward the front of the advance of their respective units as may be necessary to direct their movements with energy and rapidity in the attack. . . . All officers will push their units forward with all possible energy." He also authorized condign measures against leaders who did not respond effectively. Corps and division commanders received authority "to relieve on the spot any officer of whatever rank who fails to show in this emergency those qualities of leadership required to accomplish the task that confronts us."[17]

Information from the three corps confirms Bullard's view. On 27 September, I Corps, next to the Argonne forest, reported: "We progressed against strong resistance." On the 28th, "infantry advancing . . . met with determined resistance. The line was practically unchanged." On the 29th, the enemy was reported as "harassing our forward troops with machine-gun and artillery fire,

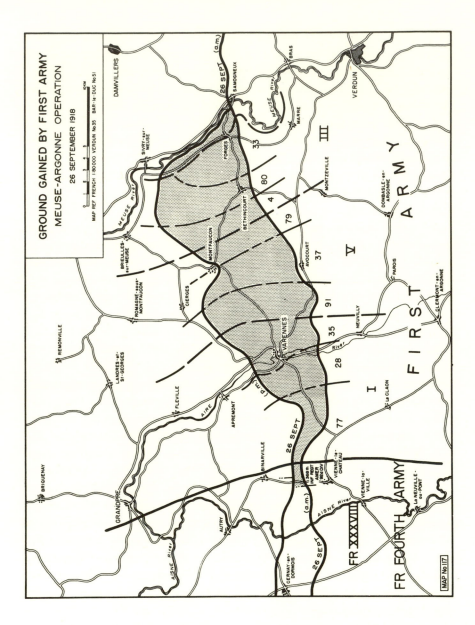

GROUND GAINED BY FIRST ARMY
MEUSE-ARGONNE OPERATION
26 SEPTEMBER 1918

MAP REF FRENCH 1:80,000 VERDUN No.35 BAR-le-DUC No.51

MAP No.117

particularly from the east edge of the Foret d'Argonne." Bullard's III Corps reported that, on 27 September it "continued to encounter heavy M.G. fire from the left flank . . . also artillery fire from the northwest and heavy M.G. fire from the front. Early this morning [28 September] our line remained approximately the same as last night." On 28–29 September, "the infantry met considerably more resistance. Very heavy M.G. and artillery fire prevented further advance during the day." On 30 September, II Corps noted that an attack by the 4th Division had failed "because of heavy artillery fire. . . . No advance of our line. . . . Our line at present stabilizing." V Corps, attacking in the center, noted the capture of Montfaucon, reporting that "the enemy had but few troops engaged in the defense of Montfaucon. . . . they relied heavily upon machine-gun fire to check our forces. . . . The advance of our troops was hindered everywhere by machine-gun fire and intermittent shelling by the enemy." During the period 28–29 September, the reports remained the same: "Small machine gun groups, favorably located have proved a constant hindrance to the attackers. Artillery activity of the enemy is on the increase." On 30 September, this refrain was repeated: "The enemy is strongly resisting the advance of this corps. His line has been reinforced and volume of hostile artillery fire has increased. . . . The enemy is making stubborn resistance along entire front."[18]

Pershing continued to exhort his troops to advance, but he was eventually forced to suspend his forward movement. By 30 September, he had gained about 8 miles and reached a line facing the enemy's third and strongest line of fortifications, the Kriemhilde Stellung. This obstacle was supposed to have been overwhelmed on the second day of the attack. On 29 September, Field Order No. 32 indicated that the attack would resume later. For the moment the three corps were to organize a defensive along the line Bois de la Cote Lemont–Nantillois–Apremont–southwest across the Argonne. Veteran divisions relieved the most exhausted units at the front: the 1st Division replaced the 35th Division in I Corps, and the 2d and 3d Divisions replaced the 37th and 79th Divisions in V Corps. The 91st Division was withdrawn to the corps reserve, so that the V Corps after that functioned with an entirely new group of organizations. These changes further complicated difficult problems of supply. Donald Smythe summarizes the circumstances graphically. "Whether because of incompetence or inexperience or both, the First Army was wallowing in an unbelievable logistical tangle. It was as if someone had taken the army's intestines out and dumped them all over the table."[19]

German explanations for their successful defense emphasized American inexperience and flawed tactics. An officer from the 5th Reserve Corps who observed the action wrote: "American infantry is very unskilful [*sic*] in attack. It attacks with closed ranks in numerous and deep waves, at the head of which come the tanks. Such forms of attack form excellent targets for the activity of our artillery, infantry, and machine guns, if only the infantry does not get scared on account of the advancing masses and loses its nerve." Methods of coping with tanks had been identified. "The infantry allows them to approach closely and then fires upon them with machine guns, with rifles . . . , and with artillery. Thereupon, the tanks generally turn back." Hand grenades also proved effective. If the tanks continued to advance, the infantry left them to the artillery.[20]

The pause in the offensive was all the more galling to the Americans because the French on the left had made significant progress. Gouraud's Fourth Army was held up initially, but on 29 September, it overran the line of the Py River. Then on 1 October, it seized the strong point at Notre-Dame-des-Champs and on 3 October, another, Blanc Mont, this time with the valuable help of the American 2d Division. Pershing had released the experienced organization for this purpose. On 30 September–1 October, the French Fifth Army, operating farther west between the Vesle and the Aisne, pushed the Germans across the Aisne-Marne canal. By 7 October, the German defenders had retreated to positions behind the Suippe River and the line of the Arnes. However, the French seem to have paced their advance to match the progress of the American First Army on their right and the British Expeditionary Forces on their left.[21]

Pershing put the best face on what was surely a severe disappointment. Writing to Secretary of War Baker on 2 October, he claimed that "operations here have gone very well, but, due to rains and the condition of the roads have not gone forward as rapidly nor as far as I had hoped. . . . Our losses so far have been moderate." In his memoirs, he argued that the enemy had to weaken its order of battle elsewhere to hold the hinge of his defense on the western front, although he conceded that the enemy had fought well. "In this dire extremity the Germans defended every foot of ground with desperate tenacity and with the rare skill of experienced soldiers."[22]

What had stopped the American attack, the first in the series that made up Marshal Foch's general counteroffensive? No one explanation is sufficient to explain the check administered to the First Army. Several complications combined to force suspension of the attack in front of the Kriemhilde Stellung.

Adhering to Foch's instructions, the First Army sought to gain surprise, but this effort did not succeed. Attempts to convince the enemy that the Americans would attack eastward toward Metz had some effect, but information about the Meuse-Argonne attack fell into enemy hands several days in advance. This misfortune allowed the German command to alert reinforcements who were able to move promptly into position soon after the beginning of the attack.[23]

Of much greater significance was the inexperience of the American divisions. Pershing had to rely on undertrained troops during the initial phase of the Meuse-Argonne offensive, having used his battle-tested divisions at St. Mihiel. From a tactical point of view, the principal difficulties resulted from failure to coordinate infantry attacks and artillery fire. Methods developed elsewhere on the western front to deal with machine-gun nests were often ignored, leading to unnecessary casualties. Too often, green commanders and staffs ordered mass frontal attacks against well-sited weapons. Pershing had discounted warnings from the Allies that his divisional and corps commanders were not yet prepared for the challenge of the western front, but events of 26–30 September proved him wrong.[24]

The most obvious of Pershing's difficulties was the extraordinary logistical tangle that soon developed behind the lines. Only two roads of any consequence led to the battlefield, and these traversed spongy soil that could not withstand heavy traffic. Congestion in the bottleneck between the First Army's depots and the huge force pinned down in front of the Kriemhilde Stellung prevented efficient supply of ammunition and food. It also inhibited forward displacement of artillery batteries. Hunter Liggett described conditions on the line. "The miserable roads began to have their effect on the second day. As the infantry advanced it lost the proper support of the artillery, which was unable to follow. The engineers and pioneers toiled furiously, but the task was an appalling one. Four years of shell fire had left the spongy soil of No Man's Land a troubled sea. . . . The rest of the region—a succession of half-obliterated trenches, water-filled shell holes and tangles of wire—defied transport; and when the artillery did slug its way through, it found itself at a disadvantage, at first, in the blind country."[25]

Other critics have questioned Pershing's plan. Liddell Hart drew attention to the distance the attack must carry through difficult terrain before encountering the principal German fortifications. The German elastic defense based on clever use of machine guns and well-placed artillery, an expedient so beneficial to the French and British during their defensive battles from March to July, proved most effective, halting the Americans after their initial success. Braim stresses the ability of the defenders to concentrate fire on the Americans from three locations: the high ground in the Argonne forest, the hogback running north-south through the center of the narrow sector, and the heights east of the Meuse. He argues that Pershing should have included the entire Argonne forest in his sector or better still attacked east of the Meuse to neutralize the heights. Whatever one makes of these criticisms, it is certain that Pershing's plans did not give sufficient attention to the difficulties associated with advancing on a narrow front in difficult terrain against very strong positions that afforded excellent cover and concealment, many in flanking locations on high ground.[26]

The check administered to the First Army after a promising beginning energized Allied criticism of General Pershing. Haig complained privately about the difficulties that the First Army had encountered, which struck him as like those of the Belgian army operating to his north. After noting reports that congestion had forced a halt in offensive operations for several days, he exploded: "What very valuable days are being lost! All this is the result of inexperience and ignorance on the part of the Belgian and American Staffs of the needs of a modern attacking force." Gen. Jean-Henri Mordacq, a member of Clemenceau's entourage who observed Pershing after the battle bogged down, recorded some striking impressions. "I could read clearly in his eyes that, at that moment, he realized his mistake. His soldiers were dying bravely, but they were not advancing, or very little, and their losses were heavy." Mordacq agreed with Haig's views on the causes of the American failure. "All that great body of men which the American Army represented was literally struck with paralysis because the 'brain' didn't exist, because the generals and their staffs lacked experience. With enemies like the Germans, this kind of war couldn't be improvised."[27]

Foch shared these negative evaluations and attempted to retrieve matters by making significant changes in command. After informing Petain that the Americans had been stopped more by the failure of their staff to manage logistical matters than by enemy action, he sent his principal staff officer, General Weygand, to Pershing with a devastating proposal. He wanted to send two or three American divisions to the French XXXVIII Corps operating on the right wing of the French Fourth Army just to the west of the American I Corps. A similar force would relocate east of the Meuse and join the French XVII Corps. A new French Army, the Second, would direct the troops located near the Argonne. Pershing would retain command of a reduced army on both sides of the Meuse. Weygand specified that the objectives assigned earlier would remain the same, but Pershing was to use his expanded force east of the Meuse to seize the heights between Damvillers and Dun-sur-Meuse. "The result would secure the flank of our general offensive toward the north and afford greater liberty of movement to our armies through the possession of the roads and of the railroad in the Valley of the Meuse."[28]

Pershing immediately rejected this proposal. To accept it would have been tantamount to admitting failure, but to Foch he adduced other reasons for his opposition. Among them were his long-held objection to placing American troops under French generals; his intention to avoid "dismemberment of the American First Army at a moment when its elements are striving for success under the direction of American command"; and the logistical confusion that would result from the establishment of mixed commands. He assured the generalissimo that he would immediately launch attacks both west and east of the Meuse. Foch could only bow to Pershing's wishes, making the proviso that the American operations "start without delay and that, once begun, they be continued without any interruptions such as those which have just arisen."[29]

Privately Pershing expressed great irritation at Foch's initiative, attributing it to Premier Clemenceau. He wrote at the time: "I will not stand for this letter which disparages myself and the American Army and the American effort. He [Foch] will have to retract it or I shall go further in the matter." Pershing presumably thought that Foch had overstepped his authority, which did not extend to local operational matters. In any event, Foch pulled back, and Pershing was left to galvanize his forces for a resumption of his offensive. A few days later, when Foch described this episode to Haig, the British commander opined that he could reach Valenciennes in forty-eight hours with three fresh American divisions. Foch responded that "it was impossible to get any troops from Pershing at the moment." After the war, Pershing admitted that serious shortages of transport had arisen, but he blamed the War Department for this circumstance. "After nearly eighteen months of war it would be reasonable to expect that the organization at home would have been more nearly able to provide adequate equipment and supplies, and to handle shipments more systematically." He admitted that "serious trouble, if not irreparable disaster" might have resulted, if the Allies had not met many of his needs.[30]

Lack of progress on the Franco-American front disappointed Foch, but extraordinary events on the British front in Picardy, the other main element of the general counteroffensive, brought him the greatest satisfaction. On 27 September, the British First Army (Horne) and Third Army (Byng) attacked the Hindenburg line between the Sensee River and Villers-Guilain. The Canadian Corps burst across the Canal du Nord, the assault penetrating four miles into the German defenses on the first day. On the second and third days, the offensive broke completely through the Hindenburg line and reached the outskirts of Cambrai, a critical center of communications. Again, efficient combined operations, this time including armor, provided the margin of victory. The Hindenburg line was designed to resist bombardment but not tanks; it succumbed to attacks by infantry and armor closely coordinated with artillery fire.[31]

On 29 September, another British Army, the Fourth (Rawlinson), struck to the south between Vendhuile and Holnon on a 12-mile front against the German Second and Eighteenth Armies and moved swiftly across the St. Quentin Canal. General Debeney's French First Army, located to Rawlinson's right, also launched an attack, which made a less spectacular but measurable gain. Again, the Hindenburg line was breached completely, and the victorious Allied armies now conducted a pursuit of the enemy.[32]

The American II Corps (Maj. Gen. George W. Read), which included the 27th and 30th Divisions, was attached to the Fourth Army during the attack across the St. Quentin Canal. It made a flawed but signal contribution to this success. Read's troops were located between the British III and IX Corps. They faced a difficult stretch of the Hindenburg line constructed over the Bellicourt tunnel that carried the St. Quentin Canal underground for almost 6 kilometers. Two days before the main attack, the Americans failed in an attempt to seize three German redoubts that protected the fortifications of the tunnel. Some attacking troops were cut off. Therefore, the assault of 29 September was made without artillery support. As in operations elsewhere, inexperience dogged the Americans, the 27th Division in particular becoming disorganized in a fog after losing many officers. German counterattacks either repulsed or pinned down the American infantry. Fortunately the 3d Division of the Australian Corps, ordered to pass through the 27th Division and to continue the assault to the Beaurevoir line of German fortifications (a reserve position behind the main line of resistance), eliminated German resistance.

The 30th Division fared somewhat better, crossing the ground above the Bellicourt tunnel and seizing the town of Bellicourt, although it was stopped short of its objectives. It also benefited from the support of the Australian Corps; the Australian 5th Division passed through and continued the attack successfully. Again, American divisions serving as part of a European command had encountered initial trouble but had acquitted themselves honorably. To the right of the 30th Division, the British 46th Territorial Division took advantage of the fog that had confused the Americans and crossed the St. Quentin Canal just below the southern exit of the tunnel. This success greatly compromised the German position. Further assaults extended the initial penetration. By 4 October, the Fourth Army had smashed through the Beaurevoir defenses.[33]

Meanwhile, on 28 September, the Flanders Group of Armies struck still another of Foch's blows in Flanders between Dixmude and the Lys River on a

17-mile front against a depleted force of about five German divisions. Success came immediately. The German first line of defenses fell on the first day and the second line came under strong attack. On the second day, Dixmude was taken. So were Passchendaele Ridge, the scene of desperate fighting in 1917, and the Messines–Wytschaete line. The attack on the Lys then slowed, but just to the south, General Birdwood's British Fifth Army captured La Bassee, Lens, and Armentieres. These actions soon forced Ludendorff to give up the channel ports, and they threatened indispensable rail communications. No American units participated in this action, but two divisions were sent to the Flanders Group of Armies for future operations.[34]

On 29 September, French and British troops attacked the center of the German line between La Fere and Peronne. The Allies now were engaged all along the western front from Dixmude to the Meuse, a distance of 250 miles. Everywhere the German army had suffered defeat, although in one sector, the Meuse-Argonne, it had prevented a breach of its principal fortifications. Signs of exhaustion appeared everywhere. For example, the German Eighteenth Army, retreating to a line of defenses east of the Hindenburg line, felt that it must receive a reinforcement of five divisions. Otherwise it could assume "no responsibility . . . for holding the position" that it was supposed to defend. The American 30th Division reported that German prisoners of war were "quite fed up and glad to be out of the war. The opinion of the men was that Germany is on its last legs." Ludendorff was confronted with the greatest crisis of the war.[35]

Thus Haig's forces accomplished what Pershing's First Army had failed to achieve: a rapid, complete breach of the enemy's principal fortifications guarding the Lille-Strasbourg railroad lines. The British success was all the more remarkable because it came against the strongest concentration of German forces on the western front. Ludendorff had thinned his defenses elsewhere to strengthen the positions in front of the British First, Third, and Fourth Armies. Liddell Hart noted that forty British divisions and two American divisions faced thirty-seven German divisions between St. Quentin and Lens. Maurice counted only thirty-one British and two American divisions against thirty-nine enemy divisions on the front of the three British Armies. The Allies enjoyed a much more pronounced margin in the south. Ludendorff had only twenty divisions to cope with thirty-one French divisions and thirteen double-strength American divisions, the latter equivalent to twenty-six of the enemy, a disadvantage to the defenders of about three to one. Haig had urged the American attack on Foch in the hope that it would force Ludendorff to move divisions from the front of the British, but the Field Marshal's forces crossed the Hindenburg line before any German troops were transferred to the American front.[36]

The combined impact of the Allied attacks between 26 and 29 September, but most especially the British smash through the Hindenburg line toward Maubeuge, elicited a rapid response from Ludendorff. Already convinced that Germany could not win the war, Ludendorff fell completely apart at the news of the British victories, which came as the Bulgarian army collapsed on the Salonika front. He professed to attribute his panicky actions of 28–29 September mainly to the Bulgarian defeat. This explanation was in all likelihood a means of shifting the onus of military failure from his army to that of a lesser ally. On 1 October a foreign office representative at Spa noted: "I get the impression that they [the high command] have all lost their nerve, here, and that, if things come to the worst, we can justify our action to the outside world by Bulgaria's behavior." On 28 September, Ludendorff informed Hindenburg that he deemed it necessary to make a peace offer immediately and to seek an early armistice. "The position could grow only worse, on account of the Balkan position, even if we held our ground in the West. Our one task now was to act clearly and firmly, without delay." Hindenburg then said that he had come to the same conclusion and concurred with Ludendorff's suggestion. They agreed that the armistice must permit a "controlled and orderly evacuation of the occupied territory and the possible resumption of hostilities on our own borders." They did not believe that Germany would have to abandon territory conquered in the east, "thinking that the Entente would be fully conscious of the dangers threatening them as well as ourselves from Bolshevism."[37]

On the same day, Foreign Minister Paul von Hintze in Berlin skillfully executed what was later called a "revolution from above" by negotiating with Reichstag leaders. He recognized that significant changes must take place in the German government, if it wished to approach President Wilson in search of an armistice and peace negotiations. Certain leaders favored this course. Klaus Schwabe argues that von Hintze and his supporters believed Germany "had to entrust the role of peace mediator to Wilson alone because his conditions were more favorable than anything which Germany could expect from its European opponents and because the interests of Germany and the United States coincided on the issues of freedom of the seas and freedom of trade." Besides, the American peace terms were well known, and it would be difficult for Wilson to ignore an initiative from Berlin. Governmental changes would allow the established regime to survive the difficult process of obtaining an armistice and negotiating a peace settlement. Above all, it was necessary to initiate parliamentary government.[38]

On 29 September, a crown council held at Spa with Kaiser Wilhelm, Foreign Minister von Hintze, Ludendorff, and Hindenburg attending, made the necessary arrangements. It was decided to make an appeal to President Wilson, bypassing France and Britain, because the American peace program was much less draconian than that of the Entente Powers. On the same day, unbeknownst to the High Command, the kaiser decided to propose establishment of parliamentary government. The chancellor, Hertling, refused to concur in this measure, but von Hintze remained firm, and his views prevailed. Hertling's resignation cleared the way for a new premier, the moderate Prince Max of Baden, who was acceptable to Wilson. One of Ludendorff's officers, Maj. Baron Erich von dem Bussche, was sent to Berlin to explain matters to the Reichstag leadership. Hindenburg left the front, going with the kaiser to Berlin. Ludendorff explained why he remained behind: "I was, unfortunately, indispensable at Spa, owing to the position in the field." Ludendorff was anxious to hasten the peace process, but he denied that extreme military exigency was the reason, citing instead his wish to "avoid further loss of life" and his assumption that "the earlier we began [the process required to arrange peace] the more favorable would our position be at the commencement of negotiations." He was among those who believed that Wilson would resist the more damaging Entente war aims. Meanwhile, if his troops gained a breathing space, they could regroup on the German border for a possible resumption of hostilities.[39]

On 2 October, the final step was taken to inaugurate peace negotiations: it was decided to send a message to President Wilson proposing an end to the war. Von dem Bussche explained the High Command's views to the Reichstag leadership. He observed that although Germany had used up its reserves, the army could continue to fight. It could for "an incalculable period, inflict heavy losses on our enemies and leave a desert behind us, but we could not win that way." This consideration explained why Hindenburg and Ludendorff had decided that "an effort should be made to bring the fighting to an end so that the German nation and its allies might be spared further sacrifices." Von dem Bussche was at pains to discuss the role of the American troops. They had provided the necessary bulge in manpower, although they *were not in themselves of any special value or in any way superior to ours.* At those points where they had obtained initial successes, thanks to their employment in mass, their attacks had been beaten off in spite of their superior numbers." Their contribution was "to take over large sections of the [inactive] front and thus make it possible for the English and French to relieve their own veteran divisions and create an almost inexhaustible reserve."[40]

The acting chancellor, Friedrich von Payer, adopted Prince Max's view that Germany should avoid a request for an immediate armistice because it was a sign of weakness. He asked Hindenburg to clarify the reasons for the shaken

High Command's insistence on immediate action. Hindenburg gave oral answers to several questions. How long could the army keep the Allies out of Germany? The field marshal was uncertain, but he hoped that the enemy could be held until the coming spring. Should the government expect an early collapse? Hindenburg did not think so. Was the emergency so critical that immediate action was necessary to obtain an armistice? Hindenburg noted his letter of that day to the chancellor in which he had urged action without delay. Was the field marshal aware that territorial losses might result, especially Alsace-Lorraine and the purely Polish areas of the eastern provinces? Hindenburg recognized that Germany might lose French-speaking areas of Alsace-Lorraine, but he saw no need to surrender territory in the east. Payer also wanted Hindenburg to review a draft of the note to be sent to President Wilson. This document did not reach the field marshal, or so it was claimed.[41]

On 3 October, Prince Max became chancellor, and he immediately signed the peace note to President Wilson, which proceeded through Swiss channels to its destination on 6 October. It proposed an armistice and peace negotiations based on the Fourteen Points and other presidential pronouncements, an act that led to further correspondence between Washington and Berlin. Wilson responded on 8 October, posing some questions. Did Germany accept the entire American program in principle? Did Prince Max speak for his people only or for those who had so far conducted German policy? The president specified that Germany would have to remove its army from all occupied territories. Schwabe summarizes the main purposes of the document. "It tried to commit Germany irrevocably to the Wilsonian peace program. It precluded the Central Powers from deriving a military advantage from a possible armistice. It expressed doubts about the authority of the new German government to conduct the proposed negotiations." Prince Max quickly responded on 12 October: Germany accepted the Fourteen Points in principle; the peace conference would deal only with details of their application. He spoke both for the German government and its people.[42]

Meanwhile, the Entente leaders, purposefully excluded from the discussion, manifested anxiety and even irritation. Wilson's demands were much less stringent than those contained in the confidential understandings between the Allied Powers known as the "secret treaties." On 8 October, a joint meeting of the Allied Naval Council and the Permanent Military Representatives specified various terms of armistice. General Bliss, the American Military Representative, refused to sign the terms, pleading lack of instructions. Privately he was critical of them. "Judging from the spirit which seems more and more to actuate our European allies, I am beginning to despair that the war will accomplish more than the abolition of German militarism while leaving *European* militarism as rampant as ever."[43]

On 14 October, President Wilson made a stern reply to the second German communication, but it eventually led to a German-American deal. In this note, Wilson stated that the Allies would decide upon procedures for evacuation of occupied territories, rejecting some proposals on this question from Prince Max, and would not agree to an armistice that might permit resumption of hostilities. He also included a broad hint that the kaiser should abdicate and that others responsible for German policy should resign. The president thus reflected the Allies' wish that he take a firm position, but he also kept open the door to peace negotiations.

Wilson's stiff note created great alarm in Berlin, but Prince Max decided that Germany's best hope remained the American leader. He was anxious to reach agreement; he wanted to place the president "in the position of *arbiter mundi* and further give him the opportunity of trying to moderate the fanatical aspirations of his 'Associates.'" On 20 October, Prince Max agreed to Wilson's conditions, outlining a program of electoral reform and enhanced powers for the Reichstag. This response satisfied Wilson, although it greatly annoyed the British. On 23 October, the president notified Prince Max that he would now submit the correspondence to the Allies. Germany accepted this note on 27 October.

The stage was now set for climactic negotiations in Paris. To represent the United States in these deliberations, President Wilson dispatched Colonel House to Paris.[44]

The battles of October and November that followed the triumphs of the American, British, French, and Belgian armies in September were fought with awareness on both sides that peace negotiations were under way. This circumstance surely buoyed the spirits of Foch's command and depressed those of Ludendorff's forces, but despite the harbingers of peace that came from time to time, both sides continued to fight bitterly. Foch constantly emphasized the necessity of keeping pressure on the enemy. Ludendorff called for a stubborn defense, recognizing that a military collapse would greatly lessen Germany's ability to moderate the terms of peace. However, after Ludendorff's actions of 28–29 September, the end was practically foreordained, and both armies and civil populations gradually sensed this truth. Liddell Hart insists that Ludendorff's initiative was an "open confession of defeat." The remaining combat merely confirmed the stark reality of Germany's failure, but the fighting was unforgiving.[45]

7

FOCH'S GENERAL COUNTEROFFENSIVE, PART II: 4 OCTOBER–11 NOVEMBER 1918

While the British Expeditionary Force and the Flanders Group of Armies gathered themselves early in October to exploit the advantages they had gained to the north, the American First Army prepared to resume its offensive between the Meuse and the Argonne, acting in concert with the French Fourth Army to its left. On 3 October, Marshal Foch made representations to General Petain about the slow pace of the French Fourth Army, complaining especially about ineffective leadership. He urged unrelenting pressure. "By striking full force, with uniformity, in favorable weather, we conserve the troops and we obtain important results economically, instead of conducting a lagging battle wherein men, munitions and good days are wasted and minor results achieved." These comments were also aimed at the American First Army; Foch diplomatically noted that his observations about the French Fourth Army also applied to "several others." Such criticisms stung Pershing, and he responded by ordering a general attack.[1]

Plans for the American attack of 4 October emphasized the seizure of three enemy strong points: Cunel heights, Romagne heights, and the elevations on the eastern edge of the Argonne forest around Chatel-Chehery and Cornay. Artillery and other weapons sited in each of these areas with others on the heights east of the Meuse River had stopped the American advance. Further progress depended on clearing the enemy from these positions. The III Corps (Bullard) and the V Corps (Cameron) were assigned the task of carrying the heights of Cunel and Romagne. "The main effort was to be directed against the western flank of Cunel heights, in order to avoid enemy fire from the east flank of the Meuse River, and against the eastern flank of Romagne heights." On the left, Liggett's I Corps was given two missions: neutralization of enemy

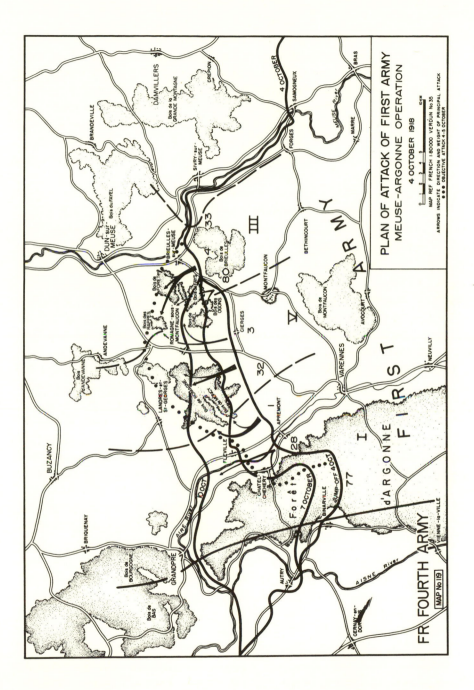

PLAN OF ATTACK OF FIRST ARMY
MEUSE-ARGONNE OPERATION
4 OCTOBER 1918

MAP REF FRENCH 1:80000 VERDUN No 35

ARROWS INDICATE DIRECTION AND WEIGHT OF PRINCIPAL ATTACK
●●● OBJECTIVE ATTACK 4-5 OCTOBER

MAP No 119

fire from the eastern edge of the Argonne forest and support for Cameron's move against the western portion of Romagne heights. The latter operation would create a favorable position for a surge westward through Cornay and Chatel-Chehery. It sought to outflank the German defenders inside the Argonne and force their retirement. To inhibit the enemy artillery, the plan emphasized counterbattery fire, including gas shells. Smoke screens were ordered to conceal the attack from German artillery positions east of the Meuse. Several veteran divisions brought from St. Mihiel strengthened the three American corps.[2]

The attack of 4 October was unsuccessful; none of the objectives were attained despite powerful infantry assaults. Operations reports for the first days of the battle summarized the conditions well. On 6 October, the enemy was "maintaining himself stubbornly. He has many well organized machine-gun nests. He was evidently on a strong line of defense which he is determined to hold." More of the same came on 7 October. "The enemy still resists stubbornly and shows no signs of yielding." Despite considerable effort, the Americans did not silence the artillery and machine-gun fire that poured from the several heights. Only the I Corps made a useful advance, positioning itself to penetrate the Argonne.[3]

General Pershing observed that the German defenders benefited from reinforcements. The number of enemy divisions on the First Army front, he wrote later, increased to twenty-seven in line and seventeen in reserve. By 4 October, the divisions directly involved in the defense had expanded from twenty on 26 September to twenty-three against fifteen American divisions. Numerical comparisons of this nature are misleading because the German divisions, much below complement, varied greatly in strength, and the American divisions, much closer to full complement, were double-sized. Braim estimates that in this attack the Americans had an advantage of nine to one in manpower. Although the First Army did not reach its objectives, it took comfort in the mistaken belief that its operations held some of the enemy's best divisions in the Meuse-Argonne sector. The Operations Report claimed that the "continuous blows" of the Americans were "reflected in German retirements on other fronts, since to yield on this front would imperil the enemy's whole Army. Our previous conclusion that we must maintain the battle until the enemy was worn out was now fully confirmed."[4]

Despite overwhelming superiority in manpower, the American attack failed because of what Braim calls "uninspired tactics." Was the battle turning into an "American Somme," a repetition of the extraordinarily bloody battle between the British and the Germans that took place in July 1916? By 6 October, the First Army had taken about 75,000 casualties because it had depended on massed infantry attacks without effective coordination with other arms. Col. George Marshall acknowledged after the war that the First Army depended on mass instead of maneuver. "Our men gave better results when employed in a 'steamroller' operation, that is, when launched in any attack with distant objectives and held continuously to their task without rest or reorganization until unfit for further fighting. Their morale suffered from delays under fire, their spirits were best maintained by continued aggressive action, even though the men themselves were approaching the point of complete exhaustion." This unimaginative tactical doctrine, a consequence of inadequate training, was far from the open warfare that Pershing espoused so fulsomely before the First Army went into battle. It was equally alien from the sophisticated use of combined arms that characterized British and French operations. Braim notes that about 200,000 Americans attempted to advance in a small area no more than 12 miles wide against preregistered artillery and machine-gun fire. They paid dearly. "Such a trade-off—bodies for bullets—was not intended, but the restrictiveness of the terrain, the quality of the defenses, and the poor training of the massed attacking forces brought about that result."[5]

Pershing now recognized that he must seize the high ground in the Argonne and east of the Meuse before he could expect to break through the Kriemhilde Stellung. On 7 October, General Liggett drove his I Corps northwest into the Argonne, and by 10 October, he forced the German defenders to withdraw. Among other accomplishments, this operation led to the relief of the "Lost Battalion," several companies of the 77th Division that had been surrounded by the enemy. On 8 October, the French XVII Corps with the American 29th and 33d Divisions attacked east of the Meuse to seize the heights that provided the German artillery with excellent observation westward as far as Cunel. This operation did not succeed in occupying the heights, but it at least caused some attenuation of the German fire. An attack by the V Corps against the Romagne heights on 9 October and a more general attack on 11 October yielded only local gains.[6]

According to General Pershing, these operations produced "some of the most bitter fighting of the war." The First Army forced its way "through dense woods, over hills and across deep ravines, against German defense conducted with a skill only equalled by that of the French in front of Verdun in 1916." Gone was the illusion that the enemy would not offer tenacious resistance. Pershing now argued that his purpose was "to increase the fighting front of the army and thus consume the maximum number of German divisions. In this latter respect, the attack was particularly successful, aimed as it was directly at the pivot of the German line on the Western Front." The commander-in-chief thus at least temporarily abandoned his earlier purpose: to smash through the Hindenburg line and seize the Carignan-Sedan railroad. The principal result of these operations was to exact German losses, although at the sacrifice of more Americans. An attack by the III Corps on 12 October generated ten thousand American casualties. Ludendorff acknowledged that the Americans had applied severe pressure, but he observed that despite their numerical superiority, "the attacks of the youthful American troops broke down with the heaviest losses." In spite of this terrible beating, Pershing gave no thought to suspending his operations. To have done so, as Allan Millett notes, would have been to admit that his goal of creating an independent American army was a horrendous error.[7]

Although the Americans remained stalemated in front of the Kriemhilde Stellung, other armies recorded significant gains elsewhere on the western front. These successes were a consequence of Foch's insistence on maintaining strong pressure on the German army wherever possible. Haig warned his command against "insidious rumors" about peace and "the disturbing influence of such peace talk. . . . at no time has there been a greater need of relentless effort or fairer promise of great results." On 5 October, the British Fourth Army crossed the Scheldt River and seized the plateau of Beaurevoir-Montbrehain. On 8 October, the British Third Army joined the Fourth Army, which still included the American II Corps, for a successful assault on the next line of German fortifications. The French First Army supported this movement with an advance to the south. On the same day, the French Fourth, Fifth, and Tenth Armies scored significant gains between the Oise and the Aisne. The net result was a general German withdrawal in front of the British lines between the Sensee and Oise rivers to the Hermann positions behind the Selle River and in front of the French lines between the Oise and the Aisne to the Hunding-Brunhilde fortifications. Meanwhile, the Group of Armies of Flanders continued to advance. By 16 October, the German army had abandoned the Belgian coast; Ostend was reoccupied on 17 October and Zeebrugge two days later.[8]

On the night of 9–10 October, General Pershing undertook a thorough evaluation of his circumstances, considering the entire western front with the Meuse-Argonne sector. He did so partly because he needed about 90,000 replacements to restore his divisions to full strength. He would have available only 45,000 men for this purpose before 1 November. His G-3 reports Pershing's decision. "The general situation demanded that the attack on the First Army front, and that of the Allies farther west, should be pushed to the limit. But if the First Army was to continue its pounding, this action must be coordinated with that of the Allies, and we must not only bring our divisions then with the French to the First Army, but we must break up incoming divisions to furnish, in part at least, the replacements so urgently needed." On 10 October, Pershing discussed these matters with Marshal Foch who accepted the AEF's analysis. The French agreed to release the Americans serving with them gradually–the 2d, 6th, 36th, 81st, and 88th Divisions–although two other divisions, the 37th and the 91st, were eventually sent to reinforce the Flanders Group of Armies in the north. Haig retained the 27th and 30th Divisions.[9]

Pershing adopted several expedients to ease the replacement problem. First, he reduced the size of infantry companies from 250 men to 175, a step similar to those taken in other armies after a period of engagement on the western front. More important, he broke up several divisions arriving in France, among them the 34th, 38th, 84th, and 86th Divisions. He also reduced the number of depot divisions from two of every six arriving to one in every six and broke up one, the 31st Division. Pershing blamed the War Department for not following a program of shipments that included sufficient replacements, but he was at least partially at fault. He had failed to anticipate the huge losses that occurred in the offensives on the Marne and the Vesle in August and those that came during the Meuse-Argonne battle.[10]

On 10 October, Pershing reached another decision of great importance; he reorganized the AEF and made some changes in command, including his relief as the commander of the First Army. In his memoirs, Pershing recalled that the period 1–11 October "involved the heaviest strain on the army and on me." He found it difficult to move troops in and out of the line without presenting the enemy with an opportunity to regroup. This consideration prevented him from ordering a delay while he repaired roads and resupplied his units. Also the inclement weather did not "inspire energetic action on the part of troops unaccustomed to the damp, raw climate." One of Pershing's officers observed of the commander at this time: "The strain was too great; this last battle had overloaded him." He was also smarting from extensive criticism of his army's failure to advance rapidly while important gains were made elsewhere. He gave as his reason for making the changes the growth in the responsibilities of the AEF, especially the opening of an offensive east of the Meuse, which would overstrain him and his staff. Accordingly, on 10 October he created the American Second Army, assigning Maj. Gen. Robert L. Bullard to its command. This organization, which began to function on 12 October, occupied the line from the Moselle to Fresnes-en-Woevre established after the reduction of the St. Mihiel salient. Bullard immediately began to plan operations toward the east. Most important, Pershing turned over the First Army to General Liggett, who delayed his assumption of command until 16 October. Pershing made himself commander of a group of armies with his headquarters at Ligny-en-Barrois. Other changes were made among the corps commanders.[11]

At Foch's insistence, Pershing remained active, closely supervising his command from a train near the First Army's headquarters at Souilly. He spent "a portion of each day at official headquarters giving directions regarding operations and deciding other important questions." The rest of the time he remained "at the front in close touch with corps and divisions." As commander of a group of armies, he reported directly to Marshal Foch, but he continued to discuss his use of French units with General Petain.[12]

Frank Vandiver, one of Pershing's biographers, believes that Foch sent General Weygand to Souilly on 12 October with an order relieving Pershing of command of the First Army and putting a French general in his place. Pershing supposedly was to command a quiet sector around Pont-a-Mousson. The implacable Clemenceau forced this initiative, but the American commander-in-chief rejected it out of hand. As evidence for this episode, Vandiver cites a memorandum of a conversation held at the Army War College in 1920 with Col. Jacques de Chambrun, a French liaison officer on Pershing's staff. No other information has turned up to corroborate this account. It seems most unlikely that Foch would have given such an order without consultations such as those that took place on other occasions at the beginning of September and again at the beginning of October, when he had attempted to reduce Pershing's responsibilities.[13]

The subject of relief did not arise when Pershing explained his command changes to Foch on 13 October, although on that occasion the generalissimo was unsparing in his criticism of the stalemate in the First Army sector. Foch sharply noted that "on all other parts of the front the advance was very marked; that the Americans were not progressing as rapidly as the others; that he would like to see them advance." Pershing defended his forces, arguing that "the fighting which is being done by the Americans facilitates the advance of the armies because we are drawing to our front from in front of the others a number of German divisions." Later he claimed that twenty-six enemy divisions had engaged his troops since 26 September, to which Foch took exception. When Pershing commented on the challenges of the terrain, Foch unkindly responded that "he realized the . . . [difficulties] of the ground and it was for this reason that he had proposed to General Pershing to make his attack west of the Argonne Forest, but that General Pershing had wished to attack where he is now attacking and he had, consequently, allowed him to do so." When Pershing observed that he had done so to avoid dividing his command by allowing a French force to operate between two American groups, Foch ended the colloquy by saying: "This was now of no importance. . . . all he wanted was results."[14]

Clemenceau's antipathy toward Pershing resurfaced on 21 October, when, perhaps remembering the long dispute over amalgamation, he wrote to Foch proposing "nothing less than to effect a change in the chief command of the American Army." After commenting on Pershing's "invincible obstinacy," he noted that the Americans had been "marking time ever since their forward jump the first day; and in spite of heavy losses, they have failed to conquer the ground assigned them as their objective. Nobody can maintain that these fine troops are unusable; they are merely unused." Clemenceau recognized that Foch had attempted to persuade Pershing to change his ways. He wondered "whether, after the failure of fruitless conversations, the time has not come for changing methods." He was aware of shifts in American command arrangements. If these did not produce results, he thought it would be "high time to tell President Wilson the truth and the whole truth." To this scathing criticism, Foch replied on 23 October, stating that he intended to deal with the American difficulties by moving divisions between the independent American force and Allied armies elsewhere. He recognized the inexperience of the American commanders and staffs but commented that "this crisis is the sort from which all improvised armies suffer, and which always considerably impairs their effectiveness at the start." Finally, he repeated certain arguments that Pershing had used in their meeting of 13 October to explain the delay on the American front, especially the difficult terrain and the determined German resistance. This episode ended Clemenceau's campaign to remove Pershing, but if the war had continued into 1919, the French premier might have renewed his proposal to raise the question with President Wilson.[15]

One distressing sign of a sharp decline in the morale of the First Army was the growth in the number of "stragglers," a euphemism for deserters, behind the front line. An American veteran of the war, Joseph Douglas Lawrence of the 29th Division, estimated that stragglers "amounted to an average of four or five to a company for every major assault. Many men cannot muster the courage to jump from a trench and rush the enemy in the open, whether they wear an American uniform or not." Pershing mentions this difficulty only once in his memoirs, quoting from his diary on 20 October: "Some straggling reported; directed energetic measures against it." When Liggett assumed command of the First Army he discovered that the number of stragglers was around a hundred thousand. "It was essential, first of all, to gather up the army as a team and round up the stragglers that our full weight be felt in one concerted blow." To deal with this problem, he "established straggler's posts on all the roads, tightened the military policing of back areas and sent out officers with patrols to search the woods and dugouts, and thousands of strays and hideaways poured in." General Bullard also dwelt on this problem. "The hardest work that I did or saw done by others in France was the holding of men to duty in service and battle." Some "theorists" who had not fought at the front wanted to reduce the numbers of military police, but "as our fighting increased these military police had to be augmented in every way possible. An unbroken line of them now followed our attacks."[16]

By the middle of October, the panic that had consumed the German High Command subsided because the advance of the Allies had slowed. Ludendorff now attempted to regain control of the great battle raging along the western front by conducting a fighting retreat. He still desired an armistice but only to ease a withdrawal to a defense line between Antwerp and the Meuse River. He hoped to hold out until the spring of 1919. This plan required the troops farthest from the Meuse on the German right wing, those in Flanders, to make the longest retreat. Those closest to the Meuse on the left of the active front opposed to the Americans would have to offer the strongest resistance. Ludendorff also planned a gradual retreat from the Laon bulge in the center, a move that became imperative after Haig smashed through the Hindenburg line to the north.[17]

The shortage of reserves to bolster threatened sectors of the German line remained exceedingly worrisome, but after the initial penetration of the Hindenburg fortifications, the Allied advance slowed everywhere. This hesitation stemmed in part from the necessity to repair communications and to reorganize and resupply victorious but tired troops. It also came from tenacious German resistance, allowing a disciplined withdrawal to prepared fortifications in the rear, particularly the Hunding-Brunhilde Stellung. The Belgian army moved to within 2 miles of Roulers by 2 October but did not seize the town until 14 October. The British enveloped Cambrai by 30 September but did not take it until 9 October. Debeney's French First Army occupied St. Quentin on 1 October but advanced only 10 miles farther by 10 October. Gouraud's French Fourth Army to Pershing's left was also stalled. The most significant gains of this period occurred in the British sector between Cambrai and St. Quentin.[18]

American troops of the 89th Division loading 75 mm shells at Remonville in November 1918. Logistical tangles limited the pace of the final American offensive, one of the reasons why Foch relied on attrition rather than maneuver.

The German High Command's returning optimism contrasted with the pessimism of military and civilian leadership in Berlin. On 17 October, Ludendorff objected strenuously after Prince Max, responding to pressure from President Wilson, decided to halt submarine warfare and to pledge not to devastate evacuated territories. He also called for a "war of endurance in defense of the fatherland" while negotiations continued with the Americans. Meanwhile, Crown Prince Rupprecht sent Prince Max a most gloomy assessment of military prospects. "We cannot sustain a serious enemy attack, owing to a lack of all reserves. If we succeed, by retreating behind the serious obstacle of the Meuse, in shortening our front considerably, we can hold out there under favourable circumstances for one or two months, but only if the enemy does not violate Holland's neutrality or drive her to take sides against us, and if the Austro-Hungarian troops are not withdrawn from the Western Front." He doubted that the defense could hold out through December because the Americans were arriving in France at the rate of about 300,000 men per month. He did not rule out a sudden catastrophic collapse. Stating that Ludendorff did not recognize the truth, he concluded dramatically. "Whatever happens, we must obtain peace before the enemy breaks through into Germany; if he does, woe on us!"[19]

Prince Rupprecht proved a sound prophet. Ludendorff's personal position depended on stopping the Allied advance, but a new set of Allied attacks on the western front penetrated the Hermann and Hunding-Brunhilde defenses and destroyed his last ounce of credibility. On the British front, Haig fought the battle of the Selle. Debeney's First French Army and Rawlinson's British Fourth Army, which included the American II Corps, struck on 17 October. In two days these forces drove the enemy across the Sambre River and the Oise Canal. On 20 October, elements of the British First and Third Armies crossed the Selle River, storming the heights on its east bank. This success penetrated the Hermann position, the last German defenses short of the Antwerp-Meuse line. Again Haig gained a striking victory without marked superiority in manpower. Twenty-six Allied divisions, including the American 27th and 30th Divisions, bested thirty-one German divisions while capturing 20,000 prisoners and seizing 475 guns.[20]

General Read, the commander of the II Corps, commented on the behavior of his troops during the battle of the Selle. After praising Anglo-American command relationships, he claimed for his divisions an "essential contribution to the operations of the Fourth Army." He also noted that while his men displayed initiative and dash, otherwise they "had no advantage over the British whose extensive experience kept units well in hand, and whose liaison was excellent where the Americans tended to become too scattered and to neglect at times, in the heat of battle, to keep the higher command closely informed of the chain of minor developments." If the II Corps should fight again, Read believed that it would attain objectives at a lesser cost in lives. "Objectives were consistently gained, but only at the end of the [combat] phase were battalion and company commanders generally using their auxiliary arms to the fullest extent and to the most economical saving of men and junior officers." The chief failing of regimental and higher commands was inexperience. "While the staffs as a rule functioned efficiently, there was a tendency for them to lose the remarkably close touch with combat units that all British headquarters maintained." Despite these deficiencies the II Corps earned high commendation from Field Marshal Haig. In a special order of the day he informed the Americans: "It does not need me to tell you that in the heavy fighting of the past three weeks you have earned the lasting esteem and admiration of your British comrades in arms, whose successes you have so nobly shared." In this instance, as in others, American divisions operating in larger Allied formations experienced early difficulties but generally made important contributions, a result contrary to the expectations of General Pershing.[21]

Meanwhile, the American First Army prepared to resume the offensive. On 11 October, Petain ordered the Franco-American forces fighting on the Champagne-Meuse front to advance their line by outflanking the German positions along the Aisne River. This measure would adjust to the gains that had been made to the left between the Sensee and the Oise. Pershing was directed to move through the Kriemhilde Stellung to the region of Buzancy. On 12 October, Petain issued instructions to the French Fourth Army. "As long as American First Army is less advanced than Fourth Army, Fourth Army will not limit its operation on Aisne right bank strictly to the area assigned to it as zone of action . . . in order to overcome successively resistance opposing left wing of American First Army." Stung by the implication that his forces were lagging, Pershing informed Petain that he intended to attack the German third position vigorously on 14 October. "The situation is fully appreciated and all efforts are being and will be exerted for decisive results." He planned to continue the attacks east of the Meuse while the III and V Corps drove salients on both sides of the Bois de Romagne and the Bois de Bantheville farther north. After clearing these wooded areas, the two corps would join and continue their advance. Meanwhile the I Corps would hold on its left while supporting the advance of the V Corps on its right. As Pershing's army moved forward, the French Fourth Army would attempt to outflank enemy troops opposing the American left. Pershing excused delays on his front by stressing the importance of the Meuse-Argonne sector to the enemy and arguing that his operations had forced enemy retirements elsewhere on the western front.[22]

Like the previous general attacks of 26 September and 4 October, that of 14 October fell short of its objectives, although it eventually brought the First Army roughly to the position it had planned to occupy on 27 September. Veteran divisions participated in this effort. The V Corps, now commanded by Maj. Gen. Charles P. Summerall, who replaced General Cameron, seized the Cote Dame Marie, the strongest point in the Romagne heights. The town of Romagne and the Bois de Romagne also fell to the Americans, bringing them to the southern edge of the Bois de Bantheville. The Kriemhilde Stellung had finally been partially breached, and the American lines now flanked those of the Germans to the east and the west. This was a significant accomplishment, but the German defenders continued to dispute every inch of ground. By 19 October, Pershing was forced to suspend the general attack. Liddell Hart considered this operation a failure. It had gained little at great cost; "even the Higher Command realized that the offensive had reached stalemate. An attempt to press on, with exhausted troops and disordered communications, could exercise no pressure adequate to be any appreciably greater relief to the

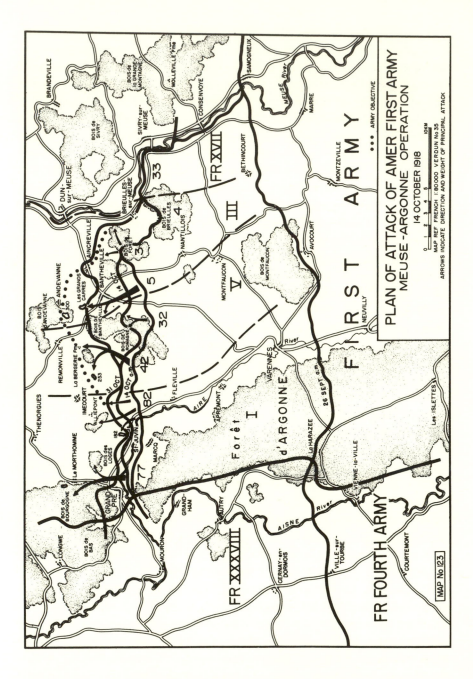

PLAN OF ATTACK OF AMER FIRST ARMY
MEUSE-ARGONNE OPERATION
14 OCTOBER 1918

••• ARMY OBJECTIVE

MAP REF FRENCH 1:80,000 VERDUN No 35
ARROWS INDICATE DIRECTION AND WEIGHT OF PRINCIPAL ATTACK

MAP No 123

other Allied armies." Pershing later claimed that the penetration of the Kriemhilde Stellung after almost a month of effort was "the outstanding glory of our service in France." Ludendorff did not share this appraisal, stating on 17 October: "We must not overrate the Americans. They are certainly smart. But we have beaten them hitherto, even when we were very inferior in numbers. . . . our men are not anxious about the Americans; they are about the English. We must not let our troops feel isolated."[23]

General Liggett, now in command of the First Army, wisely devoted two weeks to reorganizing and retraining his command. He also conducted limited operations designed to improve starting positions for the next general attack. The most important assignments during this period fell to the I Corps, commanded by General Dickman, which attempted to clear the Bois de Loges to improve the position of the French Fourth Army. Although Dickman did not succeed, he managed to capture Grandpre, which allowed Gouraud to advance his right flank to a position favorable for resumption of the general offensive. Meanwhile, the First Army prepared effective artillery plans to support infantry attacks and to suppress enemy fire, including extensive use of gas. Of equal importance was special training for infantry "assault teams" to prepare them to engage machine-gun nests successfully while other infantry elements bypassed them. Finally, the First Army took advantage of tactical innovations that had served the British and French armies well during the battles of July–October.[24]

Pershing believed that his advance could have continued unabated, but given "a certain loss in cohesion," it was "deemed advisable to take a few days for the replacement of tired units, the renewal of supplies, and the improvement of communications." In his final report, he boasted of the American accomplishments between 26 September and 31 October, claiming that the First Army's "spirit of determination . . . made it impossible for the enemy to maintain the struggle until 1919." This presumptuous view gave short shrift to the achievements of the Allies elsewhere on the western front, and it obscured both operational shortcomings and more than 100,000 casualties.[25]

While the First Army restored itself, Marshal Foch prepared another round of general inter-Allied attacks to begin toward the end of October. His directive of 19 October, destined to be his last, provided for continuation of the movements inaugurated on 26 September. The Group of Armies of Flanders on the left was ordered to advance toward Brussels across the Escaut (Scheldt) and Dendre rivers. The BEF and the French Fourth Army were to continue their efforts to force the enemy back to the Ardennes, moving toward Maubeuge. To the south, Foch ordered an attack intended to cause "the fall of the line of the Aisne by a maneuver of two wings." The French Fifth Army

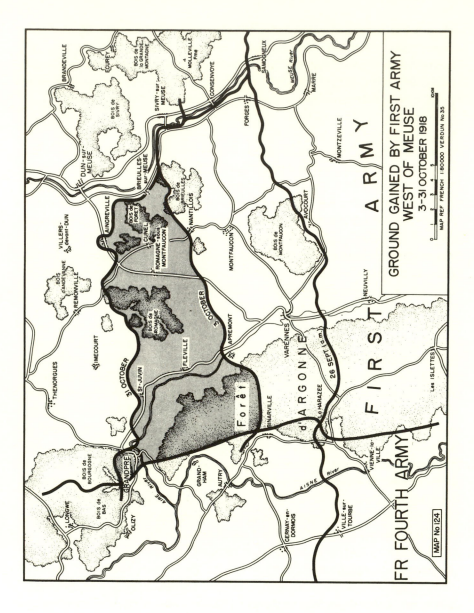

GROUND GAINED BY FIRST ARMY
WEST OF MEUSE
3-31 OCTOBER 1918

MAP REF FRENCH 1:80000 VERDUN No 35

MAP No 124

on the left would attack toward Chaumont–Porcien. On the right, the French Fourth Army and the American First Army would attack in the direction of Buzancy–Le Chesne. As before, these movements were designed to gain control of the railroad between Mezieres and Aulnoye, an accomplishment that would force a general German retreat.[26]

As the German army braced for Foch's new offensive amid indications of general collapse, Prince Max's government completed its bilateral negotiations with President Wilson. This outcome doomed Ludendorff, who proved unwilling to accept responsibility for the defeat. Hindenburg precipitated matters by issuing a provocative order of the day on 25 October without the approval of the civil authority. "Wilson's answer means military capitulation. It is therefore unacceptable to us soldiers. Wilson's answer can be for us soldiers only a challenge to continue resistance to the utmost of our power. When the enemy realizes that the German front is not to be broken through in spite of every sacrifice, he will be ready for a peace which ensures Germany's future." Prince Max then threatened resignation, and the kaiser supported him. On 26 October, Ludendorff resigned to avoid removal. Hindenburg remained in command; General Wilhelm Groener took Ludendorff's place at Spa.[27]

The crisis of the Central Powers extended to the lesser partners, now on their last legs. Bulgaria had already signed an armistice on 29 September, after suffering a smashing defeat on the Salonika front. In Palestine, General Allenby destroyed a Turkish army at Megiddo on 19 September, leading to Turkey's capitulation on 30 October. Austria-Hungary addressed a peace proposal to President Wilson as early as 16 September and, on 7 October, requested an armistice. On 24 October, the Italian army attacked on the line of the Piave River, soon gaining a great victory at Vittorio Veneto. Vienna sought an armistice on 30 October and was granted one on 3 November. Most revealing were emphatic intimations of political and social unrest within Germany. As Liddell Hart put it, "The 'home front' began to crumble later, but it tumbled quicker than the battle front."[28]

The prospect of an early end to the war now stimulated discussions of armistice terms, the basis on which the German army might lay down its arms. Recommendations of terms of armistice lay within the province of the military, unlike the terms of peace, which were the responsibility of the civil governments. As early as 8 October, Foch enunciated three prime conditions that Germany must accept: liberation of all occupied territory; assurance of a basis for crushing Germany, should it attempt to renew hostilities; and arrangements to ensure collection of reparations. He added six specific conditions intended to prevent the enemy from removing or destroying materials of war and military facilities. At Lloyd George's instigation, a letter went to Wilson on 9 October from the British and French leaders warning against German trickery and noting that the military experts must consult about the terms of an armistice. Foch and General Wilson, the British chief of the Imperial General Staff, feared that the American correspondence with Prince Max would create complications. President Wilson made certain that prudent operational safeguards would accompany a cease-fire. His letter of 12 October stated that the military counsellors must decide terms of armistice and that these must ensure "the present superiority of the armies of the United States and of the Allies on the battlefield." Foch was quick to define his understanding of the term "military counsellors," which he thought meant the commanders-in-chief of the several Allied armies. The generalissimo remained suspicious of President Wilson, especially after Prince Max's note of 20 October intimated that the evacuation of occupied territories would reflect "the proportion now existing between troops at the front." He thought it undesirable that "the Germans should come to consider President Wilson as a sort of arbiter between the Entente governments and the Central Powers. In such a game the Entente had everything to lose and nothing to gain; it was advisable, therefore, that without delay the military counsellors be given the floor." Meanwhile, Haig presented his views on armistice terms to Lloyd George. He proposed that the British only ask in the armistice for "what we intend to hold, and that we set our faces against the French entering Germany to pay off old scores. In my opinion, the British Army would not fight keenly for what is really not its own affair." He was much less demanding than Foch, believing that unduly stringent demands would lead to continuing German resistance.[29]

Evidence of Entente alarms did not escape the observant General Bliss, still manning his post at Versailles. On 14 October he wrote mordantly to General March. "I think I told you some time ago that I heard a gentleman in high position here say that the United States was building a bridge for the Allies to pass over; that the time for the United States to secure acquiescence in its wishes was while the bridge was building; that after the Allies had crossed over the bridge they would have no further use for it or its builders. This may be true or not. I do not know." Haig's comment on Wilson's independent course confirmed Bliss's suspicions. "Feeling was strong against the President," he complained. "He does not seem to realise our requirements, so a telegram was sent to him pointing out that in addition to retreating to the pre-war frontier, the enemy must hand over territory as guarantees, and *at least* Alsace-Lorraine."[30]

To find out the views of Petain, Haig, and Pershing about armistice terms, Foch convened a conference at Senlis on 25 October. Haig led off, repeating the views he had expressed earlier to Lloyd George. He proposed that Germany evacuate the occupied areas and Alsace-Lorraine, deliver Metz and Strasbourg to the Allies, return rolling stock, and repatriate French and Belgian citizens taken to Germany. Petain wanted to occupy the left bank of the Rhine from the Dutch border to the French frontier and to establish bridgeheads on the right bank. He also asked for five thousand locomotives and a hundred thousand railway cars. Pershing came next. Thinking that the military prognosis was most favorable, he advocated severe terms. Besides the proposed exactions of Haig and Petain, he wanted a guarantee that Germany would not interfere with the transportation of American troops and supplies to Europe; the delivery of submarines and their bases to the Allies or a neutral power; and the return of all rolling stock taken from France. He said nothing about unconditional surrender.[31]

Foch did not accept Haig's somewhat pessimistic views, and his recommendations reflected this outlook. The Germans had been pounded unceasingly since 15 July, losing over a quarter of a million prisoners and over four thousand guns. The enemy was "physically and morally, a thoroughly beaten army." He recognized that the British and French troops were tired and that the American army was a "young army." Still, it was "full of idealism and strength, and ardour; it has won victories and is now on the eve of another victory; and nothing gives wings to an Army like victory." His terms reflected these observations. They included immediate evacuation of occupied territories and repatriation of inhabitants; surrender of five thousand cannon, thirty thousand machine guns, and three thousand trench mortars; evacuation of territory on the left bank of the Rhine and creation of four bridgeheads on the right bank; prohibition of destruction in the evacuated area; delivery of five thousand locomotives and one hundred and fifty thousand railway cars in good condition; delivery of one hundred and fifty submarines, withdrawal of the German fleet to Baltic ports, and occupation of Cuxhaven and Heligoland; and maintenance of the blockade for the period necessary to fulfill the conditions of the armistice.[32]

The Senlis conference stimulated a brief tiff between Haig and Pershing; it stemmed from the British commander's criticism of the American army. On 19 October, Haig had expressed himself candidly to the prime minister and others about the state of the Allied armies; their condition suggested moderate terms of armistice. He thought the French worn out and the British fighting hard but facing a period of diminishing success. The American army, he continued, "is not yet organised; it is ill-equipped, half-trained, with insufficient supply services. Experienced officers and N.C.O.s are lacking." At Senlis he repeated these views. Pershing became angry at Haig's remarks, which he deemed disparaging to his forces. Haig claimed to have had no such intention. His purpose was to ensure that his colleagues recognized "the difficulties which confront our Forces before we can make the Germans accept 'Unconditional Surrender.'" The Americans were "very touchy" because the French had criticized them so much. He wrote soothingly to Pershing, but his private opinion did not change. On 29 October, he recorded Lloyd George's comment on his statement at Senlis. "L. G. was very pleased that I had spoken about the real state and present military value of the American Army. . . . Foch reported in the same way to him but would not tell Pershing to his face what he thought of the American Army and its present fitness for war."[33]

Pershing was agitated. The disappointing performance of the First Army preyed on his mind, and his reaction was to insist upon onerous treatment of the defeated enemy. On 28 October, the First Army's chief of staff, Brig. Gen. Hugh Drum, recorded Pershing's thoughts. "He is convinced that if civilization is to receive the full benefit of this terrible war, it must end only with the unconditional surrender of Germany. The military situation is such that in his judgment there can be no excuse for not obtaining unconditional surrender." It is possible, even probable, that Pershing hoped the war would continue for a while so that he and his army could make a major contribution to victory. This accomplishment would erase the bitter memory of the check in the Meuse-Argonne sector and confound critics such as Haig, Lloyd George, Foch, and Clemenceau.[34]

Pershing's disturbed spirit may help to account for an otherwise unaccountable breach of his authority, a display of differences with civil authority on the way to end the war. Pershing conveyed to the War Department the views on the terms of armistice that he had expressed at Senlis, an act that promptly elicited a message from Secretary Baker containing the president's reaction. Wilson desired terms of armistice that would prevent resumption of hostilities, but he did not wish to humiliate the German government. Such an outcome might play into the hands of militarists in Berlin. This message constituted an implied rebuke of Pershing and a strong hint that he should desist from advocating unduly severe terms of armistice. Colonel House had arrived in Paris to attend the meetings of the Supreme War Council that would decide both terms of armistice and the political basis of postwar peace negotiations. Wilson explained to his emissary the reasons for taking a moderate stand. "My deliberate judgment is that our whole weight should be thrown for an armistice which will prevent a renewal of hostilities by Germany but which will be as moderate as possible within those limits, because it is certain that too much success or security on the part of the Allies will make a genuine peace settlement exceedingly difficult if not impossible." Baker invited Pershing to inform Wilson of any considerations that "ought to be weighed before settling finally his views."[35]

On 30 October, General Pershing sent an unsolicited letter to the Supreme War Council that advocated unconditional surrender instead of an armistice. He neglected to discuss its contents beforehand with Colonel House or his superiors in Washington. This initiative aroused a considerable reaction. When Pershing dispatched the message to the Supreme War Council, he sent a copy to House and cabled its contents to the War Department. Pershing thus placed himself on record as advocating a position contrary to that of his political superiors. He was within his authority in responding to a request from the Supreme War Council for his views on terms of an armistice. He was far outside it in opposing an armistice and calling instead for unconditional surrender, a position that directly contradicted that of his civilian superiors. In taking this action, Pershing stepped out of character; normally he was careful to defer to civilian leadership.[36]

Pershing's action dismayed Colonel House and outraged Secretary Baker, normally a staunch supporter of the general. House wondered whether Pershing realized that he was dealing with "a political rather than a military question." In Washington, Baker notified the president that Pershing had placed himself "on record one way with you and another way with the Supreme War Council. It is really tragic." Baker then prepared a strong reprimand for delivery to Pershing, but Colonel House retrieved matters. First he asked Foch on 31 October whether it was preferable to continue fighting or to make an armistice. Foch replied: "I am not waging war for the sake of waging war. If I obtain through the Armistice the conditions that we wish to impose on Germany, I am satisfied. Once this object is attained, nobody has the right to shed one drop more of blood." This view undercut Pershing. On 3 November, House met with the general, who apologized for acting without prior consultation with civilian authorities. House then recommended to the president that he drop the matter because Pershing's letter was no longer under consideration at the Supreme War Council. This tactful advice was accepted, and Pershing escaped censure. After the war Baker chose to suppress the affair. He claimed in his annual report for 1919 that "no shadow of misunderstanding had arisen between him [Pershing] and his Commander in Chief." Despite his surrender to House, the general did not change his personal opposition to an armistice.

He said shortly after the war: "What I dread is that Germany doesn't know she was licked. Had they given us another week, we'd have *taught* them."[37]

The Supreme War Council rapidly reached agreement on the critical issues before it, the political basis of the postwar peace negotiations, and the military, naval, and air terms of armistice. The Entente leaders were loathe to accept Wilson's Fourteen Points and associated pronouncements, which contradicted many provisions of the so-called secret treaties. They were forced to do so when House intimated that otherwise the United States might withdraw its army from the war. In the pre-armistice agreement reached on 4 November, the Allies declared "their willingness to make peace with the Government of Germany on the terms of peace laid down in the President's Address to Congress of January 8, 1918, and the principles of settlement enunciated in his subsequent addresses." Only two exceptions were specified, although both were of great significance. Britain reserved its views on freedom of the seas, and France obtained agreement that Germany would have to pay reparations for damage to civilians and their property. Meanwhile, Foch's recommendations of armistice terms generally prevailed, although the naval terms were made more severe at the instance of the British Admiralty. There remained only for Germany to accept the terms of the armistice.[38]

The inter-Allied general offensive scheduled for 1 November began as the civilian governments moved to end the war, a circumstance bound to weaken the resolve of the German defenders. Foch's main objective remained the critical rail communications that served the German army along the western front. British and French attacks toward Maubeuge proved entirely successful against disintegrating German resistance; the Allies soon reached points on the lateral railroad. On 8 November, the British occupied Avesnes and the next day, the fortress of Maubeuge. Simultaneously, the French took Hirson. By coincidence, Canadian forces entered Mons on 11 November, the last day of the war, where British troops had first seen action in 1914. Meanwhile, the Group of Armies of Flanders crossed the Scheldt River and drove toward Ghent. The French Army of Belgium, which included the American 37th and 91st Divisions, participated in this advance.[39]

While the inter-Allied attacks from the west toward Ghent and Maubeuge gained ground, the French Fourth Army and the American First Army resumed their northward movement toward Mezieres and Sedan. These operations were intended to force the withdrawal of the Germans from the Brunhilde fortifications on the line of the Aisne. The French Fourth Army would push toward

Le Chesne and the American First Army toward Buzancy, their flanks meeting at Boult-aux-Bois. Foch wanted Pershing to attack westerly toward the Bois de Bourgogne, lying north of the Argonne, but the Americans had seen enough of French forests. Instead Liggett decided to move across the last formidable barrier to its north, the wooded Barricourt heights. He expected to occupy the Bois de Bourgogne after the Franco-American advance had forced the Germans to withdraw. On 1 November, the V Corps (89th and 2d Divisions with 1st and 42d Divisions in reserve) would make the principal thrust, assaulting the Barricourt heights. On the left, the I Corps (80th, 77th, and 78th Divisions with 82d Division in reserve) would move to Boult-aux-Bois and link with the French Fourth Army. The III Corps (5th and 90th Divisions with 3d Division in reserve) would advance on the right. The French were to lend extensive artillery support, including the use of gas shells to neutralize German fire from the eastern edge of the Bois de Bourgogne. Foch thought the initial plan unduly restrictive. He urged concentration simply on the direction, speed, and depth of the assault, a concern that led to some flexibility in the specifications for the advance. In contrast to the initial operations in the sector launched on 26 September, the divisions in this movement were experienced and well-prepared organizations. Infantry-artillery coordination was much improved, and commanders were emboldened to attempt complicated maneuvers such as night attacks. The confident Americans faced exhausted German divisions that were far below normal strength.[40]

The German army was on its last legs. Ludendorff claimed that, after the initial setbacks, his forces had resisted the general Allied attack effectively. As time passed, he recognized that "now we were weaker, and first one and then another division failed to fight. The number of shirkers behind the front increased alarmingly." Commanders found it necessary to exhort their troops. Maj. Gen. Freiherr Quadt, commanding the 76th Reserve Division, recognized the hardships his troops had to endure, but he told them that the "general situation necessitates holding out. The political leaders of England and France refuse to consent to a reasonable peace, which Germany has suggested and made every effort to bring about. They want to destroy us and devastate our country." He spoke especially of effective opposition to the French and the Americans around Grandpre, which he thought proved that "in spite of the tremendous strain we are still in a position to offer an energetic resistance to the enemy at points where our leaders think it advisable." Others were more realistic. One officer from Supreme Headquarters noted that the "need of rest led to the peace offer 4 weeks ago. The enemy has recognized this fact and will not allow us any rest. He is attacking continuously, first here, then there,

German troops under an American gas attack during the Meuse-Argonne offensive. Note gas masks and casualties.

and the [enemy] reserves are constantly on the move. No more [German] reserves are available." Reporting a mutiny in a German division, its commander cited as reasons for it a difficult march and the breakdown of transport, agitation of the local population that affected troops from Alsace-Lorraine, and "unfavorable political news [that] probably had a strong influence on the morale of the troops."[41]

The High Command, recognizing that Foch planned an early offensive, accelerated preparations for a retreat to the Antwerp-Meuse line. Concern for the evacuation of essential material and wounded troops caused delays, but preparatory orders for the movement were issued on 30 October. Hindenburg protested fruitlessly when the civilian government objected to orders that specified the destruction of various facilities located on the path of the retreat. The Supreme Command planned an orderly fighting withdrawal to strong positions in occupied territory at a reasonable pace, but Foch's pressure precluded anything other than a headlong sprint to unfinished fortifications. Hindenburg recognized that the American attacks had contributed to his defeat, but he could not resist a last word. "The experience of these massed [Americans] will have taught the United States for the future that the business of war cannot be learnt in a few months, and that in a crisis lack of this experience costs streams of blood."[42]

The American attack of 1 November was generally successful, surely the most efficient of the campaign. Only seven German divisions opposed this advance, four of which had been on line for a long period. The V Corps in the center quickly gained control of the Barricourt heights, while on the right the III Corps captured Andevanne and Aincreville. On the left, the I Corps made little progress, German troops offering strong resistance in the Bois de Loges. This result was of no consequence, because the seizure of the Barricourt heights and the advance of the French Fourth Army placed the German Fifth Army in an untenable position. It must now counterattack or retreat north of the line Boult-aux-Bois–Buzancy. It chose to withdraw, fleeing to crossings of the Meuse in the Dun-sur-Meuse–Stenay area. The I Corps occupied Buzancy on 2 November and soon moved into Boult-aux-Bois and a junction with the French Fourth Army. This achievement, which turned the Bois de Bourgogne, forced the Germans to abandon the Brunhilde fortifications.

The advance continued as fast as the French and American armies could displace artillery and supplies forward. By 3 November, the First Army "Summary of Intelligence" reported that "the hostile front has seemed practically to have disappeared and contact has been maintained with difficulty." On 4 November, the advance extended to the heights of the Meuse, where the French XVII Corps and other units made gains. By that night, the III Corps occupied the left bank of the Meuse as far north as Stenay. Meanwhile, heavy artillery was brought forward to fire on the Carignan-Sedan railroad and the rail junctions at Longuyon and Conflans, although with its defenses broken, the rail line itself had lost much of its significance. The German army abandoned it and retreated to the east as it had earlier abandoned the line of the Aisne. On the left of the First Army, the French Fourth Army moved through the undefended Brunhilde position and toward the Sedan-Mezieres district.[43]

The successes of 1–4 November reflected the growing experience of the First Army. Artillery directed by corps and army headquarters applied successive "concentration fires" that produced a danger zone of 1,000 meters in depth. Special units were detailed to attack strong points while other troops pressed on. Changes also were made in the employment of aircraft. According to the after-action report of the First Army, "the bombing squadrons attacked the hostile infantry and artillery in close cooperation with our advancing infantry. This resulted in direct material and moral assistance to the infantry during the critical stages of the attack." Improved staff work under General Liggett's supervision produced a decision to bypass the formidable wooded regions on the left flank instead of accepting many casualties in attempts to overrun excellent

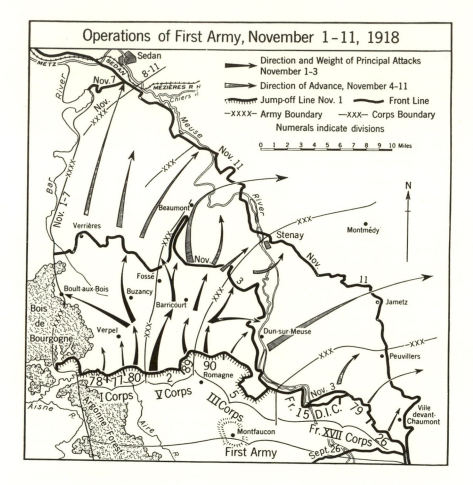

Operations of First Army, November 1–11, 1918

Direction and Weight of Principal Attacks November 1–3
Direction of Advance, November 4–11
Jump-off Line Nov. 1 — Front Line
–xxxx– Army Boundary   –xxx– Corps Boundary
Numerals indicate divisions

0 1 2 3 4 5 6 7 8 9 10 Miles

defensive positions. The First Army executed a complicated wheel to the right, positioning itself for a move toward Metz.[44]

General von Gallwitz's headquarters quickly recognized the extent of the German defeat. One observer noted that the German defenders were "fighting courageously but just cannot do anything"; therefore the army must withdraw to the rear of the Meuse River. Von Gallwitz immediately reported his predicament to his superiors, insisting that "only a timely withdrawal to a rearward line which is stronger and better secured can for a certainty strengthen the front and release the reserves required for the pivot and other threatened points." At Supreme Headquarters, Gen. Wilhelm Groener, Ludendorff's replacement, noted the advantages of a move to the Antwerp-Meuse position but also the disadvantages. It would produce "a more widespread critical depression at home, a triumph for the enemy," and it would be difficult to support the defense because a "faulty railroad net east of the line" would preclude "lateral shifting of the reserves." The next day he noted the availability of French and American divisions for a thrust toward Sedan. Hindenburg recognized the weakness of the Antwerp-Meuse position, most of which existed only on paper. It was necessary for the Fifth Army to hold south of the Meuse not only to avoid untoward political consequences at home but to buy time for preparation of the Antwerp-Meuse position.[45]

On 4 November, the German army began its *Kriegsmarsch*, an attempt to break contact with the Allied armies and to conduct a general withdrawal to the north bank of the Meuse. The First Army quickly recognized the state of affairs, noting on 5 November that west of the Meuse "the enemy continued his hasty withdrawal, which amounts almost to a collapse." Intelligence information did not change on the next day: "No definite information secured [about the enemy]. His retirement west of the Meuse on Sedan appears to have been hasty and rapid." By 6 November, the left bank of the Meuse was occupied as far north as Allicourt, and the Carignan-Sedan railway was but 2 kilometers distant. Meanwhile the III Corps crossed the Meuse. On 7 November, it stood 10 kilometers east of the river, at last forcing the Germans to abandon the heights that provided them with strong artillery positions and excellent observation to the west. The only real constraint on Liggett's forward movement was the need to support the forward echelons, no easy task because the Americans had reached the devastated Verdun battleground. As the *Kriegsmarsch* began, revolution broke out within Germany, fueled by recognition that should the Americans continue to advance in Lorraine, the next effective line of resistance must be on the Rhine instead of the Meuse. General von Gallwitz despairingly reported the circumstances on the left flank of the active line to Supreme Headquarters. "The west bank of the MEUSE could not be held by the tired divisions. . . . The enemy has seized a foothold at an important point on the east bank; he will continue his attack with fresh masses."[46]

Pershing later discerned in these American operations the cause of the German appeal for an armistice on 6 November: advancing 41 kilometers since 26 September, the First Army "had cut the enemy's main line of communications. Recognizing that nothing but a cessation of hostilities could save his armies from complete disaster, he appealed for an immediate armistice." This overblown claim neglected the fact that the German army had escaped east of the railroad line before the Americans reached it. The inter-Allied agreements concluded in Paris decided the timing of the German appeal. The decisions of 4 November were communicated to Germany on 5 November. From a military point of view, the German decision to request an armistice reflected the brilliance of Foch's operational plans and their execution by the several armies fighting on the western front since 26 September, especially the British army's advance toward Maubeuge. The American campaign, more one of attrition than of maneuver, made a significant contribution to the inter-Allied achievement, but it was not the only or even the most important national effort.[47]

Whatever the ebullience that Pershing manifested in postwar accounts of the final campaign, at the time he concocted a thoroughly misguided and ultimately unsuccessful scheme to deprive the French army of the honor of occupying Sedan. There Napoleon III had been forced to surrender his army to Moltke in 1870. On 4 November, an order from Foch drew the boundary between the First Army and the French Fourth Army to a point on the Meuse 3 kilometers south of Sedan. On 5 November, General Conner, a member of Pershing's staff, went to First Army headquarters. General Liggett was not there, but Conner encountered the G-3 of the First Army, Col. George C. Marshall, Jr. He said to him: "It is General Pershing's desire that the troops of the First Army should capture Sedan, and he directs that orders be issued accordingly." Marshall then drafted an order to Summerall, commanding V Corps, and Dickman, commanding I Corps. "General Pershing desires that the honor of entering Sedan should fall to the American First Army. He has every confidence that the troops of the I Corps, assisted on their right by the V Corps, will enable him to realize this desire." Later the First Army's chief of staff, General Drum, added another sentence. "In transmitting the foregoing message, your attention is invited to the favorable opportunity now existing for pressing our advance throughout the night. Boundaries will not be considered binding." Marshall did not succeed in stopping this unorthodox transaction, made when his commander was absent.[48]

The 42d Division, a part of the I Corps located to the left of the V Corps, should have made the main movement, but Summerall of V Corps, an enemy of Dickman, decided literally to steal a march. He ordered his old division, the 1st under Gen. Frank Parker, not only to move across the front of the 42d Division but over the boundary between the French and American armies and to enter Sedan ahead of all other troops. This strange decision complicated an already disreputable enterprise. On the night of 6–7 November, elements of the 1st Division moved across the front of the 42d Division. On the way, a detachment mistakenly captured a brigade commander of the 42d, Douglas MacArthur, who wore a hat that looked like those of German officers.[49]

General Liggett did not learn of this affair until 7 November, but when he did, he immediately canceled Summerall's operation. Upon receiving reports from the French of the 1st Division's movement, he went immediately to the Corps headquarters, noting later that "this was the only occasion in the war when I lost my temper completely." The march had exhausted the 1st Division, which Liggett had deliberately held back for use on the east bank of the Meuse. It also could have created an excellent opportunity for an enemy counterattack, which fortunately was not possible. Liggett called the movement an "atrocity" and ordered an investigation. He later decided to drop the matter, no doubt because the truth would have been a serious embarrassment to General Pershing. Liggett did not mention his superior in his postwar account of this affair. When he and Pershing discussed the incident on 9 November, the commander-in-chief appeared undisturbed. In his memoirs, Pershing wrote blithely: "Under normal conditions the action of the officer or officers responsible for this movement of the 1st Division directly across the zones of action of two other divisions could not have been overlooked, but the splendid record of that unit and the approach of the end of hostilities suggested leniency."[50]

On 5 November, Pershing issued orders to both the First and Second Armies about projected operations. Arguing the need to sustain pressure on the enemy west of the Moselle, Pershing espoused the principle of the offensive in Foch-like tones, throwing in mention of open warfare methods. His goal was the "complete destruction of the enemy's armed forces"; his intention was to drive beyond the German frontier toward the Briey-Longwy region, long a prime preoccupation of American planners. The First Army was ordered to complete its present operations, crossing the Meuse and clearing the district between the Bar and Chiers rivers before striking toward Longwy, while the Second Army concerted plans for an attack on the axis Fresnes–Conflans–Briey. Meanwhile Foch ordered the French general Charles Mangin to prepare a separate offensive east of the Moselle River in the direction of Chateau-Salins. This movement was intended to weaken the stubborn German defense of the right bank of the Meuse. On 10 November, Pershing agreed to provide six divisions, then a part of Bullard's Second Army, to support Mangin's twenty French divisions during their attack in the Moselle region. The American force would become the Second Army, and the old Second Army would become the Third Army. These efforts were in line with Foch's determination to maintain the general offensive until Germany accepted an armistice of the Allies' devising.[51]

These plans guided the final operations of the AEF. Gains were steady but slow on the American front and elsewhere. Roads were crowded; bridges required repair; efforts had to be made to supply civilians; and bad weather inhibited air operations. These circumstances kept the German retreat from turning into a rout. For its part, the First Army completed clearance of the heights east of the Meuse, and by 11 November, it had moved to the line Fresnes-en-Woevre–Stenay–Pont-Maugis, encountering little opposition. The Second Army launched its initial attacks on 10 November and made some progress. Mangin's plans for operations in the Moselle region were never executed. On 8 November, Foch informed Pershing that hostilities would halt at a time not yet determined and that, when the end came, he should report carefully on his location. On 9 November, Kaiser Wilhelm abdicated and fled to Holland. Early on 11 November, Foch notified Pershing that the armistice would begin at 11 a.m. The American First and Second Armies continued to advance until the appointed hour, when the guns fell silent.[52]

8

THE MEANING OF 1918

When the United States entered the First World War, President Wilson made political and strategic decisions that committed the nation to a major mobilization, including an enormous expansion of the United States Army. Given little prewar preparation, the nation would require an extended period to acquire military personnel and equipment, to train organizations that could fight on equal terms against powerful European enemies, and to deploy a huge army to Europe. This circumstance greatly influenced the operations of the American Expeditionary Forces in 1918.

President Woodrow Wilson went to war with an established *policy*, those basic goals or war aims for which the nation would expend its blood and treasure. During 1915–1916, he had defined his conception of a just and lasting peace, which he sought fruitlessly to attain by making himself a disinterested mediator of the Great War. Even before the intervention of April 1917, Wilson stated his purposes publicly in his speech of 22 January. He called for "peace without victory" to end the conflict in Europe and "some definite concert of power" to banish war permanently. Thus Wilson signified America's intention to secure an equitable territorial settlement based on self-determination and a new world order based on collective security. This agenda was at considerable variance from those of either the Allied Powers or the Central Powers. The United States shared the Allies' wish to preclude German hegemony in western Eurasia, but in many ways, Wilson's policy ran counter to the provisions of the "secret treaties" that recorded the multifarious postwar desires of the antihegemonic coalition.

Shortly after entering the war, the president decided upon his *strategy*, that is, the comprehensive design to guide the use of American power in all its guises—political, economic, psychological, and military—to gain his political end, which was to dominate the peace settlement and gain acceptance of his scheme for a new world order. Wilson's decisions about *military* strategy, the design to guide the use of the American armed forces, were generally consistent with the wishes of the European Allies, although he entertained vastly different war aims. Wilson recognized that an essential preliminary to any peace settlement, whether European or American in character, was a decisive victory over the Central Powers. He concluded that the basic military strategy of the Allies would serve American policy. Accordingly he acquiesced in the British proposal that the United States Navy augment the Royal Navy's anti-submarine campaign against Germany's U-boats. Germany had invited American belligerency by undertaking a campaign of unrestricted submarine warfare against neutral and noncombatant commerce. Its leaders gambled that this maritime strategy would bring victory before the United States could mobilize sufficiently to influence the outcome of the war. Wilson also accepted the Allied view that the way to impose a decision on the Central Powers was to concentrate land power on the western front and destroy the German army.

In one fundamental respect President Wilson's strategy diverged from the wishes of the Allies. He decided that the United States would mobilize an independent army that would fight under its own flag and in its own sector of the western front, according to its own doctrine, with its own commanders, staffs, and services of supply. When in position, the independent American army would strike a decisive blow, giving Woodrow Wilson the leverage needed to dictate the terms of peace. The United States rejected the alternative urged by the Allies, which was to deploy troops to Europe organized in divisions or even smaller organizations for service in the French and British armies. This scheme, which became known as "amalgamation," would bring American fighting power to bear on the western front in a short time because it would be unnecessary to train higher-level commanders, to provide support troops, and to build logistical facilities.

The decision to field an independent army, a consequence mainly of political considerations, meant postponement of full-scale American operations until 1919 at the earliest, since it would take at least two years to mobilize a large army that could deal with the German army. General Pershing was sent overseas to create the American Expeditionary Forces and mould them into a powerful army. He enjoyed unusually strong support from his civilian superiors, who gave him the time and freedom of action needed to complete his task.

The decision to form an independent army entailed substantial risk because the Central Powers might prevail before the United States could influence the outcome, but neither the War Department nor the president gave serious thought to any other course. Various considerations influenced this decision.

Amalgamation would prove enormously unpopular among the American people; the army itself would object for reasons of pride; technical difficulties would arise given organizational, doctrinal, and other types of asymmetry between American and European practice; and above all, an independent army that forced victory would ensure Wilson's domination of the postwar peace negotiations.

Despite the strenuous efforts of the War Department and the commander of the AEF, only a few American divisions arrived in France by January 1918. None were ready for combat, a cause of great concern because the war had gone badly for the Allied and Associated Powers in 1917, and prospects were dim for 1918. The helter-skelter American mobilization necessarily produced considerable confusion and delay, enough to stimulate a serious congressional inquiry. Fortunately the home government attained much improved efficiency by the summer of 1918. There was, to be sure, one important inter-Allied achievement in 1917. Germany's attempt to gain victory at sea was frustrated, although the U-boats sank millions of tons of merchant shipping, because the adoption of the convoy system kept losses within manageable limits. On land the Central Powers defended themselves well, rebuffing powerful offensives launched by the French, the British, and the Russians. Besides, they won two great victories: Russia was knocked out of the war, and Italy almost collapsed after a catastrophic defeat at Caporetto. Germany's triumph on the eastern front released many experienced divisions for service in the west. The maritime strategy having failed in 1917, the German High Command composed of Field Marshal Hindenburg and First Quartermaster General Ludendorff decided to stake everything on a great land offensive in 1918. They intended to destroy the British and French armies on the western front before the United States could dispatch sufficient reinforcements to decide the outcome.

Germany's purpose, which became apparent late in 1917, stimulated various responses on the Allied side. The necessity for improved inter-Allied cooperation forced the Allied and Associated Powers to form a Supreme War Council and several other coordinating agencies to make the most of their remaining resources. Also, the Allies revived proposals for the amalgamation of American troops into their armies to cope with the expected German offensive. General Pershing, who continued to receive firm support from his government, strongly resisted this course. He was prepared to permit temporary service by American divisions in quiet sectors of the French and British fronts primarily for training. He viewed this measure as a part of the process by which he would create an independent force to conduct separate operations at the earliest possible time. Pershing opposed combat service by American divisions under British and

French commanders not only because of his divergent views on training and doctrine but because he believed that, if committed to battle, his troops would be so weakened that they would become unfit for service in an independent American army. He relaxed his resistance only to obtain British shipping needed to transport American divisions to Europe. In return he condoned severely limited forms of temporary amalgamation.

Unfortunately for Pershing and his troops, the German offensive, which began late in March 1918, severely disrupted plans to field an independent army. Ludendorff directed five powerful strikes against the British and French armies and created a desperate emergency, retaining the initiative until July. In March and April, British forces on the Somme River in Picardy and the Lys River in Flanders endured a terrible beating, and the French suffered similarly during offensives in May and June against the Chemin des Dames ridge and the line between Montdidier and Noyon. Pershing was forced to condone temporary amalgamation of some American divisions not only for training but for combat. He was also compelled to accept Allied proposals that the United States send to France only combat soldiers, infantrymen, and machine gunners, in return for needed shipping. This expedient delayed the arrival of supporting elements such as artillery and engineers. The Allies promised to make up these deficiencies from their resources, and they did so during the concluding months of combat.

On 15 July, Ludendorff launched the last of his offensives, but it was quickly contained, and the Allied generalissimo, Ferdinand Foch, immediately recaptured the initiative. During July, August, and September, he conducted a series of limited counteroffensives against the salients that the Germans had driven into the Allied lines. These attacks were intended to restore the elan of his troops, improve rail communications, consume the German reserves, and secure positions from which to launch a general offensive. Offensive operations became possible because, by July, American troops had arrived in sufficient numbers to give Foch a narrow but constantly growing superiority in manpower. The German command committed most of its available reserves between March and July, and those remaining were soon sacrificed in efforts to defend against Foch's limited counteroffensives.[1]

Foch organized a French counterattack on the Marne during July, a British offensive on the Somme River in August, and operations on the German flanks in Belgium and Lorraine during September. He hoped to prevent Ludendorff from shifting troops to threatened points. Petain attacked on 18 July between the Aisne and the Marne and reached the Vesle River by 6 August. On 8 August, Haig inflicted a devastating defeat on the Germans at Amiens, the most impressive of the limited offensives, which led to German discussions about ending the war. Anticipating an Allied attack in Flanders, Ludendorff decided to refuse battle there, withdrawing eastward and shortening the front to conserve his dwindling manpower.

Meanwhile General Pershing finally forced Foch to allow the formation of the initial independent American force, the First Army. It was assigned as its first task the last limited counteroffensive, reduction of the St. Mihiel salient in Lorraine. Ever since his early months in France, Pershing had planned independent operations in Lorraine, which was at the right of the active western front. He built up his services of supply with operations in this sector in mind. Hoping to strike a decisive blow intended to win the war, he proposed to drive toward Metz and interdict the lateral railway that supplied the bulk of the German army located to the west. This achievement would force the German army to withdraw from the occupied territories and would move the struggle across the German border. Pershing envisioned as the first step in this operational design the reduction of the St. Mihiel salient, which had been created in 1914 and had long been a quiet sector. At the last minute Foch decided that Pershing should undertake as his main effort an attack with the French Fourth Army northward from positions west of the Meuse River toward Mezieres, another location on the lateral railroad. This thrust would be one pincer of a mighty converging attack on Ludendorff's depleted forces that Foch wished to make late in September.

When the commander of the German Composite Army C, which held the St. Mihiel salient, realized that an American attack was imminent, he ordered his forces to withdraw to the Michel Stellung, a line of fortifications at the base of the salient. This movement was only in its initial stages when, on 12 September, the First Army attacked in overwhelming force. Pershing's blow confused the German withdrawal and also accelerated it. The First Army captured only about 16,000 prisoners, not having cut off most of the retreating enemy because of inexperience, but it was a solid victory that improved Allied morale. Pershing gained control of the railroad between Nancy and the west and eliminated a threat to the rear of the Allied forces operating west of the Meuse.

Foch then prepared a general inter-Allied offensive, hoping to expel the German army from France and Belgium and to seize good positions from which to force a decision in 1919. He chose to attack both faces of the huge salient that had been driven into France and Belgium, aiming to interdict a section of the lateral railroad that ran behind the German lines between Lille and Strasbourg. Haig's troops would attack the west face of the salient in the direction of Cambrai and Maubeuge, seeking to cut the railroad at Aulnoye. Simultaneously a Franco-American force would launch another powerful attack against the south face of the salient aimed at Mezieres. Two other attacks would prevent Ludendorff from maneuvering his reserves to block the move against the Aulnoye-Mezieres region. One of these would come in Belgium on the line of the Lys River where the Group of Armies of Flanders commanded by Albert, king of the Belgians, would move on Ghent. The French in the center of the Allied lines would advance toward Laon against the nose of the salient.

The American First Army was assigned the task of penetrating a strong section of the Hindenburg line, the Kriemhilde Stellung, located between the Meuse River and the Argonne forest, while west of the Argonne the French Fourth Army advanced against the line of the Aisne toward Mezieres. Pershing was forced to move his divisions into line in the short space of ten days. Initially he had to rely almost entirely on inexperienced troops, having committed his veterans at St. Mihiel. Pershing drew heavily on the French and British armies for artillery, aircraft, armor, and many types of support troops. His operational plans prescribed a quick penetration of three distinct German bastions located in difficult terrain, including the Kriemhilde Stellung, during the first two days of battle. He depended on surprise and spirit to break through before German reinforcements appeared in strength.

On 26 September, the First Army with nine divisions in the front line attacked between the Meuse River and the Argonne forest, only to encounter stubborn resistance from five weak enemy divisions. Well-sited machine-gun and artillery positions on high ground repulsed the American frontal attacks short of the Kriemhilde Stellung. The French Fourth Army west of the Argonne forest also advanced slowly. Neither the French nor the Americans moved more than a few miles toward Mezieres during the initial phases of Foch's great converging operation. Again, American inexperience contributed to what amounted to a check in the Meuse-Argonne sector. Both civil and military leaders of the Allies voiced considerable criticism of Pershing because of the AEF's failure to breach the German position.

Meanwhile, on 27 September Haig assaulted the Hindenburg line between the Sensee River and Villers-Guilain, and this attack gained immediate success. In three days the British reached the outskirts of Cambrai. On 29 September, another British attack farther south also penetrated the Hindenburg line, making excellent progress across the St. Quentin Canal. Haig had originated the plan to have the Americans attack north toward Mezieres instead of east toward Metz so that Ludendorff would have to transfer troops from the British sector to the Meuse-Argonne, but the British Army gained its main purpose before the German High Command could take such action.

As the British and Franco-American forces carried out converging operations against the German salient, the Group of Armies of Flanders attacked in Belgium, and a Franco-British force in the center of the line moved toward La Fere–Peronne. Everywhere from Dixmude in Flanders to the Meuse River in Lorraine, Foch kept his armies on the move, straining Ludendorff's depleted resources along a front of about 250 miles.

At this juncture, the German High Command, recognizing that the war was lost, pressed the civil government to seek an armistice and arrange for peace negotiations. The British success against the Hindenburg line forced Ludendorff's hand, although the collapse of Bulgaria and intimations of Austrian and Turkish breakdowns also influenced him. During October, a new German chancellor, the liberal-minded Prince Max of Baden, conducted a bilateral correspondence with President Wilson. He sought to end the war based on the least onerous enemy statements of war aims, the American Fourteen Points and associated pronouncements. These negotiations, from which the Allies were purposefully excluded, ended on 23 October, when Wilson accepted Prince Max's proposal to negotiate peace based on the American war aims. Meanwhile Foch prepared the terms of an armistice, a separate matter properly delegated to the military. Representatives of the Allies and the United States then met in Paris, sitting as the Supreme War Council, to decide whether to endorse Wilson's arrangements with Prince Max and Foch's military, naval, and air terms of armistice. Colonel House, Wilson's delegate, forced the reluctant Allies to accept the American program for the peace settlement with but two modifications when he announced that otherwise the United States would withdraw its army from the war. The Supreme War Council also acquiesced in the onerous armistice terms that Foch had drawn up after consulting with Haig, Petain, Pershing, and the Belgians.

Thus operations during the last six weeks of the war unfolded while the German government moved rapidly toward peace negotiations, a circumstance that lifted the morale of Foch's armies and depressed those of the Central Powers. However, the German army offered stubborn resistance in all sectors. The dispirited Ludendorff recovered his balance sufficiently to attempt a fighting withdrawal to a line between Antwerp and the Meuse River from which he hoped to hold out through the winter. This desperate effort, which proved unacceptable in Berlin, led to his forced retirement on 26 October.

The American First Army sustained its costly frontal attacks against the Kriemhilde Stellung throughout the first three weeks of October. Finally it managed to penetrate the German defenses and to gain favorable positions for future operations, although it suffered over 100,000 casualties. By this time, Pershing had become commander of an American army group. He relinquished command of the First Army to General Liggett and established the American Second Army under General Bullard. During the last two weeks of October, Liggett devoted himself to resting and reorganizing the First Army while planning a resumption of the offensive.

On 1 November, the First Army launched an attack coordinated with others on the western front that immediately proved successful. Liggett routed the enemy and outflanked the Hindenburg fortifications before the French Fourth Army to the west. The Germans then began a general withdrawal from the line of the Aisne to the Antwerp–Meuse line. Accordingly the American First Army engaged in a pursuit during the remaining days of the war.

Pershing, upset by his failure to gain a brilliant victory, vented his frustration in two ways. First, he advocated unconditional surrender instead of a negotiated armistice, sending an unauthorized letter to the Supreme War Council urging this course. Colonel House quickly neutralized this insubordinate initiative, and Pershing escaped a reprimand. Next, during the last days of the war, the AEF commander authorized the capture of Sedan, scene of the great French disaster of 1870. This action would deprive the French army of this honor. Fortunately General Liggett put a stop to this misconceived enterprise, an operational and political monstrosity.

The war ended on 11 November at the eleventh hour. Foch's general offensive had succeeded far beyond its author's expectations, showing the validity of his aphorism that nothing gives wings to an army like victory. His coordinated and sustained attacks imposed terrible attrition on the German army, which used its last reserves in the defense of the Hindenburg line. He did not force a general breakthrough and envelopment, but the unrelenting operations of July–November finally broke the will of the German army, the German people, and the German leadership. At the end, resistance simply melted away.[2]

The AEF conducted itself as might have been expected of an army that lacked experience and was thrown into battle prematurely. The decision to create an independent army and conduct separate operations ensured that Pershing's command could not fight efficiently on a large scale until at least two years after the intervention of April 1917. The emergency that developed on the western front during March–July 1918, when Ludendorff sought a decision through massive offensives, forced premature employment of American troops, an unavoidable change of plan. This unexpected outcome led initially to temporary amalgamation of some American divisions into the Allied armies, mostly in quiet sectors for training. Some of these brigaded units entered combat, acquitting themselves well under French and British command after undergoing bruising baptisms of fire.

The performance of the American First Army, created only three months before the armistice, was less impressive than those of the amalgamated divisions. During the Meuse-Argonne offensive, this organization, only a rudimentary version of what had been planned, suffered from incomplete organization, inadequate training, unsound logistical support, and inexperienced commanders and staffs. In many ways, the difficulties that the AEF encountered during its brief interlude of service in 1918 paralleled those of the European armies in the first stages of the war. The improvement of the First Army during the bloody Meuse-Argonne campaign, especially after Liggett assumed command, suggests that it would have fought with growing confidence and success, if the struggle had carried over into 1919.

The AEF never fulfilled the mission established for it in 1917, the delivery of a decisive blow to assure Wilson of a dominant position at the postwar peace conference, but it contributed significantly with the French, British, and Belgian armies to Foch's huge joint offensive that finally broke the German army. In the end, the most important service of the AEF was to appear in France. Its presence allowed release of veteran Allied divisions from quiet sectors and gave Foch the superiority in manpower he needed to make a success of his coordinated and sustained operations. Although Pershing never struck a knockout punch, the AEF's achievements were more than sufficient to guarantee President Wilson's control of the postwar peace negotiations, the purpose for which the AEF fought in France. When the Germans decided to end the war, the Allies were unable to prevent Wilson from committing both the Central Powers and themselves to a settlement based on the American war aims and peace proposals.

As in most American wars, the overwhelming military reality was the unpreparedness of the United States Army. Delay in committing American divisions to battle and the brevity of American operations tended to obscure the bitter truth of the dubious victory in the Meuse-Argonne sector, one that was long deferred and most costly. The sudden end of the war headed off what might have become serious criticism of the AEF. Pershing's inflated claims of success have been too often accepted without careful study.

Pershing was surely a flawed commander. If the war had continued into 1919, he might well have fallen from grace. No American theater commander ever received more support from his civilian superiors. President Wilson and Secretary Baker backed him unswervingly during the long controversy over amalgamation. Pershing's stubborn self-righteousness, his unwillingness to correct initial misconceptions such as those that marred the doctrine and training of the AEF, and his stormy relationships with Allied military and civilian leaders hurt the AEF.

Pershing considered his sustained resistance to amalgamation a great achievement, but his intransigence is open to criticism. Given the extent of the emergency in 1918, he ought to have considered extensive brigading of American divisions and corps on a temporary basis for both training and combat. The experience gained from this exposure would have greatly benefited the AEF, when organized for independent operations. General Bliss, the most judicious American soldier in France during 1918, privately held this view but did not choose to undermine the commander-in-chief. Pershing should not have accepted long-term amalgamation, but no one ever proposed that he do so. His conviction that combat service by amalgamated divisions would render them unfit for future operations under American command was in error. Organizations such as the 1st, 2d, 28th, and 42d Divisions absorbed rough treatment during tours in other armies but emerged with considerable experience that was put to excellent use during later service in the American First Army. Despite postwar accolades conferred on Pershing, close study of the controversy over the shipment and employment of American troops during 1918 reveals that Baker and Wilson had begun to sense some of the general's limitations, which accounts for proposals made in July 1918 to confine his responsibilities to field command. Pershing's personal shortcomings were revealed briefly during the last days of the war. He overstepped his military authority in advocating unconditional surrender and foolishly attempted to deprive the French army of the honor of occupying Sedan. The unexpected victory of November 1918 masked these transgressions. What reason was there to dwell on such matters in the glow of Foch's great victory? Pershing railed at what he considered the premature end of the war. He wanted to fight on so that the AEF could prove with deeds the excellence that he had claimed for it, but it seems probable that the armistice spared him growing difficulties later.

Marshal Foch served superbly as generalissimo in 1918. He realized that the key to victory was attrition instead of maneuver. He was able not only to coordinate an ultimately successful containment of Ludendorff's tremendous attacks but to organize limited counteroffensives and eventually a general counteroffensive that imposed irreplaceable losses of men and material on the German army and finally broke its will and that of the German people. He made effective use of all the national contingents under his authority, including the American Expeditionary Forces, despite the difficulties that arose in dealings with the timorous Petain, the unimaginative Haig, and the stubborn Pershing.

In measuring the American contribution of 1918 to the defeat of Germany it is well to bear in mind comparisons such as one made by John Terraine. Between 18 July and 11 November, the armies under Foch captured enemy troops and guns as follows:

British Army	188,700 prisoners	2,840 guns
French Army	139,000 prisoners	1,880 guns
American Army	43,000 prisoners	1,421 guns
Belgian Army	14,500 prisoners	474 guns

As these statistics suggest, the most important American contribution in 1918 was not combat operations, although the inexperienced AEF for the most part fought bravely. The principal American offering was to provide the margin in manpower and material that allowed Foch to wage his war of attrition successfully during the last four months of the war.[3]

Gen. Frederick Maurice, a perspicacious British observer who wrote a cogent postwar analysis of Foch's remarkable campaign, thought it idle to dispute about who won the war. He argued correctly that no one army, leader, or event decided the outcome. "Germany could not have been beaten in the field, as she was beaten, without the intimate cooperation of all the Allied armies on the Western Front directed by a great leader, nor without the coordination for a common purpose of all the resources of the Allies,—naval, military, industrial, and economic."[4] The prime lesson of 1918 is that coalition warfare is a most difficult enterprise. Victory comes to allies who persevere in the trying but essential effort to cooperate effectively in the common cause despite inevitable conflicts of interest and outlook.

NOTES

1. For Pershing's final report see U.S. War Department, *War Department Annual Reports, 1919*, vol. 1, part 1 (Washington, D.C.: Government Printing Office, 1920). For his memoirs see *My Experiences in the World War*, 2 vols. (New York: Frederick A. Stokes, 1931). Pershing's view also appears in Frank Vandiver's *Black Jack: The Life and Times of John J. Pershing*, 2 vols. (College Station and London: Texas A & M University Press, 1977). For the two histories of the AEF see Edward M. Coffman, *The War to End All Wars: The American Military Experience in World War I* (New York: Oxford University Press, 1968); Harvey A. DeWeerd, *President Wilson Fights His War: World War I and the American Intervention* (New York: Macmillan, 1968). For a recent evaluation of Pershing that departs from the traditional view of the AEF see Donald Smythe, *Pershing: General of the Armies* (Bloomington: University of Indiana Press, 1986).

2. Arthur S. Link et al., eds., *The Papers of Woodrow Wilson*, vol. 40: *November 20, 1916–January 23, 1917* (Princeton, N.J.: Princeton University Press, 1982), pp. 536, 539. Hereafter this collection is cited as Link, ed., *WP*, with volume number and page number. The quotation from the war message is in ibid., vol. 41: *January 24–April 6, 1917* (Princeton, N.J.: Princeton University Press, 1983), pp. 526–27.

3. Link, ed., *WP*, 41:526–27.

4. Memorandum by John Howard Whitehouse, 14 April 1917, in Link, ed., *WP*, vol. 42: *April 7–June 23, 1917* (Princeton, N.J.: Princeton University Press, 1983), p. 66.

5. For Wilson's comment to Whitehouse on his desire to remain detached in outlook see ibid., p. 65. For his statement on the Allies see Wilson to House, 21 July 1917, Papers of Colonel Edward M. House, Yale University, New Haven, Connecticut. For the Wilson-Balfour conversation see Link, ed., *WP* 42:141.

6. Baker is quoted in Daniel R. Beaver, *Newton D. Baker and the American War Effort 1917–1919* (Lincoln: University of Nebraska Press, 1966), p. 13. For other comments on Wilson's view see I. B. Holley, Jr., *General John M. Palmer, Citizen Soldiers, and the Army of a Democracy* (Westport, Conn.: Greenwood Press, 1982), p. 268; Timothy Nenninger, "American Military Effectiveness during the First World War," in Allan R. Millett and Williamson Murray, eds., *Military Effectiveness*, vol. 1: *The First World War* (Boston: Allen & Unwin, 1988), p. 117.

7. For the size of the army see American Battle Monuments Commission, *American Armies and Battlefields in Europe: A History, Guide, and Reference Book* (Washington, D.C.: Government Printing Office, 1928), p. 15. The statistics about the size of the senior

officer corps are in Allan R. Millett, *The General: Robert L. Bullard and Officership in the United States Army, 1881–1925* (Westport, Conn.: Greenwood, 1975), p. 308.

8. For the War College recommendation see Marvin A. Kreidberg and Merton G. Henry, *History of Military Mobilization in the United States Army, 1775–1945* (Washington, D.C.: Government Printing Office, 1955), p. 293. This is Department of the Army Pamphlet no. 20-12. For the observation of Gen. Peyton C. March see his *The Nation at War* (Garden City, N.Y.: Doubleday, Doran, 1932), p. 2. Nenninger observes: "Essentially it [the army] was a constabulary force. . . . It was not suited for the war being waged in Europe. . . . With the regular army small and ill-fitted for sustained combat on the Western Front, and with no reliable reserve component available, clearly the Western Front was not consistent with the resources at hand." "American Military Effectiveness during the First World War," p. 130.

9. Bliss's views are in Bliss to Secretary of War Newton D. Baker, 25 May 1917, in the Papers of General John J. Pershing, Library of Congress, Manuscript Division, Washington, D.C. Bridges's proposal is in Bridges to Major General Hugh L. Scott, 30 April 1917, Papers of General Tasker H. Bliss, Library of Congress, Manuscript Division, Washington, D.C. See also Smythe, *Pershing*, p. 8. For an incisive summary of the results of the Balfour mission see Kathleen Burk, *Britain, America, and the Sinews of War, 1914–1918* (Boston: George Allen & Unwin, 1984), pp. 134–35.

10. Joffre's views are in Joseph J. C. Joffre, *The Memoirs of Marshal Joffre*, trans. T. Bentley Mott, vol. 2 (London: Geoffrey Bles, 1932), 2:568. For Joffre's report to the French minister of war see Historical Section, Department of the Army, *United States Army in the World War 1917–1919*, vol. 2: *Policy-forming Documents American Expeditionary Forces* (Washington, D.C.: Government Printing Office, 1948), especially pp. 4–7 (hereafter *USAWW*, with volume number and page number). This volume is one of seventeen that have been reprinted by the United States Army Center of Military History without alteration in the pagination, although the type is changed. Therefore citations to the original volumes are valid for the reprinted volumes. President Wilson's decision is in Wilson to Baker, 3 May 1917, Link, ed., *WP* 42:202.

11. For a brief analysis of the president's policy and strategy during World War I see David F. Trask, "Woodrow Wilson and International Statecraft: A Modern Assessment," *Naval War College Review* 36 (March–April 1983): 57–68. Some scholars maintain that President Wilson in 1917 did not believe that he would have to deploy the independent army that was projected at the beginning of the American intervention. He hoped that the war would end before any such measure became necessary. This conjecture may well be accurate, but if so, it does not mean that the United States would not move energetically to prepare an independent force.

12. For this episode see Beaver, *Newton D. Baker*, pp. 45–46. The quotation is on p. 46.

13. Undated memorandum from Wiseman, "Some Notes on the Position in August 1917," House Papers; Lloyd George to Wilson, 3 September 1917, in David Lloyd George, *War Memoirs of David Lloyd George*, vol. 4: *1917* (Boston: Little, Brown, 1934), pp. 518–34; unsigned memorandum on Italy, Macedonia, and Turkey, forwarded to Wilson, 11 October 1917, Papers of President Woodrow Wilson, Library of Congress, Manuscript Division, Washington, D.C. General Bliss, by this time the chief of staff, forwarded the War College Division's study to the secretary of war with his concurrence. Bliss to Baker, 11 October 1917, Bliss Papers, box 222. Secretary Baker also supported the study. Baker to Wilson, 11 November 1917, Link, ed., *WP*, vol. 45: *November 11, 1917–January 15, 1918* (Princeton, N.J.: Princeton University Press, 1984), pp. 4–6. For a study of this episode see David F. Trask, *The United States in the Supreme*

War Council: American War Aims and Inter-Allied Strategy, 1917–1918 (Middletown, Conn.: Wesleyan University Press, 1961), pp. 14–15. For March's view see his *The Nation at War*, p. 113.

14. For the ALBERICH MOVEMENT see Erich von Ludendorff, *Ludendorff's Own Story: August 1914–November 1918* (New York and London: Harper & Brothers Publishers, 1919), 2:4, 8, 24. Micheler is quoted in S. L. A. Marshall, *World War I* (New York: American Heritage, 1985), p. 292.

15. For Sharp's report see his message to Wilson, 5 May 1917, Link, ed., *WP* 42:230–31. Petain's statement is in his letter to Armies of the North and Northeast, for Commanders of Groups of Armies and Armies Alone, 19 May 1917, *USAWW* 2:1.

16. For the Foch-Robertson meeting see Ferdinand Foch, *The Memoirs of Marshal Foch*, trans. T. Bentley Mott (Garden City, N.Y.: Doubleday, Doran, 1931), pp. 223–24. For the defensive posture see Report of the G-3, *USAWW*, vol. 14: *Reports of Commander-in-Chief, A.E.F., Staff Sections and Services* (Washington, D.C.: Government Printing Office, 1948), p. 10. See also Foch memorandum, 27 July 1917, calling for a defensive on secondary fronts while hastening "in every possible way the creation of an American army and its transport to France." Foch, *Memoirs*, p. 224.

17. Erich Ludendorff, *The General Staff and Its Problems: The History of the Relations between the High Command and the German Imperial Government as Revealed by Official Documents*, trans. F. A. Holt (New York: E. P. Dutton, 1920), 2:470–71. For Hindenburg's explanation of the necessity to adopt a defensive posture on land, see his *Out of My Life*, trans. F. A. Holt (London: Cassell, 1920), 2:249, 361–64. For Admiral Capelle's statement of 1 February 1917 see *Geheime Akten*, Records of the German Foreign Office Received by the Department of State from St. Antony's College, reel 14, vol. 65, frame 162. For a comprehensive collection of documents on the naval warfare during 1917 and 1918 see Michael Simpson, ed., *Anglo-American Naval Relations, 1917–1919* (Aldershot, Eng.: Scolar Press for the Navy Records Society, 1991).

18. Smythe explains the choice of Pershing in *Pershing*, pp. 2–3. For Baker's selection of Pershing and Wilson's approval see Baker to Wilson, 8 May 1917, and Wilson to Baker, 10 May 1917, Link, ed., *WP* 42:249–51, 263–64.

19. Smythe discusses the considerations of the executive branch in *Pershing*, pp. 6–7, quoting Baker's remark to Pershing on two orders. Baker described his views in his Report of the Secretary of War, in U.S. Department of War, *War Department Annual Reports, 1919* 1, 1:8. Pershing received two sets of orders. Acting Chief of Staff Bliss signed one drafted by Pershing's chief staff officer, Col. James G. Harbord. It made no mention of the independent army. Maj. Gen. Francis J. Kernan drafted a second set approved by Bliss and signed by Baker, which reflected the War Department's contacts with the Allied missions. It included the provision that Pershing was to maintain the independence of the American army. Smythe surprisingly minimizes the importance of these orders. "Both letters went to France, were put into a safe, and never consulted again. Perhaps their chief significance is in revealing the confused, disorganized condition of the General Staff in the early days of the war when apparently its right hand did not know what its left was doing." Smythe, *Pershing*, p. 12. See also Frederick Palmer, *Bliss, Peacemaker: The Life and Letters of General Tasker Howard Bliss* (New York: Dodd, Mead, 1934), p. 163; John J. Pershing, *My Experiences* 1:38–39; March, *The Nation at War*, p. 244.

20. For the Pershing-Baker accord on amalgamation see Smythe, *Pershing*, p. 8. For the Pershing-Wilson conversation see ibid., p. 11.

21. For Baker's statement on the reasons for an independent army see his introduction to Thomas G. Frothingham, *The American Reinforcement in the World War* (Garden City, N.Y.: Doubleday, Page, 1927), p. xxx.

22. George Marshall's recollection of St. Nazaire was recorded in 1957. It is in Larry I. Bland and Sharon K. Ritenour, eds., *The Papers of George Catlett Marshall*, vol. 1: *"The Soldierly Spirit," December 1880–June 1939* (Baltimore, Md.: The Johns Hopkins University Press, 1981), p. 111. For Marshall's observations about the 1st Division see Forrest C. Pogue, *George Marshall*, vol. 1: *Education of a General, 1880–1939* (New York: Viking, 1963), p. 147.

23. John Dickinson, *The Building of an Army: A Detailed Account of Legislation, Administration, and Opinion in the United States, 1915–1920* (New York: Century, 1922), pp. 271–72; James E. Hewes, Jr., *From Root to McNamara: Army Organization and Administration, 1900–1963* (Washington, D.C.: U.S. Army Center of Military History, 1975), p. 22. Bullard's observation is quoted in Coffman, *War to End All Wars*, p. 49. Cf. the reaction of Col. Peyton C. March at about the same time as recounted in Edward M. Coffman, *The Hilt of the Sword: The Career of Peyton C. March* (Madison, Milwaukee, and London: University of Wisconsin Press, 1966), p. 44. For the contributions of the War College Division see Beaver, *Newton D. Baker*, p. 49. Hewes argues that the War College Division, which set up five functional committees and a military intelligence section, became a de facto general staff. *From Root to McNamara*, p. 27.

24. For Baker's views see Beaver, *Newton D. Baker*, pp. 52–53. For Wilson's attitudes see Robert Cuff, *The War Industries Board: Business-Government Relations during World War I* (Baltimore, Md., and London: Johns Hopkins University Press, 1973), pp. 5–6, 67. These two volumes are essential standard works on mobilization during World War I. For a different view see Paul A. C. Koistinen, *The Military-Industrial Complex: A Historical Perspective* (New York: Praeger, 1980), pp. 23–46. Cuff writes of such analyses: "It is the tendency of some first to conceptualize the political economy of the war years as a fully integrated institutional order and then to make it a paradigm for future historical development." He contends that "fuller attention to the details of industrial mobilization, treated primarily in the context of the war years, requires that serious qualifications be made about the thoroughness and permanency of structural integration between business and government before, during, and after World War I. . . . the keynotes of business-government relations during the war are complexity, hesitancy, and ambiguity." Cuff, *The War Industries Board*, pp. 6–7. For a useful summary of Wilsonian attitudes toward mobilization in 1917 see Hewes, *From Root to McNamara*, pp. 29–31.

25. For Secretary Baker's view of the Council of National Defense see *War Department Annual Reports, 1917* 1:45. See also ibid., pp. 46–49. For the War Industries Board see Cuff, *War Industries Board*, pp. 1–2. This account of the WIB's deficiencies follows ibid., pp. 104, 113.

26. For the draft see Russell F. Weigley, *History of the United States Army* (New York: Macmillan, 1967), p. 354. For the Wilson-White exchange see White to Wilson, 26 April 1917, and Wilson to White, 3 May 1917, Link, ed., *WP* 42:139, 200. For similar views see Wilson to Paul Oscar Husting, 3 May 1917, ibid., pp. 200–201. A capsule description of selective service and its result is in the report of General Peyton C. March, Chief of Staff, in *War Department Reports, 1919* 1, 1:257–58. For Pershing's view see Pershing to Gen. Hugh L. Scott, 1 May 1917, Link, ed., *WP* 42:225. Baker sent this letter to Wilson, who responded: "This is indeed a most interesting letter from General Pershing and I thank you warmly for having let me see it. It is reassuring and it throws an interesting light upon Pershing himself." Wilson to Baker, 8 May 1917, ibid., p. 242. Pershing was frequently associated with Theodore Roosevelt, who wanted to organize a volunteer regiment for service in France on the lines of the Rough Riders. His letter to Scott suggested that he was an independent thinker who was not blindly subservient to elements antagonistic to the administration. For an outstanding recent

study of conscription during World War I see John Whiteclay Chambers II, *To Raise an Army: The Draft Comes to Modern America* (New York: Free Press, 1987).

27. National Guard cantonments were McClellan, Kearny, Cody, Fremont, Greene, Hancock, MacArthur, Wadsworth, Wheeler, Logan, Sevier, Sheridan, Doniphan, Beauregard, Shelby, and Bowie. National Army cantonments were Lewis, Funston, Custer, Devens, Dix, Dodge, Gordon, Grant, Jackson, Lee, Meade, Pike, Sherman, Travis, Taylor, and Upton. See report of the chief of staff (March), *War Department Reports, 1919* 1:277.

28. James A. Huston, *Sinews of War: Army Logistics, 1775–1953* (Washington, D.C.: Office of the Chief of Military History, U.S. Army, 1966), pp. 333–35. For a chart showing equipment of the AEF by European nations see ibid., pp. 334–35. For the General Purchasing Board and Dawes see Report of the G-1 (AEF), *USAWW* 12:81; Smythe, *Pershing*, p. 43. For a full account see Charles G. Dawes, *A Journal of the Great War*, 2 vols. (Boston and New York: Houghton Mifflin, 1921).

29. For the relationship between Baker, Bliss, and Pershing see Coffman, *The War to End All Wars*, pp. 167–68.

30. Pershing, *My Experiences* 1:319–20. For Pershing's remark about the tail wagging the dog see Smythe, *Pershing*, p. 49. Smythe cites three reasons for Pershing's complaints when he encountered resistance from the War Department. He was the field commander in the field and best informed on his needs; he was determined to assure control over the bureaus in the War Department; finally, Pershing saw himself as the head of a semiautonomous command, "virtually independent of the War Department and its bureaus." For comments by Pershing about the failings of the War Department and his own corrective measures see Pershing, *My Experiences* 1:101–2, 183, 322.

31. For the remark of Charteris see Smythe, *Pershing*, p. 39. For Smythe's comments on the problems with Pershing's staff see ibid., pp. 82–83.

32. For these documents see Report of the Chief of Staff (March), *War Department Annual Reports, 1919*, 1, 1:240; Reports of the G-1 and G-3 (AEF), *USAWW* 14:14, 134. For Pershing's comment see his *My Experiences* 1:169–70. For the six-phase program see *SAWW*, vol. 1: *Organization of the American Expeditionary Forces* (Washington, D.C.: Government Printing Office, 1948), p. 5.

33. Baker to Pershing, 10 September 1917, Pershing Papers; Pershing to Baker, 13 November 1917, Pershing, *My Experiences* 1:227. For Pershing's efforts to frustrate proposals of amalgamation see ibid., p. 165.

34. Pershing to AGWAR, 28 July 1917, *USAWW* 2:22; Bliss to T. H. Barry, 28 September 1917, quoted in Palmer, *Bliss, Peacemaker*, p. 174.

35. Smythe, *Pershing*, pp. 37–38; Coffman, *War to End All Wars*, p. 152. Bliss had favored a smaller formation, but the War Department deferred to Pershing. Palmer, *Bliss, Peacemaker*, p. 171. Rod Paschall, a discerning observer, writes that the square division was set up so that it could "sustain losses and press home an attack to reach open ground." Rod Paschall, *The Defeat of Imperial Germany, 1917–1918* (Chapel Hill, N.C.: Algonquin Books of Chapel Hill, 1989), p. 168. The correspondence of General Bliss contains numerous references to the resistance of the National Guard to reorganization. His solution to this difficulty was to send the army to France as soon as possible, where the atmosphere would lead to an emphasis on training. Also, the presence of a large American army in Europe would have a desirable psychological impact in the Allied nations. Bliss to T. H. Barry, 28 September 1917, Bliss Papers, box 223. For information on the square division see John B. Wilson, "Mobility Versus Firepower: The Post–World War I Infantry Division," *Parameters* 13, 3 (1983): 47–52.

36. Pershing, *My Experiences* 1:150–51. See also ibid., p. 259; Pershing to AGWAR,

20 October 1917, *USAWW* 14:306; Pershing Final Report, *War Department Annual Reports, 1919* 1, 1:560–61; Millett, *Bullard*, p. 317. For an authoritative analysis of Pershing's views on open warfare see James W. Rainey, "Ambivalent Warfare: The Tactical Doctrine of the AEF in World War I," *Parameters* 13, 3 (1983): 34–46. Rainey thinks that Pershing's faulty ideas suggest that he had "difficulty reconciling the realities of modern warfare with his military heritage. His professional psyche was bound to a faith in the American marksman, be they the masses of riflemen employed by Grant in his bloody battles of attrition or the more individualistic marksmen of Pershing's own experiences. This heritage contained Pershing's interpretation of American combat experience." Ibid., p. 37.

See also Paschall, *Defeat of Imperial Germany*, p. 168. He argues that the AEF did not develop an authoritative statement of doctrine for open warfare. Ibid., p. 169. It is of interest that Pershing became an advocate of small divisions after reviewing the experiences of 1917–1918.

37. Timothy Nenninger discerns two salient difficulties with the training of the AEF. One was the lack of fixed responsibility and the necessity to split training between the United States and France. The other was the "doctrinal ambiguity" between trench warfare and open warfare. Open warfare was based on the maneuvering rifleman, but the heavy square division was designed for attritional warfare. Nenninger, "American Military Effectiveness," p. 149.

38. For the reasons for choosing Lorraine as the American sector see Report of the G-3 (AEF), *USAWW* 14:6–7; Pershing Final Report, *War Department Annual Reports, 1919* 1, 1:555–57; Pershing, *My Experiences* 1:85–86; Weigley, *History of the United States Army*, p. 371; American Battle Monuments Commission, *American Armies and Battlefields in Europe*, p. 18; Coffman, *War to End All Wars*, p. 125.

39. On 3 September 1917, Pershing issued a directive to study the question of the choice of sector. *USAWW* 2:38. Maj. D. G. Nolan, Intelligence Section, Office of the Chief of Staff, provided a memorandum, "Information about Western Front," a detailed summary of the reasons for choosing the Lorraine sector and the operations that could be conducted there. Ibid., pp. 42–43. See also references in note 36.

40. Fox Conner to Chief of Staff, 24 November 1917, ibid., p. 80; Pershing memorandum, 6 February 1918, ibid., p. 196; Fox Conner memorandum, 18 February 1918, ibid., pp. 210–11.

41. Millett, "Over Where?" p. 239.

42. For information on the development of communications between the South Atlantic ports and Lorraine, see Smythe, *Pershing*, pp. 27–28; Pershing final report, *War Department Annual Reports, 1919* 1, 1:555–57; Report of the G-3 (AEF), *USAWW* 14:7; Frank Vandiver, *Black Jack*, 2:729–34; Pershing, *My Experiences*, 2:110. One of the commanders of the Services of Supply, Maj. Gen. James G. Harbord, summarized the considerations that influenced decisions about ports, routes, and the like in a memorandum written in May 1919, which is reprinted in U.S. War Department, Historical Branch, War Plans Division, *Organization of the Services of Supply, American Expeditionary Forces*, Monograph No. 7 (Washington, D.C.: Government Printing Office, 1921), pp. 122–23.

43. Bliss to Baker, 31 May 1917, Bliss Papers, box 213; Pershing to Chief of Staff, 23 August 1917, *USAWW* 2:31; Bliss to Captain Arthur Poillon, 7 September 1917, Bliss Papers, box 219; Pershing to Chief of Staff and Secretary of War, 15 September 1917, *USAWW* 2:46; McCain to Pershing, 19 September 1917, ibid., p. 48; Pershing, *My Experiences* 1:185; Pershing to AGWAR, 27 November 1917, *USAWW* 2:83; Bliss to Baker, 23 December 1917, Bliss Papers, box 224.

44. Report of the G-3 (AEF), *USAWW* 14:11.

45. For Baker's apologia see *War Department Annual Reports, 1917* 1, 1:45. Beaver's comments are in *Newton D. Baker*, p. 108.

46. For Scott's report see Coffman, *War to End All Wars*, pp. 51–52. For the problems of the WIB see Dickinson, *Building of an Army*, p. 284. The historian of the WIB, Robert Cuff, notes: "In December and January . . . it seemed increasingly unlikely that the WIB would even last out the winter. Reverberations from the general failure of the war program deepened fissures in its rickety structure and undermined its disparate functions." Cuff, *War Industries Board*, p. 136.

47. C. H. Cramer, *Newton D. Baker: A Biography* (Cleveland and New York: World Publishing, 1961), p. 146.

48. Baker testimony, 10 January 1918, in U.S. Congress, Senate, Committee on Military Affairs, *Investigation of the War Department:* Hearings before the Committee on Military Affairs United States Senate, 65th Congress, 2d Session, part 3 (Washington, D.C.: Government Printing Office, 1918), p. 1610. See also Coffman, *The Hilt of the Sword*, p. 49.

49. *Investigation of the War Department*, p. 1611.

50. Ibid., p. 1695.

51. Ibid., p. 1926.

52. For Baker's changes see Beaver, *Newton D. Baker*, pp. 95–97; Coffman, *Hilt of the Sword*, p. 50; Cuff, *War Industries Board*, p. 136; Huston, *The Sinews of War*, pp. 314–17. For Baker's summary of the reasons for selecting March, see his introduction to Frothingham, *The American Reinforcement in the World War*, p. xxvi. For March's statement and Baker's appraisal see Smythe, *Pershing*, 91.

53. Robert Cuff has traced the evolution of the War Industries Board during the winter crisis in his *War Industries Board*, pp. 141–43, 147–49.

54. Weigley, *History of the United States Army*, p. 368. Coffman notes: "After March came to power, there was an evolution toward centralization with the ultimate goal of the General Staff going beyond its supervisory role to the actual control of the handling of supplies." Coffman, *War to End All Wars*, p. 167.

CHAPTER 2. THE EMERGENCY OF 1918

1. Trask, *The United States in the Supreme War Council*, pp. 21–23.

2. For a detailed analysis of the submarine crisis during 1917 see David F. Trask, *Captains and Cabinets: Anglo-American Naval Relations, 1917–1918* (Columbia: University of Missouri Press, 1972), pp. 126–85. Much of this information is in Holger H. Herwig and David F. Trask, "The Failure of Imperial Germany's Undersea Offensive against World Shipping, February 1917–October 1918," *Historian* 33, 4 (August 1971):611–36.

3. Ludendorff, *Ludendorff's Own Story* 2:161, 165; Hindenburg, *Out of My Life*, pp. 339, 340.

4. Ludendorff, *The General Staff and Its Problems*, 2:548. For the German planning see Girard Lindsley McEntee, *Military History of the World War: A Complete Account of the Military Campaigns on All Fronts* (New York: Charles Scribner's Sons, 1943), p. 468.

5. For the formation of the Supreme War Council see Trask, *The United States in the Supreme War Council*, pp. 20–30; Lord Maurice P. A. Hankey, *The Supreme Command: 1914–1918*, 2 vols. (London: George Allen and Unwin, 1961), 2:711–23.

6. Ibid., pp. 30–32.

7. Ibid., p. 41. See also Hankey, *Supreme Command* 2:729–33.

8. For Bliss's views see ibid., p. 36. For the WCD view see War College Report, 8 October 1918, quoted in ibid., p. 57.

9. Pershing to Baker, 17 January 1918, Pershing Papers.

10. For Bliss to Mrs. Bliss, 8 November 1917, see Bliss Papers, box 244. For the early actions of the 1st Division see Smythe, *Pershing*, pp. 56, 59. For George Marshall's report of the action near Einville on 2 November 1917 see his report, 3 November 1917, in Bland and Ritenour, eds., *Papers of Marshall* 1:123–25. For the operations of the Engineer regiments during the battle of Cambrai see Historical Section, Army War College, "Major Operations of the United States Army in the World War," May 1929, preliminary draft in manuscript in the library of the U.S. Army Center of Military History, Washington, D.C., pp. 21–22,. See also *USAWW* 4:1, 3–24. A recent account of the battle of Cambrai is in Paschall, *Defeat of Imperial Germany*, pp. 103–27.

11. Conner to Harbord (memorandum), 6 November 1917, *USAWW* 3:68–69.

12. For Petain's views of 18 November see Foch, Memoirs, p. 235. For his paper of 22 December 1917 see *USAWW* 2:204. Foch's views of 1 January are in his *Memoirs*, p. 236–37. For Foch's statement of 24 January 1918 at Compiegne see *USAWW* 2:179.

13. Petain memorandum, 8 January 1918, *USAWW* 2:151–52. For his statement made at Compiegne on 24 January 1918 see ibid., p. 179.

14. *USAWW* 2:169–71. Gen. Maxime Weygand for France, Gen. Luigi Cadorna for Italy, and Gen. Sir Henry Wilson for Britain signed this document. Bliss had returned to the United States before taking up his position at Versailles and had no opportunity to contribute to this document.

15. For Foch's statement to the SWC on 2 February 1918 see Foch, *Memoirs*, pp. 239–40. See also his statement on 30 January 1918 about the general reserve: "A general reserve which could be moved from one part of the front to another was a necessary feature of a plan of defense involving so long a front with limited resources." *USAWW* 2:185. For Weygand to Clemenceau, 22 January 1918, see ibid., pp. 172–73. As early as 8 January 1918, the Advance Group of the French General Staff suggested the need to plan a counteroffensive. This document recommended that Foch should serve as a "temporary organ of supreme command, acting as delegate of the coalition for the execution of the latter's plans." Ibid., p. 142.

16. For the history of the general reserve see Trask, *The United States in the Supreme War Council*, pp. 55–62. For Haig's refusal to cooperate and his arrangements with Petain see Haig to British Permanent Military Representative, 2 March 1918, *USAWW* 2:228; Corelli Barnett, *The Swordbearers: Supreme Command in the World War* (Bloomington: Indiana University Press, 1975), p. 294; Gregory Blaxland, *Amiens: 1918* (London: Frederick Muller, 1968), pp. 23–24. For Bliss's message reporting Haig's action see Bliss to March and Baker, 5 March 1918, ibid., pp. 233–34. Haig's interview with Lloyd George is chronicled in Haig's diary for 14 March 1918. Robert Blake, ed., *The Private Papers of Douglas Haig, 1914–1919: Being Selections from the Private Diary and Correspondence of Field-Marshal the Earl Haig of Bemersyde, K.T., G.C.B., O.M., etc.* (London: Eyre & Spottiswoode, 1952), p. 292.

17. Bliss is quoted in Trask, *The United States in the Supreme War Council*, p. 57. His efforts to support it are treated in ibid., pp. 60–62. For Bliss's statement of 30 January 1918, see *USAWW* 2:186. For the end of the general reserve see Bliss to Lansing and Baker, 14 March 1918, ibid., pp. 240–41.

18. Bliss notes of meeting with House, Petain, and Clemenceau, 25 November 1918, *USAWW* 2:81–83.

19. Pershing to Bliss, 28 November 1917, Bliss Papers, box 224.

20. Pershing to Secretary of War and Chief of Staff, 2 December 1917, *USAWW* 2:88. See also Pershing, *My Experiences* 1:250.

21. Bliss to Biddle, 4 December 1917, *USAWW* 2:93, 96. Beaver believes that this cable provided the basis for what became known as the twenty-four division program. It clarified requirements, which necessitated an increase in the American effort. Bliss's memorandum to Baker, 23 December 1917, represented an official commitment to Pershing's request for twenty-four divisions. This shift reflects the growing American role in the war that Wilson had anticipated earlier. See Beaver, *Newton D. Baker*, pp. 116–18, 120. The British proposal of amalgamation is a pencilled note, Robertson to Bliss, 2 December 1917, Bliss Papers, 224. On this letter there is a written statement that it had been sealed and not opened until 1923. Bliss may simply have sought to ensure the security of the communication, but he might also have sought to conceal the reasons why he had become worried about the consequences of strict adherence to the American plan for an independent army, given the crisis in Europe.

22. Petain to representative at Chaumont, 14 December 1917, *USAWW* 2:100; Foch, *Memoirs*, pp. 233–34.

23. Final Report of G-3 (AEF), 2 July 1919, *USAWW* 14:12–13.

24. Pershing, *My Experiences* 1:278.

25. Baker to Pershing, 18 December 1917, House Papers; Pershing to Clemenceau, 5 January 1918, *USAWW* 2:137. For Clemenceau's reaction see Clemenceau to Pershing, 6 January 1918, ibid., p. 140.

26. Pershing to Chief of Staff, 1 January 1918, *USAWW* 2:132; Pershing final report, *War Department Annual Reports, 1919* 1, 1:565; Pershing to Baker, 17 January 1918, Pershing Papers.

27. Trask, *The United States in the Supreme War Council*, p. 73. Poincare's letter stemmed from a misunderstanding. The French ambassador in Washington, Jules Jusserand, reported the same information Baker had conveyed to Pershing, but it was interpreted in Paris as meaning that Pershing was under orders to amalgamate. The British ambassador in Washington, Sir Cecil Spring-Rice, conveyed the same information to London. War Cabinet Minute, 21 December 1917, *USAWW* 2:123.

28. For the six-division program see Robertson to Haig, 3 January 1918, *USAWW* 2:134; Report of G-3(AEF), ibid., 14:14; Pershing final report, *War Department Annual Reports, 1919* 1, 1:570; Trask, *The United States in the Supreme War Council*, pp. 75–78; Hankey, *Supreme Command* 2:764–65.

29. For Pershing's statement about amalgamation to his fellow commanders at Compiegne on 24 January 1918, see *USAWW* 2:81. See also Pershing to Baker, 17 January 1918, Pershing Papers; Summary of Petain-Pershing Conversation, 13 January 1918, *USAWW* 2:155–157. For the 150-battalion program see Hankey, *Supreme Command*, pp. 743–46. For the Pershing-Bliss differences about the 150-battalion program, see Pershing to Baker, 4 February 1918, Pershing Papers. Pershing's praise of Bliss is in Pershing to Baker, 24 February 1918, Pershing Papers.

30. See minutes of the third session of the Supreme War Council, 30–31 January 1918, *USAWW* 2:186–87.

31. Bliss to Baker, 2 February 1918, Bliss Papers.

32. For the discussion of strategy at the third session of the Supreme War Council, 31 January 1918, see *USAWW* 2:188. When Bliss reported on this question, he informed the acting chief of staff, General Biddle, that a British campaign in Asia Minor had been authorized with the proviso that it not have an adverse effect in the west. Ibid., pp. 191–92.

33. Pershing to Baker, 15 November 1917, Pershing Papers. See also Pershing, *My Experiences* 1:234–35.

34. For the service of American divisions during January–March 1918 see American Battle Monuments Commission, *American Armies and Battlefields in Europe*, p. 25; Pershing final report, *War Department Annual Reports, 1919* 1, 1:565. For troop arrivals see Report of the Secretary of War, ibid., p. 4.

CHAPTER 3. THE GREAT GERMAN OFFENSIVE,
PART I: 21 MARCH–31 MAY 1918

1. For Ludendorff's view see his *The General Staff and Its Problems* 2:649. For Wetzell's statement see Corelli Barnett, *The Swordbearers*, pp. 281–82.

2. Ludendorff, *Ludendorff's Own Story* 2:225–26; Basil H. Liddell Hart, *The Real War, 1914–1918* (Boston: Little, Brown, 1964), p. 368. For a detailed analysis of the political developments that led to the offensive of 21 March 1918, see Gerhard Ritter, *The Sword and the Scepter: The Problem of Militarism in Germany*, vol. 4: *The Reign of German Militarism and the Disaster of 1918*, trans. Heinze Norden (Coral Gables, Fla.: University of Miami Press, 1973), pp. 5–187.

3. Ludendorff, *Ludendorff's Own Story* 2:220–21; Barnett, *Swordbearers*, pp. 275–83; Liddell Hart, *Real War*, p. 393. For Foch's observation see his *Memoirs*, p. 251.

4. Ludendorff, *Ludendorff's Own Story* 2:222, 224, 226–27.

5. Hindenburg, *Out of My Life* 2:345; Liddell Hart, *Real War*, p. 370.

6. Ludendorff, *Ludendorff's Own Story* 2:223. The comment on the deceptive character of the concentration on the Somme is in Historical Section, Army War College, "Major Operations," p. 25.

7. For Ludendorff's description of the new tactics see his *Ludendorff's Own Story* 2:201–2. Foch described the German improvements in his *Memoirs*, p. 250. For an early American summary of this doctrine see Historical Section, Army War College, "Major Operations," p. 26. Much attention has been given to the study of German tactics in recent years. See Timothy T. Lupfer, *The Dynamics of Doctrine: The Changes in German Tactical Doctrine during the First World War* (Fort Leavenworth, Kans.: Combat Studies Institute, July 1981), Leavenworth Paper No. 4, pp. 41–54; S. J. Lewis, *Forgotten Legions: German Army Infantry Policy, 1918–1941* (New York: Praeger, 1985), pp. 11–12; Paddy Griffith, *Forward into Battle: Fighting Tactics from Waterloo to Vietnam* (Strettington, Chichester, Sussex: Antony Bird Publications, 1981), pp. 75–86; Paschall, *Defeat of Imperial Germany*, pp. 130–31.

8. Ludendorff is quoted in McEntee, *Military History of the World War*, 1943, p. 467. For Barnett's assessment see his *Swordbearers*, p. 303.

9. For Gough's difficulties see Frederick B. Maurice, *The Last Four Months: How the War Was Won* (Boston: Little, Brown, 1919), pp. 29–30. The defensive arrangements in France have been much criticized or defended. Maurice, a strong defender of concentration in France, castigates Lloyd George for withholding reinforcements to stem the impending German attack because of his fear that Haig would use them up in fruitless frontal attacks. Troops should have been sent from Palestine, but they were not. Three of the thirteen brigades in the British divisions were broken up to fill up those remaining. Ibid., pp. 18, 21–26. James E. Edmonds describes the establishment of the Fifth Army front of 42 miles on the British right wing in his *A Short History of World War I* (London: Oxford University Press, 1951), p. 277. He gives the German and British orders of battle in ibid., 279, 282. For information about the nature of the British defenses, biased toward Flanders, and a critique of this arrangement, see Barnett, *Swordbearers*, pp. 292–93, 298–300. See also Tim Travers, *The Killing Ground: The British*

Army, the Western Front, and the Emergence of Modern Warfare, 1900–1918 (London: Allen & Unwin, 1987), p. 222; Paschall, *Defeat of Imperial Germany*, p. 103.

10. For brief accounts of the attack see James B. Agnew, Clifton R. Franks, and William R. Griffiths, *The Great War* (interim text, United States Military Academy, Department of History, 1977; rev. 1980), pp. 253–54; Trevor Wilson, *The Myriad Faces of War: Britain and the Great War, 1914–1918* (Cambridge, Eng.: Polity Press, 1986), pp. 559–63; Marshall, *World War I*, pp. 352–57; Barnett, *Swordbearers*, pp. 292–93, 306–12. Barnett stresses the damage of Passchendaele in accounting for the British failure. Ibid., p. 310. A recent account is in Robert B. Asprey, *The German High Command at War: Hindenburg and Ludendorff Conduct World War I* (New York: William Morrow, Inc., 1991), pp. 368, 391. For the relief of Gough on 27 March 1918 over Haig's objections and Rawlinson's appointment, see Edmonds, *A Short History of World War I*, p. 293; Blaxland, *Amiens*, p. 114.

11. Historical Section, Army War College, "Major Operations," p. 32; Wilson, *Myriad Faces of War*, p. 562. See also Philip Neame, *German Strategy in the Great War* (London: Edward Arnold, 1923), p. 109. For Maurice's observations see *Last Four Months*, p. 35. For Barnett's critique of the decision of 23 March, which involved three movements in different directions for different purposes, see *Swordbearers*, p. 317.

12. For Haig's comment see Blake, ed., *Private Papers of Haig*, pp. 297–98. For Foch's view see his *Memoirs*, pp. 257–58. Barnett gives details of the movement of French divisions to the British sector and the meeting of 24 March 1918 between Haig and Petain. Barnett, *Swordbearers*, pp. 309, 313, 319–21. See also Millett, Bullard, p. 354. For the kaiser's view see Walter Goerlitz, ed., *The Kaiser and His Court: The Diary, Notebooks, and Letters of Admiral Georg Alexander von Mueller, Chief of the Naval Cabinet, 1914–1918* (London: McDonald, 1961), p. 345.

13. For Haig's comment see Blake, ed., *Private Papers of Haig*, p. 298. For Clemenceau's report of Petain's statement see Barnett, *Swordbearers*, p. 326. For the Foch-Clemenceau exchange see Wilson, *Myriad Faces of War*, p. 569. Partisans of Haig shortly after the war incorrectly argued that the Doullens agreement was necessary because the board created to direct the general reserve was "too slow and cumbrous." The difficulty lay elsewhere. Haig and Petain ensured that the general reserve would not work by refusing to provide troops. For an example of this fallacy see Maurice, *Last Four Months*, p. 13.

14. For the Doullens and Beauvais agreements see Trask, *The United States in the Supreme War Council*, pp. 62–64; Wilson, *Myriad Faces of War*, p. 567; Falls, *Great War*, p. 35; David Lloyd George, *War Memoirs of David Lloyd George* 6: *1918* (Boston: Little, Brown, 1937), pp. 4–12; Hankey, *Supreme Command*, pp. 791–92. The text of the Beauvais Agreement is in *USAWW* 2:277. See also Pershing report on relations with the Allies, ibid., 12: *Reports of Commander-in-Chief, A.E.F., Staff Sections and Services*, pt. 1, p. 84, which states that at Beauvais "specific powers were given to General Foch to issue orders to carry out his plans." For Foch's recommendation to upgrade his power and the support of General Bliss and Pershing see Minutes of Beauvais Conference, 3 April 1918, in ibid. 2:275–77. Foch's critique of the Doullens agreement is in ibid., p. 275. The Supreme War Council, meeting at Abbeville on 2 May 1918, extended Foch's authority to the Italian front. Ibid., p. 368.

15. For Pershing's statement see his diary, 3 April 1918, Pershing Papers. For Bliss's view see Trask, *United States in the Supreme War Council*, p. 64.

16. For Hindenburg's appreciation see his *Out of My Life* 2:349. For Ludendorff's orders to attack Arras and subsequent adjustments see Barnett, *Swordbearers*, pp. 322, 328.

17. For Foch's actions see his *Memoirs*, p. 265.

18. For the successful Allied defense of Arras and Amiens see Wilson, *Myriad Faces of War*, pp. 563–64; Liddell Hart, *Real War*, p. 371; Barnett, *Swordbearers*, pp. 329–30; Edmonds, *Short History of World War I*, pp. 294–95; Blaxland, *Amiens*, pp. 84–85. For Maurice's view see his *Last Four Months*, p. 44. For Haig's view see Blake, ed., *Private Papers of Haig*, p. 299.

19. Maurice writes of the engagement on 28 March aimed at the capture of the Vimy ridge: "When it ended the Germans had gained a portion only of our outpost positions, and our battle positions had everywhere resisted their assaults. This time there was no fog to help the enemy, and Haig's system of defense was completely successful. It is not too much to say that this costly repulse doomed Ludendorff's campaign to failure." Maurice, *Last Four Months*, p. 44.

20. The American interpretation is in Historical Section, Army War College, "Major Operations," p. 35. For Ludendorff's message see *USAWW* 2:280, and for his comment on avoiding attrition see his *Ludendorff's Own Story* 2:232. For Hindenburg's view see his *Out of My Life* 2:340.

21. Foch's summation is in his *Memoirs*, pp. 272–73. Hoffmann is quoted in Ritter, *Sword and Scepter* 4:233. For Barnett's interpretation see his *Swordbearers*, p. 330. For Ritter's reaction see his *Sword and Scepter* 4:232.

22. For the role of the 6th Engineers in the defense of Amiens see *USAWW* 4:30–51. Some American air units became involved. See ibid., pp. 52–57. For a comment on the role of "Carey's Force," the name given to the polyglot force to which the Engineers became attached, see Maurice, *Last Four Months*, p. 43. For Pershing's meeting with Petain see report of the G-3 (AEF), *USAWW* 14:19. Pershing's comment on the meeting is in his diary, 25 March 1918, Pershing Papers.

23. Pershing final report, *War Department Annual Reports, 1919* 1, 1:571–72. See also Trask, *The United States in the Supreme War Council*, pp. 80–82. For Haig's comment see Blake, ed., *Private Papers of Haig*, p. 300.

24. Bliss to Baker, 10 April 1918, Bliss Papers. See also Trask, *The United States in the Supreme War Council*, pp. 84–85.

25. Memorandum, Conner to Harbord, 6 April 1918, *USAWW* 2:283–85. For the commander-in-chief's response to this memorandum of Connor's see the report of a telephone conversation between Pershing and Conner, 8 April 1918, *USAWW* 2:290–91.

26. For the episode of 28 March 1918 and its meaning see Smythe, *Pershing*, pp. 101–2. For Marshall's statement see George C. Marshall, *Memoirs of My Services in the World War, 1917–1918*, foreword and notes by Brig. Gen. James L. Collins, Jr. (Boston: Houghton Mifflin, 1976), p. 79.

27. Historical Section, Army War College, "Major Operations," pp. 41–43.

28. Hindenburg, *Out of My Life* 2:351–52. Trevor Wilson thinks that Ludendorff turned to the north because he could not continue to gain ground on the Somme, not because of the improving weather. Wilson, *Myriad Faces of War*, p. 569.

29. For an account of the early battle see Liddell Hart, *Real War*, pp. 372, 405. See also Barnett, *Swordbearers*, p. 330. Portugal had sent two divisions to the western front, which had been combined into one division of four brigades containing 17,000 troops. This tired force was scheduled to be withdrawn on the night of 9–10 April. Edmonds, *Short History of World War I*, p. 304.

30. Haig is quoted in McEntee, *Military History of the World War*, p. 481. For Haig's adjustments on the Lys front see Maurice, *Last Four Months*, pp. 47–48.

31. Falls, *Great War*, p. 340; Foch, *Memoirs*, p. 299. Neame observes that "the salient

created by the Germans in the plain of the Lys became just such a slaughter-house for the attackers as Falkenhayn criticized in his appreciation of the unsuccessful breakthrough attacks by the *Entente* in 1915." Neame, *German Strategy*, pp. 110–11. The American analysis is in Historical Section, Army War College, "Major Operations," p. 47. For Foch's remark see Maurice, *Last Four Months*, p. 58. Ludendorff's observations on the decline of the German army are in his *Ludendorff's Own Story* 2:245–46. Edmonds reports casualty figures in his *Short History of World War I*, pp. 315–16.

32. Wilson, *Myriad Faces of War*, p. 572; Foch, *Memoirs*, p. 299. See also report of the G-3 (AEF), *USAWW* 14:17. For the seizure of Kemmel Hill on 25 April and its effects see Maurice, *Last Four Months*, p. 50. For the Haig-Wilson-Foch meeting at Abbeville on 27 April 1918 see *USAWW* 2:356.

33. For the activity of the three American units engaged on the Lys see *USAWW* 4:58–65. For the offer of the 1st Division see Pershing to Foch, 12 April 1918, ibid., p. 260.

34. Report by the Chief of the General Staff Army Unit C [German], 19 May 1918, in *USAWW* 11:297. For Lloyd George's observation see Smythe, *Pershing*, pp. 107–8.

35. Foch, *Memoirs*, p. 307; Pershing diary, 16 April 1918, Pershing Papers.

36. For this speech see Smythe, *Pershing*, p. 107.

37. Ibid., p. 150; Pershing final report, *War Department Annual Reports, 1919* 1, 1:572–73; Reading to Lloyd George, 21 April 1918, *USAWW* 2:336–37; Memorandum, Pershing conversation with Milner and Wilson, 22 April 1918, ibid., pp. 340–41. Pershing did not receive the text of the agreement cabled to Lloyd George by Reading until 26 April. See McCain to Pershing, 26 April 1918, ibid., pp. 351–52. After returning to France, Pershing met with Foch, who "seemed to think more of transportation of Infantry for service with the French and British than of the formation of an American army. I insisted that we must prepare for the latter. After showing him that I would not consider any other policy than one looking to this end, I showed him the proposition adopted by the British on this subject and he finally agreed that if the British are capable of bringing over as many troops as they state it would be satisfactory to bring over entire divisions." Pershing diary, 25 April 1918, Pershing Papers. See also report of conversation between Foch and Pershing at Sarcus, 25 April 1918, *USAWW* 2:348–50. For Lloyd George's comments on American civil-military relations, see his *War Memoirs*, vol. 5: *1917* (Boston: Little, Brown, 1936), p. 439.

38. Baker to Pershing, 29 April 1918, Pershing Papers; Baker to Bliss, 7 May 1918, Bliss Papers.

39. Minutes of the Third Meeting, Fifth Session, Supreme War Council, *USAWW* 2:361–65. Clemenceau's protest, leading to the discussion at Abbeville, is in Minutes of an Anglo-French Conference at Abbeville, 27 April 1918, ibid., pp. 355–56.

40. Continuation of Minutes of the Abbeville Conference of the Supreme War Council, 2 May 1918, ibid., pp. 368–71. Foch's memorandum of his views presented on 2 May 1918 is in ibid., pp. 372–73. For the text of the Abbeville agreement see Pershing to March and Baker, 7 May 1918, ibid., p. 379. Pershing's report of the discussion, 6 May 1918, is on p. 381. See also his diary, which contains the statement about American public opinion. Pershing diary, 2 May 1918, Pershing Papers.

41. Haig diary, 1 May 1918, Blake, ed., *Private Papers of Haig*, p. 307. It is curious that this entry for 1 May 1918 should report the Abbeville agreement itself, which was not reached until the next day. The British soldier is quoted in John Terraine, *To Win a War 1918: The Year of Victory* (London: Sidgwick & Johnson, 1978), pp. 67–68.

42. Baker to Pershing, 11 May 1918, *USAWW* 2:399; Pershing to Baker and March,

15 May 1918, ibid., pp. 403-4. Pershing and March exchanged messages on the Abbeville agreement, the commander-in-chief reiterating the views expressed at the meeting of the Supreme War Council. March responded: "I am in complete accord with your proposition for separate American divisions. I have insisted upon that solution throughout, and it will win." Pershing to March, 5 May 1918, and March to Pershing, 6 May 1918, Pershing Papers.

43. Foch, *Memoirs*, pp. 301-2.

44. For Allan Millett's observation see his definitive essay on "Cantigny, 28-31 May 1918" in Charles E. Heller and William A. Stofft, eds., *America's First Battles, 1776-1965* (Lawrence: University Press of Kansas, 1986), p. 168. Vandenberg's order is in *USAWW* 4:270. Millett discusses the motives for the attack on Cantigny in his *Bullard*, pp. 360-61. French criticisms are noted on p. 347.

45. For Colonel Ely's observations see *USAWW* 4:326. For the comment on the benefits to be gained from the attack see Historical Section, Army War College, "Major Operations," p. 51.

46. Smythe, *Pershing*, pp. 125-27; Historical Section, Army War College, "Major Operations," pp. 51-52; Millett, "Cantigny," pp. 172-73. The German report by Baron von Watter, Commanding General, XXVI Reserve Corps, to Commanding General, German Eighteenth Army, 28 May 1918, is in *USAWW* 4:341. For the plan of attack see Field Orders No. 18, 1st Division, 20 May 1918, ibid., pp. 281-84.

47. For Marshall's comment see his Memoirs, p. 97. Pershing's observation is in his final report, *War Department Annual Reports, 1919* 1, 1:578. For a succinct but detailed account of the German reaction, see Millett, "Cantigny," pp. 175-79. See also Smythe, *Pershing*, pp. 126-28; Millett, *Bullard*, p. 367. For the postbattle activity of the 1st Division see *American Armies and Battlefields in Europe*, p. 415.

48. For Pershing's report to Baker and March see *USAWW* 2:434. Marshall's observation is in his *Memoirs*, p. 96. For Millett's views see his "Cantigny," pp. 179-82. Smythe's evaluation is in his *Pershing*, p. 128.

CHAPTER 4. THE GREAT GERMAN OFFENSIVE,
PART II: 27 MAY-17 JULY 1918

1. For Hindenburg's comment on the German motives see his *Out of My Life* 2:357-59. For Falls's comment see his *Great War*, pp. 342-44. See also Barnett, *Swordbearers*, p. 322; Terraine, *To Win a War*, pp. 69-70; Asprey, *German High Command at War*, p. 412.

2. Historical Section, Army War College, "Major Operations," p. 55. Ludendorff's description of the plan is in his *Ludendorff's Own Story* 2:250-51. For the transfer of tired British divisions to the Chemin des Dames, supposedly a quiet sector, see Maurice, *Last Four Months*, p. 59. For the American intelligence estimate see Barrie Pitt, *1918: The Last Act* (New York: W. W. Norton, 1962), pp. 138-40. Liddell Hart describes the reasoning of Maj. S. T. Hubbard, a head of the order-of-battle section in the American G-2, in predicting an attack on the Chemin des Dames: "Among the reasons given were that, as surprise was the keynote of the German method, this sector was more likely to be chosen because regarded by the Allies as secure and as a resting ground for tired divisions; that its feasible frontage corresponded well with the limited German resources available at the moment, and that this hypothesis was confirmed by the ascertained location of the German troops, particularly of certain picked divisions." Liddell Hart, *Real War*, p. 412. Petain belatedly recognized the value of the American

estimate and notified Duchene, but the French commander ignored the information. Asprey, *German High Command at War*, pp. 413–14. Five British divisions that had suffered serious losses earlier had been transferred to the supposedly quiet zone in Champagne. On the day of the attack, three were on line and two in reserve. Blaxland, *Amiens*, pp. 136–38. For criticism of Duchene's dispositions and their consequences see Barnett, *Swordbearers*, p. 333.

3. Historical Section, Army War College, "Major Operations," p. 62; Falls, *Great War*, pp. 343–44; Report of the G-3, *USAWW* 14:17; Historical Section, Army War College, *The Aisne and Montdidier-Noyon Operations*, Monograph No. 13 (Washington, D.C.: Government Printing Office, 1922), pp. 7–20.

4. For Foch's statement and his response see his *Memoirs*, p. 322. For Ludendorff's view see *Ludendorff's Own Story* 2: 268–69. Hindenburg comments in *Out of My Life* 2:364. For Petain's defensive reaction see Barnett, *Swordbearers*, p. 334. For another critique see Pitt, 1918, pp. 137–38.

5. McEntee, *Military History of the World War*, p. 488; Falls, *Great War*, p. 345; Smythe, *Pershing*, p. 137. The German 231st Infantry Division contemplated an attack but decided against it because of the strength of the American defenses. War diary of German 231st Infantry Division, 2 June 1918, *USAWW* 4:251.

6. Authorities are in general agreement on the outcome of the Aisne offensive. See Liddell Hart, *Real War*, pp. 373, 417–18; *USAWW*, vol. 11: *American Occupation of Germany* (Washington, D.C.: Government Printing Office, 1948), p. 303; Historical Section, Army War College, "Major Operations," p. 59; Wilson, *Myriad Faces of War*, p. 579; Smythe, *Pershing*, p. 138. For the American comment on the German logistical problems, see Historical Section, Army War College, "Major Operations," p. 63. For comments on the lack of an objective see Neame, *German Strategy in the Great War*, p. 112. It was true, however, that the salient created problems for the Allies. It added 30 miles of front that had to be garrisoned, and the interdiction of the Paris-Chalons railroad embarrassed lateral communications. *USAWW* 11:305.

7. For the fighting at Bouresches, Belleau Wood, and Vaux during the period 6 June–1 July 1918, see Journal of Operations, 2nd Division, 6 June 1918, *USAWW* 4:383; Field Order No. 2, Fourth Brigade, United States Marine Corps (for attack on Bouresches and Belleau Wood), ibid., pp. 364–65; Journal of Operations, 2d Division, 25 June 1918 (clearing of Belleau Wood), ibid., pp. 559–60; Degoutte commendation of Fourth Brigade, 2d Division, 30 June 1918, ibid., p. 656; Operations Report, Third Brigade, 2d Division, 16 August 1918 (attack on Vaux, 1 July 1918), ibid., p. 226; Reports, various dates, for attack on Vaux, 1 July 1918, ibid., pp. 666–75. For a detailed account of these actions see Robert B. Asprey, *At Belleau Wood* (New York: G. P. Putnam's Sons, 1965). A concise account is in Allan R. Millett, *Semper Fidelis: The History of the United States Marine Corps* (New York: Macmillan, 1980), pp. 299–304. For casualties see p. 304.

8. Klewitz to GHQ, Operations Section, 12 June 1918, *USAWW* 11:312; Report of Intelligence Section, German IV Reserve Corps, 17 June 1918, 4:607–8; Report of Section for Foreign Armies, German GHQ, 2 July 1918, ibid. 11:410; Ludendorff, *Ludendorff's Own Story* 2:269.

9. Historical Section, Army War College, "Major Operations," p. 61; Smythe, *Pershing*, p. 139.

10. For the German plan see Liddell Hart, Real War, pp. 419–20; McEntee, *Military History of the World War*, p. 490; Wilson, *Myriad Faces of War*, p. 579; Barnett, *Swordbearers*, pp. 325–26, Maurice, *Last Four Months*, p. 63; Asprey, *German High Command at War*, p. 429.

11. For French awareness of German intentions see Liddell Hart, *Real War*, pp. 373–74; Historical Section, Army War College, "Major Operations," p. 66; Report of the G-3 (AEF), *USAWW* 14:17–18. For information about the attack see ibid. 11:307; Historical Section, Army War College, "Major Operations," pp. 63–65; McEntee, *Military History of the World War*, p. 491; Neame, *German Strategy in the Great War*, p. 113; Barnett, *Swordbearers*, p. 335; Historical Section, Army War College, *Aisne and Montdidier Operations*, pp. 21–33. For Ludendorff's views see his *Ludendorff's Own Story* 2:271–72; Liddell Hart, *Real War*, pp. 420. The British call this offensive the Battle of the Matz. The German code name for it was YORCK. Edmonds, *Short History of World War I*, pp. 322, 324–25. Edmonds notes that Duchene was sacked and that Petain was almost replaced by General Marie-Louise Adolphe Guillaumat, who was recalled from Salonika. Improving conditions saved Petain; Guillaumat became the military governor of Paris.

12. Ludendorff, *Ludendorff's Own Story* 2:276.

13. The Lloyd George–Pershing exchange is in Pershing diary, 1 June 1918, Pershing Papers. The Foch-Pershing discussion is in Smythe, *Pershing*, p. 135. For the abortive project to seek the removal of Pershing, see Lee Kennett, "The A.E.F. through French Eyes," *Military Review* 52 (November 1972):4.

14. For the Pershing-Milner-Foch agreement see Pershing final report, *War Department Annual Reports, 1919* 1, 1:576; Trask, *The United States in the Supreme War Council*, pp. 91–92; Smythe, *Pershing*, p. 136. For Pershing's statement concerning the limited availability of trained infantry, see Pershing to March and Baker, 3 June 1918, *USAWW* 2:450. Smythe notes that Pershing learned of this situation on 11 May 1918. Smythe, *Pershing*, pp. 118–19. For Haig's diary, 1 June 1918, see Blake, ed., *Private Papers of Haig*, p. 313. Pershing's reaction to Lloyd George's proposal concerning training and use of American troops with the BEF is in his diary, 2 June 1918, Pershing Papers.

15. For the prime minister's communication see Pershing final report, *War Department Annual Reports, 1919* 1, 1:575. Pershing's immediate response is in Pershing to March and Baker, 3 June 1918, *USAWW* 2:450. Pershing's postwar comment is in his final report, *War Department Annual Reports, 1919* 1, 1:576.

16. For the transfer of the American divisions (the 4th, 28th, 35th, 77th, and 82d), see *USAWW* 14:24; Pershing final report, *War Department Annual Reports, 1919* 1, 1:579. Pershing's comments on this decision are in Pershing to March and Baker, 16 June 1918, *USAWW* 2:467.

17. Pershing to Haig, ibid., p. 466.

18. Wilson to Foch, 15 June 1918, *USAWW* 2:466; Haig diary, 18 June 1918, Blake, ed., *Private Papers of Haig*, p. 315. For Petain's view see Petain to Clemenceau, 19 June 1918, *USAWW* 2:481.

19. Pershing-Foch conversation, 17 June 1918, *USAWW* 2:468–70; Smythe, *Pershing*, p. 145. Smythe believes that Pershing gave Foch's proposition serious consideration, an indication of the American's flexibility in an emergency. This reasoning seems strained. Pershing's conception of an emergency involved *extreme* danger, which meant that in practice he was most unlikely to authorize forms of amalgamation that would seriously delay formation of an independent American army.

20. Pershing rejected Foch's proposal of amalgamation on 23 June 1918 during a meeting at Chaumont. McEntee, *Military History of the World War*, p. 491. For Pershing's letter to Baker, 6 July 1918, see Pershing, *My Experiences* 2:189–90.

21. For the Bombon discussion of 10 July see notes of the conference, *USAWW* 2:518–20. See also memorandum by Foch, 10 July 1918, ibid., pp. 520–21. Foch gave his account in his *Memoirs*, p. 346. See also *USAWW* 14:31.

22. For Pershing to March (letter), 19 June 1918, see Pershing Papers. Pershing wrote similarly to Secretary Baker on 18 June 1918, Pershing Papers. His proposal of sixty-six divisions is in Pershing to March and Baker (cable), 19 June 1918, *USAWW* 2:476–79. The proposal of a hundred divisions is in Pershing to March and Baker (cable), ibid., pp. 482–83.

23. For the exchanges between the War Department and AEF Headquarters concerning the hundred-division plan see Smythe, *Pershing*, pp. 146–47, 172; Report on Relations with Allies, *USAWW* 12:89. The AEF's misinterpretation of the War Department plan is in Report of the G-1 (AEF), ibid., p. 111. Pershing's attempt to alter the decision is Pershing to March and Baker, 17 August 1918, ibid. 2:579–80. The secretary of war explained the confusion in the AEF to the chief of staff and asked him to clarify the program to Pershing in Baker to March, 23 September 1918, ibid., p. 610. A letter from March to Bliss, 20 September 1918, reported the War Department's conception of the 80-division plan. March, *Nation at War*, p. 304. Smythe is critical of Pershing's recommendation, arguing that no such force was needed to gain sufficient superiority over the Germans. He questions the availability of shipping and port facilities for the shipment of a hundred divisions. Smythe, *Pershing*, p. 147.

24. For House's letter to Wilson see Trask, *The United States in the Supreme War Council*, pp. 92–93; Smythe, *Pershing*, p. 162. For Baker's letter see Pershing, *My Experiences* 2:185–86; Baker to Pershing, 6 July 1918, Pershing Papers. A part of this letter is reproduced in *USAWW* 2:512.

25. Pershing to Baker, 27 July 1918, *USAWW* 2:553. For Smythe's observations see *Pershing*, p. 165. General March's version of the plan to send Goethals emphasizes the role of Colonel House. March favored the plan, arguing that Pershing was "peculiarly unfitted" for diplomatic work. March, *Nation at War*, pp. 195–96. For an account of the effort to trim Pershing's sails that emphasizes the role of Sir William Wiseman, see Wilton B. Fowler, *British-American Relations, 1917–1918: The Role of Sir William Wiseman* (Princeton, N.J.: Princeton University Press, 1969), pp. 154–56.

26. For Pershing's agreement to Bliss's role as diplomatic intermediary, see Pershing to Bliss, 28 July 1918, Pershing Papers. For Pershing's comment on Bliss see Pershing to March, 19 July 1918, Pershing Papers. Colonel House also wrote to Pershing about the need to free him "from any of the harassing drudgery of the work behind the lines." House to Pershing, 4 July 1918, Pershing Papers. Pershing replied that he had few diplomatic responsibilities except his discussions of amalgamation, an issue that he thought "largely of the past." He also stressed the importance of unity of command, his answer to the proposed appointment of General Goethals. Pershing to House (cable), 6 August 1918, Pershing Papers. The transfer of responsibility for negotiations concerning the shipment of American troops to the Permanent Military Representatives is contained in March to American Section, Supreme War Council, Versailles, 24 June 1918, *USAWW* 2:481.

27. Pershing to Baker, 28 July 1918, and Pershing to Baker, 17 August 1918, Pershing Papers.

28. Ludendorff, *Ludendorff's Own Story* 2:278. For Hindenburg's observation see *Out of My Life* 2:374. For the final planned attack between the Somme and the Marne aimed at Amiens and Paris, see Historical Section, Army War College, "Major Operations," p. 69. See also Neame, *German Strategy in the Great War*, pp. 113–14.

29. Ludendorff's order to the German Crown Prince to prepare for the Champagne operation, 14 June 1918, is in *USAWW* 5: *Military Operations of the American Expeditionary Forces* (Washington, D.C.: Government Printing Office, 1948), p. 175. For the German crown prince's instructions, 21 June 1918, see ibid. 5:177. See also McEntee,

Military History of the World War, pp. 491–92; Maurice, *Last Four Months*, pp. 90–91; Ludendorff, *Ludendorff's Own Story* 2:306–7; Edmonds, *Short History of World War I*, pp. 329, 331.

30. Ludendorff, *The General Staff and Its Problems* 2:578. The Kaiser's role is reported in War Diary, German First Army, 15 July 1918, *USAWW* 2:186.

31. For intelligence operations prior to the German attack in Champagne see American Battle Monuments Commission, *American Armies and Battlefields in Europe*, p. 331; Historical Section, Army War College, "Major Operations," pp. 71, 75; Operations Report, French Fourth Army, 18 July 1918, *USAAW* 5:151. Foch's views are in his *Memoirs*, pp. 331–32.

32. Special Instructions (Petain), 5 July 1918, *USAWW* 5:3–4. For Foch's analysis of German tactics and his prescriptions for defense, see his *Memoirs*, pp. 331–32.

33. This account is based on Historical Section, Army War College, "Major Operations," pp. 70, 78; War Diary, Army Group German Crown Prince, 15 July 1918, *USAWW* 2:331; American Battle Monuments Commission, *American Armies and Battlefields in Europe*, pp. 331–32; War Diary, German First Army, 15 July 1918, *USAWW* 5:183, 185–86; Operations Report, French Fourth Army, 18 July 1918, ibid. 5:150–55. Maurice's summary is in his *Last Four Months*, pp. 92–93. See also Falls, *Great War*, p. 349. He reports that the Germans lost twenty tanks in this attack, the victims of French artillery fire.

34. This account is based on Falls, *Great War*, pp. 348–49; McEntee, *Military History of the World War*, p. 493; *USAWW* 5:1–2; Barnett, *Swordbearers*, p. 337. For the role of the 38th Infantry see Coffman, *War to End All Wars*, pp. 224–27. See also Operations Report, 38th Infantry (Col. U. G. McAlexander), 31 July 1918, *USAWW* 5:80–82. For a favorable French impression of the American operations see the reactions of a liaison officer from the French Fourth Army in Report of J. Corbabon, 17 July 1918, ibid., p. 171. For German explanations of the reverse see War Diary, Bavarian I Army Corps, 15 July 1918, ibid., 208–9; Report of the Operations Section, Bavarian I Army Corps, 17 July 1918, ibid., 211–12; War Diary, German IV Reserve Corps, 16 July 1918, ibid., p. 200. Other reports are in ibid., pp. 213–16.

35. For the decision to suspend the offensive see Wilson, *Myriad Faces of War*, pp. 579–80; *USAWW* 5:2; Smythe, *Pershing*, p. 151; Ludendorff, *Ludendorff's Own Story* 2:310. Hindenburg's judgment is in his *Out of My Life* 2:378.

36. For the decline in Ludendorff's reserves see Liddell Hart, *Real War*, p. 423. For Ludendorff's judgment see his *Ludendorff's Own Story*, 2:323. For that of Hindenburg see his *Out of My Life* 2:378. Statistics of the German offensives are in Paschall, *Defeat of Imperial Germany*, pp. 160–61.

37. Petain is quoted in Liddell Hart, *Real War*, p. 423.

CHAPTER 5. THE LIMITED ALLIED COUNTEROFFENSIVES:
18 JULY–26 SEPTEMBER 1918

1. For Foch's early plans see his *Memoirs*, p. 308. For his instructions to Petain, 14 June 1918 and 16 June 1918, see *USAWW* 5:223, 244. Petain issued orders for the preparation of plans on 16 June 1918. Ibid., p. 224. For Mangin's initial plan see Plan of Action, French Tenth Army, 20 June 1918, ibid., pp. 225–26. See also Mangin to Fayolle, 5 July 1918, and Petain to Fayolle, 8 July 1918, ibid., pp. 233–34. For terrain information see Historical Section, Army War College, "Major Operations," p. 85.

2. This account is based on Historical Section, Army War College, "Major Operations," pp. 72–74; McEntee, *Military History of the World War*, pp. 501–5; Petain to CGs, Groups of Armies of the Reserve and of the Center, 12 July 1918, *USAWW* 5:236; Mangin to Fayolle, 13 July 1918, ibid., p. 275; Edmonds, *Short History of World War I*, p. 333. Mangin based his later planning on the principles used in a small but successful attack he conducted on 28–29 June 1918 that was intended to interfere with German communications in Soissons. Ibid., p. 329. McEntee's observation about the scope of the offensive is in his *Military History of the World War*, p. 499. The Historical Section, Army War College noted the same point. "Major Operations," p. 76.

3. Foch, *Memoirs*, p. 354. Foch recognized that the Germans were planning an attack to the north between Arras and Ypres. He decided that the attack in Champagne must precede the attack in the north. This judgment led him to request transfer of four British divisions to the French front. Ibid., pp. 352–53.

4. For this episode see Petain to Fayolle, 15 July 1918, *USAWW* 5:241; Foch telephone message to Petain, 15 July 1918, ibid., p. 242. Petain then countermanded his earlier order in Petain to Groups of Armies of the Reserve and of the Center, 15 July 1918, ibid., p. 242. The generalissimo followed his telephone message with a letter, Foch to Petain, 16 July 1918, asking him in the future to report all instructions to army group or army commanders under his orders and any changes he might think necessary in such instructions. Ibid., pp. 244–45. Foch's explanation is in his *Memoirs*, p. 338. See also Falls, *Great War*, p. 349.

5. For accounts of the American role in the offensive see Coffman, *War to End All Wars*, pp. 234–47; Smythe, *Pershing* pp. 152–60. For Pershing's arrangements relating to the III Corps, Bullard's decision to defer to the French, and Liggett's role, see Millett, *Bullard*, pp. 381–83. For summary accounts of the action see Falls, *Great War*, pp. 349–50; Liddell Hart, *Real War*, pp. 425–28; Maurice, *Last Four Months*, pp. 95–96; Edmonds, *Short History of World War I*, p. 333. See also Foch, *Memoirs*, p. 364; Wilson, *Myriad Faces of War*, p. 581; Historical Section, Army War College, "Major Operations," p. 103. McEntee quotes Hertling in *Military History of the World War*, p. 506. Pitt notes that Mangin achieved success not by adopting the methods used earlier by the Germans but by moving troops rapidly into concealed positions just prior to the assault. Pitt, *1918*, p. 185.

6. War Diary, Group of Armies German Crown Prince, 18 July 1918, *USAWW* 5:678–79. Although dated 18 July, internal evidence suggests that this carefully written document was prepared or modified at a later date. Ludendorff's comment of 22 July 1918 is in ibid. 11:345.

7. For Hindenburg's comment see his *Out of My Life* 2:383. For general descriptions of the Aisne-Marne operations between 18 July and 6 August 1918 see Historical Section, Army War College, "Major Operations," pp. 91–92, 95, 100–101; McEntee, *Military History of the World War*, p. 510; Maurice, *Last Four Months*, pp. 95–99; Ludendorff, *Ludendorff's Own Story* 2:317–22. For detailed information about German operations see *USAWW* 2:341–57; Ibid. 5:672–75, 683–89. For Allied operations consult ibid. particularly pp. 35–37, 250, 256, 263, 266, 272–73, 275–77, 290–92, 312, 323–29, 333, 335–38, 398, 415–16, 589, 590–92, 597, 631, 633, 635, 655–56.

8. *USAWW* 14:25–26.

9. The American organizations were the 1st, 2d, 3d, 4th, 26th, 28th, 32d, and 42d Divisions. Hindenburg's comment is in his *Out of My Life* 2:386.

10. For the action of the American divisions see *USAWW* 14:28–29. Millett notes the terrible casualties of the 1st and 2d Divisions in his *Bullard*, p. 383. Liggett is quoted in McEntee, *Military History of the World War*, p. 500. He apparently discounted corps

actions at Santiago de Cuba and Manila in 1898 during the War with Spain. The organizations involved in these battles numbered less than twenty thousand troops, smaller than the division of World War I.

11. For Pershing's view see his final report, *War Department Annual Reports, 1919* 1, 1:582. For the European view see report, Section for Foreign Armies, *USAWW* 11:352. For the expert evaluation see Timothy Nenninger, "Tactical Dysfunction in the AEF, 1917–1918," unpublished paper in possession of author, p. 4. Donald Smythe makes parallel observations in *Pershing*, pp. 159–60.

12. For Foch's outlook see his *Memoirs*, p. 368. For his thoughts about the attack itself see ibid., pp. 369–70. Falls quotes Foch in his *Great War*, p. 351. As early as 27 June 1918, Foch asked Petain to prepare for offensive action, emphasizing the role assigned to American divisions. Foch, *Memoirs*, p. 343. For Foch to Petain, 27 June 1918, see *USAWW*, vol. 8: *Military Operations of the American Expeditionary Forces* (Washington, D.C.: Government Printing Office, 1948) pp. 3–4. This document is also reproduced in ibid. 5:229.

13. Maurice, *Last Four Months*, pp. 83–84; Foch, *Memoirs*, p. 342.

14. Foch prepared a memorandum for presentation at the Bombon conference in which he clarified his intentions. It is reprinted in Foch, *Memoirs*, pp. 369–72. See also C. R. M. F. Cruttwell, *A History of the Great War 1914–1918*, 2d ed. (London: Granada Publishing, 1982), p. 552. For some notes of the Bombon conference see *USAWW* 2:449–50. For the account in the British official history see Brig. Gen. James E. Edmonds, ed., *History of the Great War Based on Official Documents by Direction of the Historical Section of the Committee of Imperial Defence: Military Operations France and Belgium 1918* (London: His Majesty's Stationery Office, 1947) 4:2. See also Paschall, *Defeat of Imperial Germany*, pp. 166–67.

15. Foch, *Memoirs*, p. 373.

16. For the battle of Hamel see Wilson, *Myriad Faces of War*, pp. 587–88; Maurice, *Last Four Months*, pp. 87–88; Blaxland, *Amiens*, p. 149; Terraine, *To Win a War*, pp. 86–90. For Monash's statement see ibid., p. 86.

17. For preliminary exchanges between Haig and Foch concerning preparations for the advance east of Amiens, see Foch, *Memoirs*, pp. 375–76. For Rawlinson's preparations see Historical Section, Army War College, "Major Operations," pp. 129–30; Falls, *Great War*, pp. 372–73; Liddell Hart, *Real War*, p. 431; Wilson, *Myriad Faces of War*, p. 589. Foch initially wanted Haig to attack in the north from the La Bassee canal to free the mining region around Bethune. Haig thought the region too waterlogged. Foch went along with the British desire to make an attack at Amiens. Edmonds, *Short History of World War I*, p. 338.

18. This account is based on Foch, *Memoirs*, p. 379; Paul F. Braim, *The Test of Battle: The American Expeditionary Forces in the Meuse-Argonne Campaign* (Newark: University of Delaware Press, 1987), p. 75; Liddell Hart, *Real War*, pp. 375, 429–32, 435; Edmonds, *Short History of World War I*, p. 341. Wilson, *Myriad Faces of War*, p. 591; Barnett, *Swordbearers*, pp. 349–50; Maurice, *Last Four Months*, 101–4, 106. Maurice emphasizes the role of armor. Ibid., p. 103. One regiment of the American 33d Division participated in the attack, advancing over three miles. McEntee, *Military History of the World War*, p. 513. For Foch's instruction to continue the attack see Edmonds, ed., *History of the Great War: Military Operations France and Belgium 1918* 4:583–84. For Haig's resistance see Liddell Hart, *Real War*, p. 376; Wilson, *Myriad Faces of War*, p. 594.

19. Bidwell and Graham, *Fire-power: Army Weapons and Theories at War, 1905–1945* (London: George Allen & Unwin, 1982), p. 133; Jonathan M. House, *Towards Combined Arms Warfare: A Survey of Tactics, Doctrine, and Organization in the 20th Century*,

Research Survey No. 2 (Fort Leavenworth, Kans.: U.S. Army Command and General Staff College, Combat Studies Institute, 1984), pp. 36–37. For Haig's statement see Historical Section, Army War College, "Major Operations," pp. 134–35. Foch's comment is in his *Memoirs*, p. 390. Barnett observes that the German practice of splitting divisions into "shock divisions" for the attack and "trench divisions" for the defense ultimately failed. When the shock divisions met defeat, the trench divisions proved unable to mount sound defensives. Barnett, *Swordbearers*, pp. 352–53. Tim Travers argues convincingly that British planners were divided into two groups: a group that advocated "mechanical warfare" utilizing the new technology, and a group that advocated "traditional warfare." The successes after Amiens reflected the traditional methods, modified when possible by intelligent use of tanks, aircraft, and other new weapons, and also Foch's influence. Tim Travers, "The Evolution of British Strategy and Tactics on the Western Front in 1918," *Journal of Military History* (April 1990) 54:173–200.

20. Ludendorff, *Ludendorff's Own Story* 2:323–26, 330–33. Hindenburg did not yet despair of victory, but he agreed with the Imperial chancellor, Count Hertling, that for the moment peace discussions were called for. Hindenburg, *Out of My Life* 2:396.

21. The German crown prince urged an early retirement to the Hindenburg line, arguing that Foch was seeking a decision and that the German army could make the best possible defense behind strong fortifications. Wilhelm, German Crown Prince, to Ludendorff, 26 August 1918, *USAWW* 11:375. Ludendorff accepted a more limited withdrawal, but he vetoed an early movement to the Hindenburg line. Falls, *Great War*, p. 379. In responding to the crown prince's proposal, he put his finger on one of Foch's prime calculations: "In every withdrawal conserving our forces, we must always consider that the enemy will achieve at least a similar economy in forces, and that in view of his numerical superiority he will always be able to renew his attacks somewhere else." Ludendorff to Group of Armies German Crown Prince, 27 August 1918, *USAWW* 11:376. For a summary of the German calculations and Foch's statement about Ludendorff's delay in retiring to the Hindenburg line, see Cruttwell, *History of the Great War*, pp. 552–53. For Lossberg's proposal and Ludendorff's reaction see Ritter, *Sword and Scepter* 4:233–34. See also for Lossberg's views Asprey, *German High Command at War*, pp. 439–40, 442.

22. For German adjustments see German Crown Prince, Order, 11 August 1918, *USAWW*, vol. 6: *Military Operations of the American Expeditionary Forces* (Washington, D.C.: Government Printing Office, 1948), pp. 223–25. Ludendorff's views are in Ludendorff to Group of Armies German Crown Prince, 8 August 1918, ibid. 11:364; Ludendorff order, 16 August 1918, ibid., p. 366. Maj. Alfred Niemann's comment to Admiral Mueller is in Goerlitz, ed., *The Kaiser and His Court*, p. 380.

23. Ludendorff precipitated these talks on 10 August when he informed the kaiser that the war must be brought to an end. Barnett, *Swordbearers*, pp. 354–55. Adm. Paul von Hintze participated in these exchanges as foreign minister. Ludendorff had forced the resignation of his predecessor, Richard von Kuhlmann, for having hinted in a speech before the Reichstag on 24 June that Germany should consider peace negotiations. Ritter, *Sword and Scepter* 4:311–12. For information about the discussions and decisions of 13–14 August 1918, see Ludendorff, *Ludendorff's Own Story* 2:334–35; Ludendorff, *The General Staff and Its Problems* 2:581–82; Maurice, *Last Four Months*, p. 108; Barnett, *Swordbearers*, p. 355; Martin Kitchin, *The Silent Dictatorship: The Politics of the German High Command under Hindenburg and Ludendorff, 1916–1918* (New York: Holmes & Meier, 1976), pp. 247–51. Shortly after the war, two participants confirmed Ludendorff's report of the negotiations. See the statement of Maj. Erich Baron von dem Bussche, writing to Ludendorff on 28 December 1918, and Gen. Ernst von

Eisenhart-Rothe's letter to Ludendorff, 12 August 1919, Ludendorff, *The General Staff and Its Problems* 2:587, 588. Von Hintze communicated the decision to seek peace to a group of parliamentary leaders on 21 August 1918. Ludendorff, *Ludendorff's Own Story* 2:337. Gerhard Ritter believes that these talks did not have a sufficiently decisive outcome. Ludendorff concealed the full extent of the military emergency, leading to the assumption that diplomatic steps need not be inaugurated immediately. Hintze recognized the extent of the crisis, but he failed to exert his influence. Ritter, *Sword and Scepter* 4:323–25. See also Asprey, *German High Command at War*, pp. 439–40, 442, 452–53. The Austrian emperor, Karl, and his foreign minister, Burian, appeared at Spa on 14 August to argue the need for an end to the war, informing the Germans that Austria-Hungary could not hold out through the winter. Edmonds, *Short History of World War I*, p. 351.

24. For the explanation of the German commander's actions, see Order, Group of Armies Boehn, 9 September 1918, *USAWW*, vol. 7: *Military Operations of the American Expeditionary Forces* (Washington, D.C.: Government Printing Office, 1948), pp. 373–74. See also Operations Report, Group of Armies Boehn, 24 August 1918, ibid., pp. 813–14. For the German withdrawal order see Ludendorff to Groups of Armies Gallwitz, German Crown Prince, and Duke Albrecht, 26 August 1918, ibid. 11:373–74. For information on the Ypres-Lys offensive see ibid. 6:285–86, 304–5; McEntee, *Military History of the World War*, p. 514. The American after-action reports on the pursuit are Report of CG, 27th Division (O'Ryan), 19 December 1918, *USAWW* 6:307–9; Report of CG, 30th Division (Lewis), ibid., pp. 311–13. A German report on the activity of the 27th Division drew attention to its inexperience, especially in mobile warfare, and to the lack of infantry-artillery coordination. Hamann Report, Germany 8th Infantry Division, 3 September 1918, ibid., p. 320. For British operations in Picardy see Maurice, *Last Four Months*, pp. 109, 113–14, 148–49. The British army fought a series of four battles to exploit the success at Amiens. They were: Albert (21–31 August), Scarpe (22–30 August), Bapaume (31 August–3 September), Drocourt-Queant line (2–3 September). The Germans called the fortifications that were attacked during these operations the *Wotan* position. Edmonds, *Short History of World War I*, p. 351. They withdrew about ten miles beginning on 26–27 August to the Siegfried (or Hindenburg) positions. Ibid., p. 354.

25. For the Oise-Aisne offensive see Historical Section, Army War College, "Major Operations," p. 144; Pershing final report, U.S. War Department, *War Department Annual Reports, 1919*, vol. 1 (Washington, D.C.: Government Printing Office, 1920) pt. 1, p. 583.; Millett, *Bullard*, p. 386; *USAWW, 1:37–39*. German reports on the battles between 8 August and 11 September are in *USAWW* 11:393–402. For the defensive posture of the German Seventh Army see Report of Operations Section, Seventh German Army, 3 September 1918, ibid., p. 383. In describing the Oise-Aisne offensive Coffman offers a "tragic note." On 27 August, "four companies of the 28th Division, serving with the French at Fismettes to the right of the 3rd Division, were surrounded, when the French retreated without informing them. Only a few survivors gained the Allied lines." Coffman, *War to End All Wars*, p. 227.

26. For a period of time in July and August it appeared that the American First Army might be formed in the area of Chateau-Thierry and employed in that region. Foch contemplated an American sector from Reims to the Argonne forest, but the Americans never lost interest in operations to the east. Stabilization of the front on the Vesle River early in August reduced interest in forming the American army in that area. From then on the buildup was carried out with the idea of attacking the St. Mihiel salient. For information on this matter see Smythe, *Pershing*, p. 148; Conner to Chief of Staff,

14 July 1918, *USAWW* 2:527–31; Notes of conference at Bombon, 21 July 1918, ibid. 8:4–5; Foch to Pershing, 22 July 1918, ibid., pp. 5–6; Memorandum by General Weygand, 24 July 1918, ibid. 5:258–59. For the effect of the stabilization on the Vesle River see ibid. 6:1. For Pershing's comments on this subject see his report on relations with the Allies, ibid. 12:86–89. For Foch's observations see his *Memoirs*, pp. 395–97. For the decision to leave three American divisions with Petain, see Foch to Petain, 9 August 1918, *USAWW* 8:8–9; ibid. 14:32. For the return of the III Corps to American control see Petain to Pershing, 7 September 1918, ibid., pp. 53–54. The formation and location of the First Army is covered in McEntee, *Military History of the World War*, p. 519. For the return of three American divisions from the British front, see Haig diary, 12 August 1918, Blake, ed., *Private Papers of Haig*, p. 323; Edmonds, ed., *History of the Great War* 4:171; Pershing to Foch, 15 August 1918, *USAWW* 8:12–13; Foch to Haig, Pershing, and Petain, 17 August 1918, ibid., p. 14; Foch to Pershing, 23 August 1918, ibid. 2:583. Haig's complaints about the loss of the American divisions are in Haig diary, 25 August and 27 August 1918, Blake, ed., *Private Papers of Haig*, p. 325. It was agreed that the French would take over a section of the British front to compensate for the loss of the Americans, and it was also agreed that two American divisions would be sent to either the French or the British fronts after 8 September. Foch, *Memoirs*, p. 398.

27. For information on the transfer of French units and equipment to the First Army, see Pershing to Petain, 15 August 1918, *USAWW* 8:10; Pershing to Foch, 15 August 1918, ibid., pp. 10, 12; Pershing to Foch, 15 August 1918, ibid., pp. 12–13; Foch to Pershing, 17 August 1918, ibid., p. 15. For Conner's view see Report of G-3 (AEF), ibid. 14:53. See also Braim, *Test of Battle*, p. 107. For the quotation about the lack of American artillery and tanks see American Battle Monuments Commission, *American Armies and Battlefields in Europe*, p. 19.

28. For the military geography and the significance of the St. Mihiel salient, see Historical Section, Army War College, "Major Operations," pp. 112–14; Braim, *Test of Battle*, p. 77; *USAWW* 14:36; Smythe, *Pershing*, p. 181; Liddell Hart, *Real War*, pp. 449–51.

29. For information concerning the German defenses and troops see Historical Section, Army War College, "Major Operations," pp. 113, 115; McEntee, *Military History of the World War*, pp. 521–24; Braim, *Test of Battle*, pp. 77–78. The quotation is from American Battle Monuments Commission, *American Armies and Battlefields in Europe*, p. 107.

30. Report of the First Army, *USAWW* 14:34; Braim, *Test of Battle*, p. 111. For the order of 16 August 1918 see McAndrew to Chief of Staff, First Army, *USAWW* 8:129–31. For Foch's expectations see his *Memoirs*, p. 397. Foch's instructions are in Foch to Pershing, 17 August 1918, *USAWW* 8:16.

31. For Haig's proposal see Haig to Foch, 27 August 1918, in Foch, *Memoirs*, p. 391. The generalissimo's favorable response is Foch to Haig, c. 27 August 1918, quoted in ibid. For Haig's role in shaping the plan for a double envelopment see Liddell Hart, *Real War*, p. 452; Millett, "Over Where? The AEF and the American Strategy for Victory, 1917–1918," p. 246; Cruttwell, *History of the Great War*, p. 558; Coffman, *War to End All Wars*, p. 270; Falls, *Great War*, pp. 380–81; Blake, ed., Haig diary, 27 August 1918, *Private Papers of Haig*, p. 325.

32. Foch's observation is in his *Memoirs*, p. 339. For the Foch plan see his memorandum for Pershing, 30 August 1918, *USAWW* 8:40–41. See also "Notes on Conversation between General Pershing and Marshal Foch at Ligny-en-Barrois," 30 August 1918, ibid., p. 36. Foch's account of the meeting on 30 August 1918 is in his *Memoirs*, p. 399.

33. Ibid.,pp. 39–40. See also Smythe, *Pershing*, pp. 175–76; Paschall, *Defeat of Imperial Germany*, p. 171. Pershing saw in Foch's proposal another effort to place American troops under French command. Pershing, *My Experiences* 2:247.

34. Pershing to Foch, 31 August 1918, *USAWW* 8:42–44. Pershing summarized his views at this time in his final report, *War Department Annual Reports, 1919* 1, 1:586, and in *My Experiences* 2:250.

35. For Foch's memorandum of 1 September 1918 see Foch, *Memoirs*, p. 400; Foch to Pershing, 1 September 1918, *USAWW* 8:46. For the meeting at Bombon on 2 September see Pershing final report, *War Department Annual Reports, 1919* 1, 1:586; "Notes on Conference between General Pershing, Marshal Foch, and General Petain at Bombon," 2 September 1918, *USAWW* 2:590–92; Foch, *Memoirs*, pp. 400–401; Braim, *Test of Battle*, pp. 82–83. On 3 September, Foch issued instructions for the general offensive. These included orders for the St. Mihiel operation. Foch, *Memoirs*, pp. 404–5; *USAWW* 8:50. On 4 September, Foch conferred with Haig at Mouchy le Chatel and communicated the agreement made with Pershing on 2 September. Edmonds, ed., *History of the Great War* 4:443–44.

36. For Smythe's observation see his *Pershing*, p. 177. For that of Liddell Hart see his *Real War*, pp. 453–54. Braim seems to agree that Pershing was influenced by personal and national considerations as well as more narrowly operational and tactical considerations. Braim, *Test of Battle*, p. 79. Pershing's defense of his decision to retain the St. Mihiel offensive is in *My Experiences* 2:253–54.

37. This summary of the American order of battle is based on Smythe, *Pershing*, pp. 182–83; Historical Section, Army War College, "Major Operations," p. 117; American Battle Monuments Commission, *American Armies and Battlefields in Europe*, pp. 109–10. Fuchs had seven divisions on line and two in reserve. The AEF staff estimated that the salient could be reinforced with two divisions in forty-eight hours and two more in seventy-two hours. Paschall, *Defeat of Imperial Germany*, p. 170. The comparison to other armies is in Douglas W. Johnson, *Battlefields of the World War: Western and Southern Fronts: A Study in Military Geography* (New York: Oxford University Press, 1921), p. 484.

38. For information about the Belfort ruse see McEntee, *Military History of the World War*, p. 525; Fox Conner to Commanding General VI Army Corps, *USAWW* 8:51; Report of French Military Mission, Berne, 12 September 1918, ibid., p. 62; Colonel A. L. Conger to unidentified journalist, 25 November 1926, ibid., p. 63; Pogue, *George Marshall* 1:173; Paschall, *Defeat of Imperial Germany*, p. 173. The Belfort ruse also included radio deception and tank movements.

39. For Hindenburg's observation see his *Out of My Life* 2:399. For the comment of 1 September 1918 on American intentions see "The Situation on the West Front on September 1, 1918," *USAWW* 11:391. For Ludendorff's view see his message to Group of Armies Gallwitz, 4 September 1918, ibid. 8:290. For exchanges concerning the imminent American offensive and the proper response to it between Composite Army C, Group of Armies Gallwitz, and the High Command, see Gallwitz to Composite Army C, 3 September 1918, ibid., pp. 289–90; Operations Section, Composite Army C, to Supreme Headquarters, ibid., p. 291; Operations Section, Composite Army C, to Group of Armies Gallwitz, 9 September 1918, ibid., pp. 291–93; Ludendorff to Group of Armies Gallwitz, 10 September 1918, ibid., p. 294; Group of Armies Gallwitz to Composite Army C, 10 September 1918, ibid., p. 295; Group of Armies Gallwitz to Supreme Headquarters, 10 September 1918, ibid., p. 296; Report of Intelligence Officer from Supreme Headquarters (Anker) to Headquarters, Group of Armies Gallwitz, 10 September 1918, ibid., p. 297; Group of Armies Gallwitz estimate

of the situation (signed Gallwitz), 11 September 1918, ibid. 11:390–91; Report, Foreign Armies Section, German Supreme Headquarters, 11 September 1918, ibid. 8:299–300; Order, Operations Section, Composite Army C, 11 September 1918, ibid., p. 300. See also McEntee, *Military History of the World War*, p. 523. Ludendorff describes his decision as follows: "Local commanders were confident in spite of my demurs. General Headquarters was reluctant to evacuate the salient, on account of the industrial centers lying behind it, and, unfortunately, did not order this step until September 8." Ludendorff, *Ludendorff's Own Story*, p. 361. For the inauguration of the Loki Movement on 11 September, see Historical Section, Army War College, "Major Operations," pp. 115–16.

40. For this intelligence information see "Summaries of Intelligence, First Army American Expeditionary Forces," mimeographed copies in Library, U.S. Army Center of Military History, Washington, D.C., pt. 2, pp. 1–3. For the evaluation of this information see *USAWW*, vol. 13: *Reports of Commander-in-Chief, A.E.F., Staff Sections and Services: Part 2* (Washington, D.C.: Government Printing Office, 1948), p. 14. For Pershing's views see his *My Experiences* 2:264–65.

41. For accounts of the operations on 12 September 1918 see McEntee, *Military History of the World War*, p. 525; G-3, First Army, Digest of Operations, *USAWW* 8:255; Pershing final report, *War Department Annual Reports, 1919* 1, 1:588. For the reports of the corps see Operation Report, IV Army Corps, 13 September 1918, *USAWW* 8:280–81; Operation Report, I Army Corps, 12 September 1918, ibid., pp. 284–85.

42. For the Loki movement see Historical Section, Army War College, "Major Operations," pp. 122–23; Order, Operations Section, Composite Army C, 12 September 1918, *USAWW* 8:303; Report, Composite Army C, 13 September 1918, ibid., p. 305; Two reports by Lieutenant General Fuchs, 19 September 1918, ibid., pp. 313–16, 318–19; German Composite Army C to Group of Armies Gallwitz, 20 September 1918, ibid., p. 322; Gallwitz to Supreme Headquarters, 21 September 1918, ibid., p. 324. See also Paschall, *Defeat of Imperial Germany*, p. 180. Liddell Hart noted the inflexible command arrangements and the delays that allowed most of the Germans to escape capture. See his *Real War*, p. 457.

43. For the conclusion of operations see Pershing final report, *War Department Annual Reports, 1919* 1, 1:588; Historical Section, Army War College, "Major Operations," p. 126; Operations Report, I Army Corps, 13 September 1918, *USAWW* 8:285–86; Operations Report, IV Army Corps, ibid., p. 281; First Army Field Order No. 11, 13 September 1918, ibid., p. 261; Group of Armies Gallwitz to Other Army Groups, 14 September 1918, ibid., p. 308; Gallwitz Order, 14 September 1918, ibid., p. 307; Report of Operations, Group of Armies Gallwitz to Supreme Headquarters, 14 September 1918, ibid., pp. 309–10. Smythe aptly summarizes the results of the battle in *Pershing*, p. 186. See also Paschall, *Defeat of Imperial Germany*, p. 178, 180–81. For the postbattle views of Ludendorff and von Gallwitz, see Ludendorff, *Ludendorff's Own Story*, pp. 364–65, and Operations Section, Group of Armies Gallwitz, to Supreme Headquarters, 16 September 1918, *USAWW* 8:311–12. To Gallwitz's implied request for major reinforcements, Hindenburg responded in angry language: "I am not willing to admit that one American division is worth 2 German. Wherever commanders and troops have been determined to hold their position and the artillery has been well organized, even weak German divisions have repulsed the mass attacks of American divisions and inflicted especially heavy casualties on the enemy." Hindenburg to Gallwitz, 17 September 1918, ibid., p. 312.

44. For Marshall's opinion see his *Memoirs of My Services in the World War*, p. 147. For other proponents of the attack see Smythe, *Pershing*, p. 188.

45. Hunter Liggett, *AEF: Ten Years Ago in France* (New York: Dodd, Mead, 1928), pp. 159–61; Liddell Hart, *Real War*, pp. 459–60. For a parallel analysis see Cruttwell, *History of the Great War*, p. 560.

46. Pershing final report, *War Department Annual Reports, 1919* 1, 1:589. See also Pershing, *My Experiences* 2:272–73.

47. For the gibe that the Americans relieved the Germans at St. Mihiel, see Smythe, *Pershing*, p. 185. His strictures on the American performance are in ibid., pp. 188–89. See also Johnson, *Battlefields of the World War*, p. 404. He emphasizes the weakness of the German resistance, given the Loki movement. He thought the bag of prisoners "disappointing," considering the fast pace of the American movement. For Cruttwell's view see his *History of the Great War*, p. 560. Liddell Hart notes that the withdrawal made things easy for the Americans but that delay in executing it led to great difficulties for the German units in the salient. Liddell Hart, *Real War*, pp. 456–57. For a much more favorable evaluation of the American attack see Coffman, *War to End All Wars*, p. 262. The American histories of the AEF usually follow the views of General Pershing.

48. Gallwitz to Supreme Headquarters, 21 September 1918, *USAWW* 8:324; Report of Operations Section, Group of Armies Gallwitz (telegram, Composite Army C to Group of Armies Gallwitz), 20 September 1918, ibid., p. 320. For the German critique by Captain Weniger see ibid. 11:413–14.

CHAPTER 6. FOCH'S GENERAL COUNTEROFFENSIVE, PART I: 26 SEPTEMBER–23 OCTOBER 1918

1. For the German posture see Ludendorff, *Ludendorff's Own Story* 2:348–50. The quotation about shirking is from ibid., p. 350. The statement about resistance and peace terms is in *USAWW* 11:402. For statistics about the declining number of German divisions see Maurice, *Last Four Months*, p. 119. Foch's fear of a German withdrawal are expressed in his *Memoirs*, pp. 387–88. It is of interest that later on, in October, Ludendorff developed plans for just such a move, too late to have any effect.

2. For Foch's description of his intention see his *Memoirs*, pp. 403–4. Haig was supportive of Foch's desire to end the war as soon as possible. See his comment to Lord Milner on 10 September 1918 in Terraine, *To Win a War*, p. 144.

3. For Foch's directive see *USAWW* 8:50. See also Foch, *Memoirs*, pp. 404–5. Foch reported this plan to Haig on 4 September 1918 at Mouchy le Chatel. See Edmonds, ed., *History of the Great War* 4:443–44.

4. For the plans for an attack in Flanders see Foch, *Memoirs*, pp. 417–18. See also Maurice, *Last Four Months*, pp. 143–44; Cruttwell, *History of the Great War*, p. 564.

5. For the various offensives see Foch, *Memoirs*, pp. 408–9; Cruttwell, *History of the Great War*, p. 563; Edmonds, *Short History of World War I*, p. 409. Between the British forces attacking toward Cambrai and the Franco-American forces attacking toward Mezieres were the French Fifth and Tenth Armies, a group of twenty-eight divisions. The British Fifth Army (nine divisions) was located between the forces marshaled for the British offensive in Picardy and the attack in Flanders. The total of Allied divisions on the western front was 217, including thirty-nine double-sized American divisions. (Three more were to arrive before 11 November.) The Germans had a total of 197 divisions on the western front. The British considered that only fifty-one of the reserve divisions were fit for combat. Ibid., p. 410. For the observation in the British official history see Edmonds, ed., *History of the Great War* 5:iv.

6. For the notes of 25 and 27 September 1918 see Foch, *Memoirs*, pp. 410–11. For the note of 25 September 1918 see *USAWW* 8:80. For the note of 27 September 1918 see Edmonds, ed., *History of the Great War* 5:8–9.

7. For terrain features of the Meuse-Argonne sector see Johnson, *Battlefields of the World War*, pp. 407–8; Braim, *Test of Battle*, p. 87; McEntee, *Military History of the World War*, p. 535; Pershing, *My Experiences* 2:282; American Battle Monuments Commission, *American Armies and Battlefields in Europe*, pp. 169–70. For an interesting analysis of the terrain made prior to the battle, see Report, R. T. Ward, 7 September 1918, *USAWW*, vol. 9: *Meuse-Argonne Operations of the American Expeditionary Forces*, pp. 73–75. See also Liggett, *AEF*, p. 165.

8. For information about the German fortifications see Historical Section, Army War College, "Major Operations," p. 165; Braim, *Test of Battle*, p. 89; Smythe, *Pershing*, pp. 190–91; Pershing, *My Experiences* 2:282–83, 322; American Battle Monuments Commission, *American Armies and Battlefields in Europe*, pp. 169–70; Johnson, *Battlefields of the World War*, p. 405. The names of the three main defensive positions were those of witches that appeared in an opera by Wagner.

9. For the German order of battle see Braim, *Test of Battle*, pp. 96–97; *USAWW* 9:34; Pershing, *My Experiences* 2:290; Edmonds, ed., *History of the Great War* 5:10–11.

10. For the concentration see Historical Section, Army War College, "Major Operations," p. 175; Memorandum by Col. George C. Marshall, Jr., 19 November 1918, *USAWW* 9:64–66; Pershing, *My Experiences* 2:285; Liggett, *AEF*, p. 165; Braim, *Test of Battle*, pp. 90–92; Pogue, *George Marshall* 1:175–79. For the French troops in the First Army see Historical Section, Army War College, "Major Operations," p. 173.

11. Pershing, *My Experiences* 2:286–87; Millett, *Bullard*, p. 39; Smythe, *Pershing*, p. 192. Smythe notes that many officers had been sent to a staff school at Langres. George Marshall claimed that "the confusion and mismanagement resulting from this was tremendous." Pershing's staff asked the corps commanders to convey lessons learned during the St. Mihiel operation to the new divisions: "the passage of wire, the employment of tanks in liaison with the infantry, and the circulation on the roads." Drum to Corps Commanders, 17 September 1918, *USAWW* 9:79.

12. This interpretation is drawn from Braim, *Test of Battle*, p. 93. See also Pershing final report, *War Department Annual Reports, 1919* 1, 1:590. For Petain's order of 16 September 1918 to General Commanding the French Armies of the Center and Pershing see *USAWW* 8:69. Pershing's comment on the importance of the American front is in his *My Experiences* 2:281.

13. Smythe, *Pershing*, p. 193; Historical Section, Army War College, "Major Operations," pp. 166–67. For a careful summary of the American planning for the Meuse-Argonne offensive see Special Operations Report by Col. R. T. Ward, "The Plans for the Attack," 5 January 1919, *USAWW* 9:129–30. The French units assigned to the First Army, all located east of the Meuse, were the II Colonial Corps, the XVII Corps, and the 5th Cavalry Division, a total of seven divisions. Historical Section, Army War College, "Major Operations," p. 173.

14. Field Orders No. 20, First Army, 20 September 1918, *USAWW* 2:80–88; Braim, *Test of Battle*, p. 94; American Battle Monuments Commission, *American Armies and Battlefields in Europe*, pp. 172–73. For the First Army's order of battle see Smythe, *Pershing*, p. 195; Edmonds, ed., *History of the Great War* 5:3. For the plans concerning use of the tank corps, air service, and army artillery, see *USAWW* 9:96–100 Paschall, *Defeat of Imperial Germany*, pp. 184–85. The statistics are from Pershing final report, *War Department Annual Reports, 1919* 1, 1:592. The Historical Section, Army War College described the distribution of these forces: "The First Army had about 350 long-range heavy guns

and some light and anti-aircraft artillery. Each corps had about 600 pieces of artillery of 75 mm and 155 mm calibers, and from 140 to 200 pieces of heavier caliber. Four balloon companies and four air squadrons were assigned to each corps, except the III, which was given an additional air squadron. The III Corps had no tank battalions assigned, whereas the V Corps had eleven, and the I Corps, three." "Major Operations," p. 172.

15. Coffman, *War to End All Wars*, pp. 300–301; Pershing, *My Experiences* 2:293; Braim, *Test of Battle*, p. 94. For Millett's comment see his *Bullard*, p. 399.

16. For a detailed account of the first two days of battle see Braim, *Test of Battle*, pp. 97–110. For the reports of the three corps, all of which reported early gains and then stiffening resistance, see I Corps Operation Report, Noon 26 September to Noon 27 September 1918, *USAWW* 9:166–68; V Corps Operation Report, Noon 26 September to Noon 27 September 1918, ibid., pp. 169–70; III Corps Operation Report, Noon 26 September to Noon 27 September 1918, ibid., p. 171. For Pershing's view, which noted strong enemy defenses, especially machine-gun and artillery fire, see his *My Experiences* 2:297. For the failure to capture Montfaucon see Paschall, *Defeat of Imperial Germany*, p. 186.

17. Robert Lee Bullard, *Personalities and Reminiscences of the War* (Garden City, N.Y.: Doubleday, Page, 1925), p. 269. For the G-2's estimate of the situation on 27 September 1918, which stressed the importance of enemy machine-gun and artillery fire, see *USAWW* 9:141. For Pershing's message see Drum to Corps Commanders, 27 September 1918, ibid., p. 140.

18. For I Corps Operation reports see ibid., pp. 172–73, 176–77, 181–83. For III Corps reports see pp. 175, 180, 185. For V Corps reports see pp. 173–74, 179, 183. These reports cover the period noon to noon for 27–28 September, 28–29 September, and 29–30 September.

19. For Pershing's exhortation of his troops see General Orders No. 20, 28 September 1918, *USAWW* 9:144. For the pause see Field Order No. 32, 29 September 1918, ibid., p. 157. For the relief of the exhausted divisions see Braim, *Test of Battle*, p. 111. For the organization of the defense see Historical Section, Army War College, "Major Operations," pp. 177–78. Like most official accounts, this American version says nothing about the failure to meet objectives specified in the orders for the attack of 26 September: "The first push of the French-American offensive had been successful. A brief respite of comparative quiet had been used for reorganization, relief, and improvement of communications. West of the Meuse, preparations were making to extend the offensive toward the menacing heights of the Meuse." Ibid., p. 180. For Smythe's observation see his *Pershing*, p. 200. See also Report of G-3 (AEF), *USAWW* 14:44, another document that neglects many important negative features of the battle. Ludendorff's summary of the early battle reflected satisfaction with the outcome. Ludendorff, *Ludendorff's Own Story* 2:373.

20. For the report of a German officer assigned to Battle Group East, General Command, 5th Reserve Corps see Ralph Lutz, ed., *Fall of the German Empire* (Stanford, Calif.: Stanford University Press, 1932), 1:661–62.

21. For these developments see Foch, *Memoirs*, p. 413; Maurice, *Last Four Months*, p. 152. After the successful attack of the 2d Division on Blanc Mont on 3 October 1918 led by the Marine General Lejeune, the organization was ordered to the Meuse-Argonne. For this purpose the 36th Division relieved the 2d Division on 10 October and advanced 21 kilometers to the Aisne River with the French Fourth Army. It was relieved on 28 October 1918. For the operation at Blanc Mont and subsequent events see Report of the G-3 (AEF), *USAWW* 14:51; American Battle Monuments Commission,

American Armies and Battlefields in Europe, pp. 333–35; McEntee, *Military History of the World War*, p. 539; Pershing, *My Experiences* 2:324–27; Millett, *Semper Fidelis*, pp. 313–14; Historical Section, Army War College, *Blanc Mont*, Monograph No. 9 (Washington, D.C.: Government Printing Office, 1922). For the French tendency to adjust their advance to the pace of the Americans see Liddell Hart, *Real War*, pp. 462–63.

22. Pershing's letter to Baker, 2 October 1918, is quoted in Pershing, *My Experiences* 2:313–18. For his comments on the result of the initial attack and the effective German resistance, see p. 300.

23. For American efforts to deceive the enemy concerning the whereabouts of the attack, see Buat to Commanding Generals, Group of Armies of the East, *USAWW* 8:75. A German report that dismissed the probability of an early attack either between the Meuse and the Moselle or the Meuse and the Argonne (incorrect) assumed that the French would attack in Champagne (correct) and the Americans against Composite Army C from the St. Mihiel salient (incorrect). Ludendorff report, 22 September 1918, ibid. 11:415. The First Army "Summary of Intelligence" reported information from captured Germans that indicated the enemy knew of the coming attack. "Summary of Intelligence," 25, 26 September 1918, pp. 2, 9. Smythe notes that the enemy withdrew its outposts to the first defensive position and ordered reinforcements prior to the attack. Smythe, *Pershing*, p. 194. For several days after the beginning of the offensive on the Meuse-Argonne, German intelligence sources continued to suspect that the main effort would come elsewhere, either between the Meuse and the Moselle aimed at Metz or farther south. Intelligence Officer from Supreme Headquarters at Headquarters, Group of Armies German Crown Prince, 27 September 1918, *USAWW* 9:515; Operations Section, German Fifth Army, to Group of Armies Gallwitz, ibid., p. 518; War Diary, Group of Armies Gallwitz, 28 September 1918, ibid., p. 520; Operations Section, German Fifth Army, 1 October 1918, ibid., p. 531.

24. For criticisms of American inexperience see Millett, "Over Where? The American Strategy for Victory, 1917–1918," in Kenneth J. Hagan and William R. Roberts, eds., *Against All Enemies: Interpretations of American Military History from Colonial Times to the Present* (Westport, Conn.: Greenwood, 1986), p. 249; Maurice, *Last Four Months*, pp. 184–85; Coffman, *War to End All Wars*, pp. 313–14. The report of the First Army on the Meuse-Argonne battle notes difficulties with liaison and infantry-artillery coordination. *USAWW* 9:187. See also two reports by Col. R. T. Ward, First Army G-3, 29 September 1918, "Study of the Situation Considering the Defensive Plan," *USAWW* 9:148; "Study of Changes in Zones of Action of Corps," ibid., p. 149. German observations noted the American inexperience. "Summary of Intelligence," 5, 20 October 1918, p. 7. Tanks proved helpful in the initial days, but mechanical difficulties soon reduced their numbers to insignificance. A huge air armada of 821 aircraft greatly aided the initial attack, but it became less effective as the advance took the First Army closer to enemy air fields and farther from its own. Operations Report, First Army, *USAWW* 9:186. Pershing himself noted the problems inherent in the use of inexperienced divisions. Pershing, *My Experiences* 2:303. Pershing might have used experienced divisions, if he had accepted Foch's suggestion that he forego the St. Mihiel operation.

25. For supply problems see Coffman, *War to End All Wars*, pp. 300–303, 313; report of First Army, *USAWW* 9:187; Pershing final report, *War Department Annual Reports, 1919* 1, 1:593; Maurice, *Last Four Months*, p. 186; Cruttwell, *History of the Great War*, p. 567. See also the operations reports of the three American corps cited in note 18. For Liggett's observation see his *AEF*, pp. 178–79. For an observation like that of Liggett's, see General Bullard's comment in his *Personalities and Reminiscences of the War*,

p. 271. Pershing's comment on the logistical tangle minimized its significance. Pershing, *My Experiences* 2:304.

26. Liddell Hart, *Real War*, pp. 380, 463–65; Braim, *Test of Battle*, p. 153.

27. For Haig's view see his diary, 1 October 1918, in Blake, ed., *Private Papers of Haig*, p. 329. For Mordacq's view see Smythe, *Pershing*, p. 200.

28. Petain inaugurated this episode by complaining about American delays. Petain to Foch, 30 September 1918, *USAWW* 8:82. The order to Petain to reorganize the American command is Foch to Petain, 30 September 1918, ibid. 8:81.

29. After Weygand failed to obtain acceptance of the plan, Pershing wrote to Foch, 2 October 1918, explaining his reasons for opposing it. Ibid., p. 83. Foch's concurrence and his proviso are in Foch to Pershing, 2 October 1918, ibid., p. 85. For Foch's account of this episode see his *Memoirs*, pp. 412–13. Pershing describes these events in his *My Experiences* 2:307. Haig's summary of the episode is in Blake, ed., *Private Papers of Haig*, p. 330.

30. For this information see Smythe, *Pershing*, p. 204. Smythe thinks that Foch had the authority to act because his ideas were in the "strategic" realm. This is debatable. Perhaps Smythe confuses "grand tactics" or what is now referred to as "the operational art" with strategy. In any event, Foch chose not to pursue the matter; as Smythe notes, he normally sought to persuade rather than to coerce the national commanders-in-chief. See also Coffman, *War to End All Wars*, pp. 339–40. For the Foch-Haig exchange see Haig diary, 6 October 1918, Blake ed., *Private Papers of Haig*, p. 330.

31. For the British attack see Edmonds, ed., *History of the Great War* 5:14–56, 115–23, 146–57; Foch, *Memoirs*, p. 415; Edmonds, *Short History of World War I*, pp. 412–14; Maurice, *Last Four Months*, p. 153. For the importance of combined operations see ibid., pp. 138–41.

32. Foch, *Memoirs*, pp. 415–16; Maurice, *Last Four Months*, pp. 158–60; Edmonds, *Short History of World War I*, pp. 414–15; Blaxland, *Amiens*, 231–36.

33. For the operations of the American II Corps and its two divisions, the 27th and 30th, see Summary of Operations, Fourth Army, BEF, 29 September 1918, *USAWW* 7:229–31; Operations Report, II Corps, 18 December 1918, ibid., p. 787; Operations Report, 27th Division, 29 September 1918, ibid., pp. 308–10, 313–14; Operations Report, 3 November 1918, 30th Division, ibid., pp. 325–27; Summary of Operations, British Fourth Army, ibid., pp. 249–50; Operations Report, II Corps, 30 September 1918, ibid., p. 252; Operations Report, Australian Corps, "Capture of the Beaurevoir Defenses and Montbrehain September 20 to October 6," ibid., pp. 272–74. For many years, historians accepted Monash's view that the inexperienced 27th Division had failed to take measures to prevent German troops located in the Bellicourt Tunnel from emerging after the Americans had passed and attacking them from the rear. This stratagem had cut off some American troops. However, C. E. W. Bean, the Australian official historian, believes on the basis of extensive research that the Americans simply became confused in the fog after losing their officers. The Germans forced them to retreat or cut them off by launching conventional frontal counterattacks. Charles E. W. Bean, *ANZAC to Amiens: A Shorter History of the Australian Fighting Services in the First World War* (Canberra: Australian War Memorial, 1961), pp. 491–92. Terraine accepts this interpretation. *To Win a War*, p. 174. For comments on the fortifications in front of the American corps see the observations of Maj. Gen. E. M. Lewis, commanding the 30th Division. Operations Report, 3 November 1918, ibid., p. 325. For an extensive and cogent analysis of the difficulties that the II Corps encountered in its attack, see the Operations Report by Lt. Col. Wade H. Hayes, 15 October 1918, ibid., pp. 277–81.

34. Foch, *Memoirs*, pp. 418–20; Maurice, *Last Four Months*, p. 155; Edmonds, *Short*

History of World War I, pp. 415–16. The two American units sent to the Flanders Group of Armies were the 37th and 91st Divisions.

35. For the German view see Memorandum, German Eighteenth Army, 2 October 1918, *USA WW* 7:863–64. General von Hutier signed this document. The American information is in Operations Report, 30th Division, 30 September 1918, ibid., p. 246. Maurice notes the existence of Allied pressure from Dixmude to the Meuse. Maurice, *Last Four Months*, p. 160.

36. Liddell Hart, *Real War*, p. 380, 462; Maurice, *Last Four Months*, p. 159. See also Wilson, *Myriad Faces of War*, p. 600.

37. Ludendorff, *Ludendorff's Own Story* 2:376. Liddell Hart gives the following account of Ludendorff's behavior on 29 September: "Ludendorff was studying the problem in his room at the Hotel Britannique at Spa—an ominously named choice of headquarters! Examination only seemed to make it more insoluble, and in a rising outburst of fear and passion he bemoaned his troubles—especially his lack of tanks—and berated all those whom he considered as having thwarted his efforts—the jealous staffs, the defeatist Reichstag, the too humanitarian Kaiser, and the submarine-obsessed navy. Gradually he worked himself into a frenzy, until suddenly, with foam on his lips, he fell to the floor in a fit. And that evening it was a physically as well as mentally shaken man who took the precipitate decision to appeal for an armistice, saying that the collapse of the Bulgarian front had upset all his dispositions." Liddell Hart, *Real War*, p. 378. See also Kitchin, *Silent Dictatorship*, pp. 253–59; Goerlitz, ed., *The Kaiser and His Court*, p. 397. The views of the foreign office representative, Grunau, are in Lutz, ed., *Fall of the German Empire* 2:460.

38. For the intricate discussions that took place in Berlin and their outcome see Klaus Schwabe, *Woodrow Wilson, Revolutionary Germany, and Peacemaking, 1918–1919: Missionary Diplomacy and the Realities of Power* (Chapel Hill: University of North Carolina Press, 1985), pp. 33–38. The quotation is from ibid., p. 37. See also Ritter, *Sword and Scepter* 4:242–43.

39. Ibid., pp. 379, 383–84. For Ludendorff's insistence on immediate action see Edmonds, ed., *History of the Great War* 5:113. Ludendorff later denied that he was in a great hurry because of fear that the army would collapse very soon. Ludendorff, *Ludendorff's Own Story* 2:384. For a summary of these events see Maurice, *Last Four Months*, pp. 162–63. For Ludendorff's views on Wilson's probable behavior see his *Ludendorff's Own Story* 2:374. For the acceptance of von Hintze's plan see Ritter, *Sword and Scepter* 4:344. Ritter argues that Ludendorff wanted a breathing space for his troops, but he considers that a resumption of hostilities was impossible. Ibid., p. 341.

40. For von dem Bussche's statement see Ludendorff, *The General Staff and Its Problems* 2:631–32. The statement took special note of the American role. This reinforcement allowed the enemy to replenish its ranks. "*The American troops were not in themselves of any special value or in any way superior to ours.* At those points where they had obtained initial successes, thanks to their employment in mass, their attacks had been beaten off in spite of their superior numbers. But it was a vital advantage that they could take over large sections of the front and thus make it possible for the English and French to relieve their own veteran divisions and create an almost inexhaustible reserve." Ibid., p. 631. See also Maurice, *Last Four Months*, pp. 166–69.

41. Maurice, *Last Four Months*, p. 174. See also Edmonds, ed., *History of the Great War* 5:143–45. The note to which Hindenburg referred is discussed in ibid., p. 173; Ludendorff, *Ludendorff's Own Story* 2:173.

42. For details of Prince Max's appointment see Ritter, *Sword and Scepter* 4:345–48. His explanation of the peace initiative to the Reichstag on 5 October 1918 is in Lutz, ed.,

Fall of the German Empire 2:376–82. For the Prince Max–President Wilson exchanges covered in this paragraph see James Brown Scott, ed., *Official Statements of War Aims and Peace Proposals, December 1916 to November 1918* (Washington, D.C.: Carnegie Endowment, 1921), pp. 409–14, 418–19, 420–21. Austria-Hungary had earlier dispatched a peace feeler. For the note of 16 September and the American response of 17 September see ibid., pp. 386–89, 396. For a discussion of the president's note of 8 October see Schwabe, *Woodrow Wilson, Revolutionary Germany, and Peacemaking*, pp. 44–47. Schwabe's summary is in Ibid., p. 44.

43. Trask, *The United States in the Supreme War Council*, pp. 153–54. Bliss is quoted in ibid., p. 155.

44. The notes of 14, 20, and 23 October 1918 are in Scott, *War Aims and Peace Proposals*, pp. 421–23, 429–31, 434–36. Max is quoted in Trask, *Captains & Cabinets*, p. 327. A note from the Entente leaders sent on 9 October warned Wilson not to accept any proposal for an armistice that might permit resumption of hostilities. Hankey, *Supreme Command* 2:855. For Schwabe's comments on the note of 14 October see *Woodrow Wilson, Revolutionary Germany, and Peacemaking*, pp. 54–57. The German navy opposed an end to submarine warfare, but the kaiser supported the civilians who wanted to call it off. For the German-American exchange of 20 and 23 October see ibid., 58–59, 72. Ritter is critical of Wilson's conduct during the negotiations, labeling his attitude ambiguous and contradictory. He insisted on self-determination but also on the destruction of "willful autocracy." This approach, he thinks, denied self-determination to Germany. He criticizes Wilson's preoccupation with the peace negotiations and his neglect of armistice terms, which, he alleges, gave the Allies an opening to impose a peace of vengeance. Ritter, *Sword and Scepter* 4:351–59. The difficulty with Ritter's position is that it seems unreasonable to expect Wilson to serve as defeated Germany's advocate in dealings with the Allies, even if it was in the American interest to avoid a Carthaginian peace. Wilson pursued his own agenda, which was couched in terms of American interests and aspirations, a not unreasonable position. Ritter blames Germany's defeat on excessive militarism, but he also maintains that the bitter outcome of the peace negotiations, deemed inconsistent with the Fourteen Points, stemmed from Wilson's incompetence. A suggestion from the Allies on 9 October led to the American decision to send Colonel House to Paris. He left the United States on 16 October. Hankey, *Supreme Command* 2:855.

45. For Liddell Hart's views see his *Real War*, p. 379.

CHAPTER 7. FOCH'S GENERAL COUNTEROFFENSIVE,
PART II: 4 OCTOBER–11 NOVEMBER 1918

1. Foch to Petain, 4 October 1918, *USAWW* 8:86.

2. For a description of the planning and the quotation see Operations Report, First Army, ibid. 9:227–28. See also Historical Section, Army War College, "Major Operations," p. 181; Braim, *Test of Battle*, pp. 116–17; Pershing, *My Experiences* 2:322–23. Pershing lists the order of battle as III Corps (33d, 4th, and 80th Divisions); V Corps (3d and 32d Divisions with 42d and 91st Divisions in reserve); I Corps (1st, 28th, and 77th Divisions with 82d Division and French 5th Cavalry Division in reserve). Three divisions, the 29th, 35th, and 92d, made up the army reserve.

3. The quotations are from First Army Operations Reports, 6–7 October 1918, *USAWW* 9:221, 225. For accounts of the battle see Pershing, *My Experiences* 2:323; Report of G-3 (AEF), *USAWW* 14:44; Operations Report, First Army, ibid., p. 228.

4. For Pershing's view see his *My Experiences* 2:324. He thought that the enemy lost as heavily as his own units. The increase in the number of divisions directly engaged on the German side is noted in Report of G-3 (AEF), *USAWW* 14:44. For the American estimate of the effect of operations on the Meuse-Argonne front at this time see Operations Report, First Army, ibid. 9:228.

5. For Braim's use of the term "uninspired tactics" see his *Test of Battle*, p. 122. His comments on the trade of bodies for bullets are on p. 116. Marshall is quoted in Millett, "Over Where? The AEF and the American Strategy for Victory, 1917–1918," p. 249. Millett believes that it was possible by 1918 to make limited gains against strong positions by achieving surprise and by using "sophisticated infantry tactics," but the difficulty was to sustain the attack when it moved beyond effective support from artillery. The Americans learned from experience and applied sound doctrine during the later battles, especially after Pershing turned over the command of the First Army to General Liggett. While a corps commander he recognized the futility of massed infantry advances against strong defensive positions.

6. For a general account of operations during this period see the Report of the First Army, *USAWW* 9:253–54. For the clearance of the Argonne forest see Petain Memorandum, 5 October 1918, ibid. 8:86; Field Orders No. 44, 6 October 1918, ibid. 9:222; Report of G-3 (AEF), ibid. 14:44; Operations Reports, First Army, Noon to Noon, 8–9 October and 9–10 October 1918, ibid., pp. 245, 247; Liddell Hart, *Real War*, p. 466.

These activities led to the relief of the so-called Lost Battalion, six companies of the 308th Infantry, 77th Division, two companies of the 306th Machine Gun Battalion, and one company of the 307th Infantry. This detachment was never lost; it was cut off for five days (2–7 October) in the Argonne forest near Charlevaux Mill. American Battle Monuments Division, *American Armies and Battlefields in Europe*, p. 337; Coffman, *The War to End All Wars*, pp. 323–24. Sergeant Alvin C. York, a member of the 32th Infantry, 82d Division, single-handedly captured 132 Germans near Chatel-Chehery on 8 October 1918. Ibid., p. 324.

For the attack east of the Meuse see Field Orders No. 39, *USAWW* 9:215–16; Field Orders No. 46, 7 October 1918, ibid., p. 232; Field Orders No. 47, ibid., p. 233; Report of G-3 (AEF), ibid. 14:44; Braim, *Test of Battle*, p. 123; Coffman, *War to End All Wars*, pp. 325–26; Pershing, *My Experiences* 2:331.

Pershing's statement about the severity of the fighting is on p. 337. He argues that the attack was successful in that its main purpose was "to increase the fighting front of the army and thus consume the maximum number of German divisions. In this latter respect, the attack was particularly successful, aimed as it was directly at the pivot of the German line on the Western Front." Ibid., p. 332. Pershing here identifies his main purpose in this operation: to impose attrition on the German army. Earlier his main purpose was to break through the Hindenburg line and seize the Carignan-Sedan railroad. This apparent inconsistency reflected the failure of his attempts to achieve a rapid penetration of the Hindenburg line. Whatever his intent, his principal accomplishment was attrition, but at the expense of even greater casualties among his own troops. In any event, the results of the attacks on the Argonne and east of the Meuse straightened the American line, creating an opportunity to reorganize for a continued offensive. Operations Report, First Army, Noon 8 October to Noon 9 October 1918, *USAWW* 9:245. See also Pershing final report, *War Department Annual Reports, 1919* 1, 1:593–94. Ludendorff's view is in his *Ludendorff's Own Story* 2:404. Millett notes that only the III Corps had advanced much by about 12 October 1918. Its gains on that day cost nearly 10,000 casualties. "There had been a great deal wrong with the First Army's offensive, from the tactics of its rifle platoons to the Army scheme of maneuver, but Pershing, having committed his army, his nation's honor, and his reputation to battle, would not halt the offensive. If he had done so, it would have been admission that his dream of an independent American army playing a decisive role in the defeat of Germany was nothing more than another delusion of the Great War. He would have no answers for either his own government or the Allies when they asked why more American divisions could not be placed under French and British commanders." Millett, *Bullard*, p. 411.

7. Pershing's statements are in Pershing, *My Experiences* 2:332, 337. The results of the attacks on the Argonne and east of the Meuse are in Operations Report, First Army, Noon 8 October to Noon 9 October 1918, *USAWW* 9:245. See also Pershing final report, *War Department Annual Reports, 1919* 1, 1:593–94. Ludendorff's view is in his *Ludendorff's Own Story* 2:404. For Millett's observations see his Bullard, p. 411.

8. For Haig's message see G-1, American II Corps, to CG, 30th Division, 7 October 1918, *USAWW* 7:395. For Foch's summary of the actions around 8 October 1918 see his *Memoirs*, pp. 413–17. For the operations of the 30th Division of the American II Corps in the British Fourth Army see G-3, 30th Division, to GHQ, AEF, 10 October 1918, ibid., p. 488; War Diary, 30th Division, 10 October 1918, ibid., p. 489. Ludendorff noted that the Allies made progress very slowly despite overwhelming superiority in manpower, but he also reported the withdrawal of the German forces to the line Laon–Marle–Sissone–Aisne from Rethel on his right to Grandpre on his left. Ludendorff, *Ludendorff's Own Story*, pp. 403–4. See also Foch, *Memoirs*, p. 415. Foch recounts the advance of the Flanders Group of Armies on pp. 429–30.

9. For the difficulties that developed during the period 26 September–10 October see Smythe, *Pershing*, pp. 206–7. He notes among other things the losses resulting from the great influenza epidemic of 1918. For Pershing's evaluation see Report of G-3 (AEF), *USAWW* 14:45. Haig reported the decision to keep the 27th and 30th Divisions with the British Fourth Army in his diary for 23 October 1918. Blake, ed., *Private Papers of Haig*, p. 335.

10. For the replacement problem see Pershing final report, *War Department Annual Reports, 1919* 1, 1:594; Pershing, *My Experiences* 2:328; Report of G-1 (AEF), *USAWW* 12:115–16, 148; Report of the G-3 (AEF), ibid. 14:53; Paschall, *Defeat of Imperial Germany*, p. 191. For Pershing's complaints about the War Department's failure to provide replacements see his *My Experiences* 2:310–11, and his cable of 2 November 1918 discussed in Report of G-1 (AEF), *USAWW* 12:116. For reduction of divisional strength by four thousand troops, necessitating a corresponding reduction in size of companies, see McAndrew to Liggett and Bullard, 22 October 1918, ibid. 8:99. Nenninger maintains that "the shortages occurred because the AEF expanded more rapidly than planned, casualties were heavier than expected, and the management of the replacement system was poor." Timothy K. Nenninger, "American Military Effectiveness during the First World War," in Millett and Murray, eds., *Military Effectiveness* 1:123–24.

11. Pershing's comment on the difficulties of the period 1–11 October 1918 is in his *My Experiences* 2:320. The observation by one of Pershing's officers, Terry Allen, is in S. L. A. Marshall, *World War I*, p. 445. Pershing's explanation of the reason for changes in command arrangements is in his final report, *War Department Annual Reports, 1919* 1, 1:594. For Braim's comments on these changes see his *Test of Battle*, p. 129. The changes in command were: Liggett to First Army, Hines to III Corps, Dickman to I Corps, Muir to IV Corps, Summerall to V Corps. Cameron relinquished command of V Corps and returned to the 4th Division. For the activation of the Second Army composed of the American IV Corps and the French II Colonial Corps with

Bullard in command, see Field Orders No. 60, *USAWW* 9:257, 259; Pershing, *My Experiences* 2:336; Pershing to Foch, 11 October 1918, *USAWW* 8:88; Pershing to Petain, 11 October 1918, ibid., p. 90; Report of G-3 (AEF), ibid. 14:45.

12. For Pershing's activity see his *My Experiences* 2:383; Braim, *Test of Battle*, p. 131. For the relationship with Foch and Petain see Foch to Pershing, 16 October 1918, *USAWW* 8:97.

13. For Vandiver's account of the events of 12–13 October 1918 see his *Black Jack* 2:972–76. It is conceivable that Weygand explored some such arrangement with Pershing given the difficulties that the First Army had experienced in the Meuse-Argonne offensive and the desires of Clemenceau, but it is most unlikely that he delivered an order. Surely Clemenceau would like to have seen the last of Pershing, but to have him relieved of the command of an army in the midst of a desperate battle would have constituted a powerful affront to the United States. Braim also questions Vandiver's view and reports that Donald Smythe took the same position in a conversation with him. Neither Foch nor Pershing mention the incident, but Vandiver argues that they omitted it from their memoirs out of courtesy to each other. Braim, *Test of Battle*, pp. 130–31. Of interest is that George Marshall wrote to Colonel de Chambrun on 13 October concerning the state of the new divisions that had served in the initial phases of the battle. They had "become exhausted physically more quickly than the older divisions, owing to the inexperience of the men, officers and staffs. They must be moved out into the open into adequate shelter in order to quickly rejuvenate them. These moves must be accomplished with a minimum of physical effort and in a minimum of time if the divisions are to participate further in the present battle." Bland and Ritenour, eds., *Papers of Marshall* 1:163.

14. Notes on conversation between Foch and Pershing at Bombon, 13 October 1918, *USAWW* 8:92–94.

15. For Clemenceau's letter, 21 October 1918, see Foch, *Memoirs*, pp. 434–36. For Foch's reply of 23 October 1918 see ibid., pp. 437–38. See also Coffman, *War to End All Wars*, p. 340. General Maurice echoed Foch's comments on the difficulties of new armies, comparing the trials of the First Army with those of the British army during the first battle of the Somme in 1916. Maurice, *Last Four Months*, p. 182. Secretary of War Baker had a conversation in October 1918 with Clemenceau, which suggests that the long dispute over amalgamation influenced the French leader even at this late stage of the war. See Baker's introduction to Frothingham, *The American Reinforcement in the World War*, p. xxxi.

16. Pershing, *My Experiences* 2:350; Joseph Douglas Lawrence, *Fighting Soldier: The AEF in 1918*, Robert Ferrell, ed. (Boulder: Colorado Associated University Press, 1985), p. 88; Liggett, *AEF*, pp. 206–8; Bullard, *Personalities and Reminiscences of the War*, pp. 266–67. Bullard had noted straggling during the earlier Aisne-Marne offensive. "Popular impressions to the contrary notwithstanding, we had in our army dead-beats and deserters, evaders of battle and danger. . . . It is well for posterity to know that Americans were not all model soldiers, not all faithful. At the end of the war Paris was filled with American criminals and cried out about it." Ibid., p. 252. See also Falls, *Great War*, p. 353.

17. For a good description of Ludendorff's plan for a fighting retreat to the Antwerp-Meuse line see Maurice, *Last Four Months*, pp. 189–90. The decision to fight a delaying action while retreating gradually to the Antwerp-Meuse line was foreshadowed in Hindenburg to Group of Armies German Crown Prince, 30 September 1918, *USAWW* 6:272; Orders of the German Crown Prince, 30 September 1918, ibid., pp. 525–26; Orders, German Seventh Army, 1 October 1918, ibid., p. 273; Wilson, *Myriad Faces of War*, p. 604.

18. For indications of Ludendorff's manpower problems see Report, Group of Armies Gallwitz, 9 October 1918, *USA WW* 9:546; Ludendorff to Gallwitz, 10 October 1918, ibid., p. 549. Hindenburg to Gallwitz Group of Armies, 12 October 1918, ibid. 11:432. A variant translation of the 12 October order is quoted in Edmonds, ed., *History of the Great War* 5:268. Ludendorff's intentions are evident in an order issued to Group of Armies Crown Prince Rupprecht, 15 October 1918, which was assigned the task of preparing the Antwerp-Meuse position. *USA WW* 11:441. Maurice describes the hesitation in the Allied advance during the first weeks of October and the successes between Cambrai and St. Quentin in *Last Four Months*, pp. 178–81, 196.

19. Ludendorff's position is described in Maurice, *Last Four Months*, pp. 197, 199. For Prince Rupprecht's views see Edmonds, ed., *History of the Great War* 5:327–28. See also Liddell Hart, *Real War*, pp. 380–81.

20. Maurice, *Last Four Months*, pp. 200–201. For the operations of the American II Corps during the period 17–21 October 1918 see Memorandum, Instructions for Brigade Commanders, 27th Division, 15 October 1918, *USA WW* 7:590–93; Battle Instructions Nos. 1 and 2, Series D, 30th Division, 15 October 1918, ibid., pp. 594–98; Operations Report, British Fourth Army, 17 October 1918, ibid., p. 645; Operations Report, II Corps, 18 December 1918 (concerning events on 19 October 1918), ibid., p. 791.

21. For Read's report, 17 October 1918, see ibid., pp. 791, 793–94. For Haig's order of the day, 20 October 1918, see ibid., p. 725.

22. For Petain's orders and Pershing's response see Petain to Commander of the Group of Armies of the Reserve, the General Commanding the Group of Armies of the Center, and General Pershing, 11 October 1918, *USA WW* 8:88–89; Petain to Group of Armies of the Center, 12 October 1918, and Pershing to Petain, 12 October 1918, ibid., p. 91. For the American preparations see Historical Section, Army War College, "Major Operations," p. 185; Report of First Army, *USA WW* 9:282–83; Field Orders No. 59, First Army, 12 October 1918, ibid., pp. 255–57. For Pershing's view see *My Experiences* 2:337–38.

23. For the offensive during the period 14–18 October 1918 see Report of G-3 (AEF), *USA WW* 14:45; Smythe, *Pershing*, pp. 212–14; Braim, *Test of Battle*, p. 133; Pershing, *My Experiences* 2:340–41. For Liddell Hart's view see his *Real War*, p. 467. Various operations reports and field orders reveal the course of the battle and the difficulties that developed during its course. Operations Report, First Army, 14 October 1918 (for noon 13 October to noon 14 October), *USA WW* 9:271; Field Orders No. 65, 14 October 1918, ibid., p. 268–69; Field Orders No. 67, 15 October 1918, ibid., p. 273; Operations Report, First Army, 15 October 1918 (for noon 14 October to noon 15 October), ibid., p. 275; Operations Report, First Army, 16 October 1918 (noon 15 October to noon 16 October), ibid., p. 281; Operations Report, First Army, 17 October 1918, ibid., p. 296. Pershing's praise of his troops is in his *My Experiences* 2:341. Ludendorff's view is in his *The General Staff and Its Problems* 2:669.

24. Report of First Army, *USA WW* 9:286–89; Braim, *Test of Battle*, p. 136; Pershing, *My Experiences* 2:351–53.

25. Ibid., p. 351. See also Pershing final report, *War Department Annual Reports, 1919* 1, 1:595–96; Report of G-3 (AEF), *USA WW* 14:46.

26. Foch directive, 19 October 1918, ibid. 8:97–98. This directive is also in Edmonds, ed., *History of the Great War* 5:324–25, and in Foch, *Memoirs*, pp. 431–32.

27. For Ludendorff's fall see Foch, *Memoirs*, p. 401; Barnett, *Swordbearers*, p. 359; Ritter, *Sword and Scepter* 4:365–69. Ritter explains that Ludendorff attempted to reverse the decision to seek peace, but the kaiser would not change his mind. Ludendorff's

resignation was accepted, but Hindenburg bowed to Wilhelm's desire that he remain at his post. Ludendorff immediately accused Hindenburg of betraying him, and he never forgave the field marshal.

28. For a convenient summary of the defeat of the lesser Central Powers – Bulgaria, Austria-Hungary, and Turkey – see Falls, *Great War*, pp. 383–406.

29. For Foch's outline of terms on 8 October 1918 see his *Memoirs*, pp. 451–52. For the message to Wilson instigated by Lloyd George see ibid., pp. 453–54. For Foch's fear that the Germans might dupe Wilson see notes on conversation between Foch and Pershing, 13 October 1918, *USA WW* 8:92. Foch thought at this point that the Germans were simply playing for time so that they could re-form their armies for continued resistance. See also Pershing's diary for 13 October 1918, Pershing Papers; Pershing, *My Experiences* 2:348. General Sir Henry Wilson's suspicions of President Wilson are apparent in Wilson to Haig, 13 October 1918, in Blake, ed., *Private Papers of Haig*, pp. 331–32. He was especially fearful that the Germans would succeed in confusing the distinction between peace terms and the conditions of an armistice. For Foch's clarification of his understanding of the term "military counsellors" see his *Memoirs*, p. 456. Foch's complaints about Wilson's negotiations made on 20 October 1918 are on p. 455. Haig's views on the armistice as expressed to Lloyd George on 19 October 1918 are in Blake, ed., *Private Papers of Haig*, pp. 333–34.

30. Bliss is quoted in Trask, *The United States in the Supreme War Council*, pp. 155–56.

31. For the deliberations at Senlis see Foch, *Memoirs*, pp. 459–66; Pershing, *My Experiences* 2:359–63; Edmonds, ed., *History of the Great War* 5:398–99; Smythe, *Pershing*, p. 220.

32. Foch's statement at Senlis on the condition of the German army is quoted in Edmonds, ed., *History of the Great War* 5:399. Foch's proposed terms of armistice are in his *Memoirs*, p. 461.

33. This account is derived from the Haig diary for 19, 28, and 29 October 1918. Blake, ed. *Private Papers of Haig*, pp. 333, 338, 339.

34. Coffman quotes Drum in his *War to End All Wars*, p. 342.

35. For these developments see Trask, *The United States in the Supreme War Council*, pp. 160–61; Smythe, *Pershing*, pp. 220–21; Schwabe, *Woodrow Wilson*, pp 87–89.

36. Trask, *The United States in the Supreme War Council*, p. 161; Smythe, *Pershing*, p. 221. For the letter itself see Pershing, *My Experiences* 2:366–67.

37. Trask, *The United States in the Supreme War Council*, p. 161; Smythe, *Pershing*, p. 222. For Foch's statement on the armistice see his *Memoirs*, p. 463. Smythe rejects the view that Pershing may have acted because of political ambitions or to redeem his reputation; such a view would be "to attribute motives unworthy of the man." To explain Pershing's action, he argues that his views on armistice terms were those he would hold, *if* there were an armistice, whereas his letter to the Supreme War Council dealt with whether there *should* be an armistice. The difficulty with this view is that Pershing knew that his government had already decided in favor of an armistice. He should never have sent the letter to the Supreme War Council, as he later admitted to House. Pershing dealt with the question of whether he had taken a political action by simply stating that his letter was based on military considerations. Incidentally, he remained convinced that Germany should have been required to accept unconditional surrender. Pershing, *My Experiences* 2:368–69. Baker's statement is in *War Department Annual Reports, 1919* 1, 1:8. For Pershing's postarmistice views see Smythe, *Pershing*, p. 232.

38. For discussion of the negotiations at the Supreme War Council about the terms of peace and the terms of armistice, see Trask, *The United States in the Supreme War*

Council, pp. 151–75; Trask, *Captains and Cabinets*, pp. 313–55. Wilson did not want to accept the concessions on freedom of the seas and reparations, but he did so because of his desire to end the war as soon as possible. Schwabe, *Woodrow Wilson*, pp. 84–85. On 5 November 1918, President Wilson sent notice of the prearmistice agreement to Germany. Foch, *Memoirs*, p. 465. House believed that he had gained a great diplomatic triumph, but Klaus Schwabe, a leading German authority, is critical of his actions. He believes that House gave way on armistice terms and on interpretations of some of Wilson's points in order to assure acceptance of the Fourteen Points. These concessions limited the American ability later to resist the rapacity of the Allies. Schwabe, *Woodrow Wilson*, pp. 86, 91. Two other authorities present negative views of House: Inge Floto, *Colonel House in Paris: A Study of American Policy at the Paris Peace Conference, 1919* (Princeton, N.J.: Princeton University Press, 1973), pp. 25–60; Arthur Walworth, *America's Moment: 1918: American Diplomacy at the End of World War I* (New York: W. W. Norton, 1977), pp. 32–73. This writer offers a more favorable appraisal of House, arguing that the American gains during the prearmistice negotiations far outweighed the losses. Trask, *The United States in the Supreme War Council*, pp. 170–71.

39. For British and Belgian operations see Maurice, *Last Four Months*, pp. 213–17. For the activities of the two American divisions, the 37th and the 91st, see the Report of Major General William H. Johnson, 91st Division, 9 November 1918, *USAWW* 6:406–11; Reports of Major General C. S. Farnsworth, 37th Division, 11 and 13 November 1918, ibid., pp. 412–16, 457–62.

40. For Foch memorandum, 21 October 1918, on the plan of attack, originally scheduled for 28 October 1918, see ibid. 8:98–99. For initial instructions to the First Army see Drum to Liggett, 21 October 1918, ibid. 9:309–10. See also Maistre, Commanding French Group of Armies of the Center, to Foch, 24 October 1918, ibid. 8:101–2. For the operations plan see Field Orders No. 88, First Army, ibid. 9:333–34. For the difference of view between Foch and Pershing on the direction of the initial American attack see Foch to Pershing, 27 October 1918, ibid. 8:104; Pershing, *My Experiences* 2:356–57; Braim, *Test of Battle*, p. 136. See also Report of G-3 (AEF), *USAWW* 14:46–47; Historical Section, Army War College, "Major Operations," p. 190. For artillery dispositions see American Battle Monuments Commission, *American Armies and Battlefields in Europe*, p. 187. Foch's concerns are expressed in his memorandum, 27 October 1918, *USAWW* 8:103–4. See also Foch, *Memoirs*, p. 440. For indications of flexibility in the American plan see directions from McAndrew to Liggett, 29 October 1918, calling for the farthest possible advance on the first day and continued movement on the second day, even if the French Fourth Army was delayed because of the need to move artillery across the Aisne River. *USAWW* 8:105–6.

41. Ludendorff, *Ludendorff's Own Story* 2:398–99; Captured German document, dated 21 October 1918, reported in Summary of Intelligence, 30 October 1918, p. 7; Communications by Colonel Heye, 22 October 1918, *USAWW* 11:449. For an example of a mutiny see the report of the behavior of a regiment in the 18th Landwehr Division on 29 October 1918. Operation Section, Group of Armies Gallwitz, to Supreme Headquarters, 30 October 1918, ibid., p. 455; Report of Mutiny, Major General Gadecke, to Metz Group, 2 November 1918, ibid., p. 464.

42. For German awareness of the impending attack see "Summary of Intelligence," 29 October 1918, p. 3; War Diary of German Group of Armies Gallwitz, 30 October 1918, *USAWW* 9:568; Gallwitz to Supreme Headquarters, 31 October 1918, ibid. 11:458–59. For Hindenburg's comment see his *Out of My Life* 2:436–37. For the preparatory order for the movement to the Antwerp-Meuse position see Groener No. 11080, 30 October 1918, *USAWW* 11:456. For civilian opposition to destruction on

the retreat to the Antwerp–Meuse line see Max, Prince of Baden, to von Hintze, 31 October 1918, ibid., p. 458. For Hindenburg's objection to this constraint see Hindenburg to von Hintze, 1 November 1918, ibid., p. 461. Trevor Wilson describes Ludendorff's plan for a phased withdrawal to the Antwerp–Meuse line and notes that the stage was set for a climactic battle. Wilson, *Myriad Faces of War*, pp. 604–5.

43. This account is based on Smythe, *Pershing*, pp. 223–24; Coffman, *War to End All Wars*, pp. 345–47; Liddell Hart, *Real War*, p. 468; Braim, *Test of Battle*, p.137; Pershing final report, *War Department Annual Reports, 1919* 1, 1:596–97. Report of First Army, *USAWW* 9:366–69; Report of G-3 (AEF), ibid. 14:47. For the estimate of the situation on 3 November 1918 see "Summary of Intelligence," 3 November 1918. See also Operations Report, First Army, 1 and 2 November 1918, *USAWW* 9:371–72, 375–79; Field Orders No. 99, First Army, 3 November 1918, ibid., pp. 377–78; Field Orders No. 101, 4 November 1918, ibid., p. 381; Operations Report, First Army, 4 November 1918, ibid., p. 383. Foch wrote that actions by the French Fourth Army from 13 October east of Vouziers, which established bridgeheads across the Aisne, drew some German troops from the Argonne, relieving some of the pressure on the First Army and creating desirable conditions for the attack of 1 November. Foch, *Memoirs*, p. 441.

44. Report of First Army, *USAWW* 9:66–67; Liddell Hart, *Real War*, p. 468. For comments on specific tactical adjustments that helped to deal with the deadly German machine guns and to improve management of logistical support, see Coffman, *War to End All Wars*, p. 345.

45. War Diary, Group of Armies Gallwitz, 2 November 1918, *USAWW* 9:576; Gallwitz's estimate of the situation, 2 November 1918, ibid. 11:463; "Conference with His Excellency Groener," 2 November 1918, ibid., p. 462; "Situation on the West Front on November 2, 1918," ibid., p. 465; Hindenburg to Group of Armies Gallwitz, 3 November 1918, ibid., p. 466.

46. Braim, *Test of Battle*, p. 137; Operations Reports, First Army, 5 and 6 November 1918, *USAWW* 9:385–86, 389. The report for 5 November noted that German troops still resisted strongly east of the Meuse. Liddell Hart drew attention to the coincidence of the American attack and the outbreak of violent revolution in Germany and its operational consequence. Liddell Hart, *Real War*, p. 383. For evidence of declining German morale see Douglas Johnson, *Battlefields of the World War*, pp. 413–14. For Gallwitz's view see his report to Supreme Headquarters, 7 November 1918, *USAWW* 11:471–72.

47. For Pershing's claim see his final report, *War Department Annual Reports, 1919* 1, 1:598. Pershing ungallantly neglected to emphasize or praise the role of General Liggett, whose leadership of the First Army during the successful phase of the Meuse-Argonne offensive was no small part of the reason for victory. For the relative unimportance of the movement across the Carignan-Sedan portion of the rail line by this juncture see Liddell Hart, *Real War*, p. 468. Pershing's claims for the First Army might have been understandable when made in 1919, although in error, but it is difficult to understand why he should have repeated them in his memoirs of 1931. Pershing, *My Experiences* 2:382.

48. For this episode see Marshall, *Memoirs of My Services in the World War*, pp. 189–90; Smythe, *Pershing*, p. 228; Coffman, *War to End All Wars*, p. 348. The order, 5 November 1918, is in *USAWW* 9:385.

49. Smythe, *Pershing*, p. 228–29; Coffman, *War to End All Wars*, pp. 349–50. Summerall's contorted explanation of his action is in his report to Liggett, 7 November 1918, *USAWW* 9:391–92. For the role of Douglas MacArthur see D. Clayton James, *The Years of MacArthur*, vol. 1: *1880–1941* (Boston: Houghton Mifflin, 1964),

pp. 227–37. On 7 November 1918, the I Corps sector was transferred to the French Fourth Army, and the corps went into reserve on 10 November. *USAWW*, Report of G-3 (AEF) 14:49.

50. For Liggett's account see his *AEF*, pp. 227–30. His anger is reflected in his demand for an investigation of the event. Drum to Grant, 7 November 1918, *USAWW* 9:391. See also Coffman, *War to End All Wars*, pp. 352–53. Pershing's version of events, which makes no apology for his order to capture Sedan ("It was the ambition of the First Army and mine that our troops should capture Sedan, which the French had lost in a decisive battle in 1870"), is in his *My Experiences* 2:381. Liddell Hart treated the episode in his *Real War*, p. 469.

51. Pershing to Liggett and Bullard, 5 November 1918, *USAWW* 14:48. See also Braim, *Test of Battle*, p.139; Historical Section, Army War College, "Major Operations," pp. 203–4. The six organizations committed for the attack east of the Moselle toward Chateau-Salins were the 3d, 4th, 28th, 29th, 35th, and 36th Divisions. Report of G-3 (AEF), *USAWW* 14:50; Pershing, *My Experiences* 2:386–87. For Foch's account of the plans to attack in the Moselle region see his *Memoirs*, pp. 444–47.

52. For the difficulties that slowed the final operations see Edmonds, *Short History of World War I*, pp. 422–23. For the final activities of the American First Army see Operations Reports, First Army, 7 and 10 November 1918, *USAWW* 9:395, 410; Field Orders Nos. 108 and 111, 7 and 10 November 1918, ibid., pp. 390, 408; Report of G-3 (AEF), ibid. 14:49. For the brief operations of the American Second Army on 10–11 November see Millett, *Bullard*, p. 425. Bullard was cautious because he was short of "battle-ready infantry." Ibid., p. 421. For the armistice see Foch to Pershing, 8 November and 11 November 1918, ibid., pp. 111, 113–14. For the events that led to the German acceptance of the armistice see Ritter, *Sword and Scepter* 4:384–85. For Hindenburg's announcement of the armistice to his troops see *USAWW* 9:598. It was an early aspect of the effort to establish the view that a civilian stab in the back had brought about the defeat.

CHAPTER 8. THE MEANING OF 1918

1. Holger Herwig notes that German tactical innovations ultimately failed to produce victory because Ludendorff vastly underestimated the ability of the Allies to resist his attacks and because the Germans lacked sufficient technology. Efforts to probe for and exploit weaknesses in the Allied front wore down the attack divisions and the inadequate logistical system. Of particular importance was the lack of motorized transport and armored vehicles. Also, the Germans were not yet sensitive to the possibilities of combining an infantry, armored, and air attack. Conservative Wilhelmian Germany had not modernized sufficiently to conduct a modern war of a nation in arms. Holger Herwig, "The Dynamics of Necessity: German Military Policy during the First World War," in Allan R. Millett and Williamson Murray, eds., *Military Effectiveness*, vol. 1: *The First World War* (Boston: Allen & Unwin, 1988). Andreas Hillgruber discerns in the political objectives of the Hindenburg-Ludendorff tandem the roots of Germany's war aims under Hitler a generation later. The dictatorship of 1917–1918 emphasized political hegemony in eastern Europe rather than merely an economic sphere of influence. "A basic axiom of the 1918 eastern policy held that it was entirely possible for Germany to take all of Russia in its grasp and keep the giant empire in an enduring state of dependency." This stance was the opposite of the earlier German view, which

stressed Germany's weakness compared to Russia. Andreas Hillgruber, *Germany and the Two World Wars* (Cambridge, Mass.: Harvard University Press, 1981), pp. 44–45.

2. General Edmonds provides a sensible evaluation of the Foch offensive. Neither the British nor the Franco-American attacks achieved a breakthrough, but the Germans were pushed back essentially to the base of the great salient. The best opportunity fell to the Franco-American forces, but in that sector the least experienced troops, the Americans, had to attack over the most difficult ground. "A huge slice of occupied territory had been regained, but no large portion of the enemy's forces had been cut off; nor had his communications been reached." The Germans relied on their "super counterattack (*Eingreif*) divisions" but lacked sufficient troops. The special divisions were soon used up, and no more reserves were left to deal with threatened spots. Edmonds, *Short History of World War I*, p. 411.

3. Terraine, *To Win a War*, p. 258. Cf. the comment of Lord Hankey: "The war was won primarily by a tremendous combined system of co-ordination and goodwill, which focused all the efforts of all the Allies on the supreme task of defeating the enemy, but which only reached its maximum in the last year of the war." Hankey, *Supreme Command* 2:855.

4. Maurice, *Last Four Months*, p. 245.

SELECTED BIBLIOGRAPHY

PRIMARY SOURCES

Blake, Robert, ed. *The Private Papers of Douglas Haig, 1914–1919: Being Selections from the Private Diary and Correspondence of Field-Marshal the Earl Haig of Bemersyde, K.T., G.C.B., O.M., Etc.* London: Eyre and Spottiswoode, 1952.

Bland, Larry I., and Sharon K. Ritenour, eds. *The Papers of George Catlett Marshall*, vol. 1: *"The Soldierly Spirit," December 1880–June 1939.* Baltimore: Johns Hopkins University Press, 1981.

Bullard, Robert Lee. *Personalities and Reminiscences of the War.* Garden City, N.Y.: Doubleday, Page, 1925.

Dawes, Charles G. *A Journal of the Great War.* 2 vols. Boston and New York: Houghton Mifflin, 1921.

Foch, Ferdinand. *The Memoirs of Marshal Foch.* Trans. T. Bentley Mott. Garden City, N.Y.: Doubleday, Doran, Inc., 1931.

Goerlitz, Walter, ed. *The Kaiser and His Court: The Diaries, Notebooks and Letters of Admiral Georg Alexander von Mueller, Chief of the Naval Cabinet, 1914–1918.* London: McDonald, 1961.

Hankey, Lord Maurice P. A. *The Supreme Command: 1914–1918.* 2 vols. London: George Allen and Unwin, 1961.

Hindenburg, Paul von. *Out of My Life.* Trans. F. A. Holt. London: Cassell, Ltd., 1920.

Historical Section, Department of the Army. *United States Army in the World War, 1917–1919.* 17 vols. Washington, D.C.: Department of the Army, 1948. [The United States Army has reprinted this series.]

Joffre, Joseph J. C. *The Memoirs of Marshal Joffre.* Trans. T. Bentley Mott. Vol. 2. London: Geoffrey Bles, 1932.

Lawrence, Joseph Douglas. *Fighting Soldier: The AEF in 1918.* Robert H. Ferrell, ed. Boulder: Colorado Associated University Press, 1985.

Liggett, Hunter. *A.E.F.: Ten Years Ago in France.* New York: Dodd, Mead, 1928.

Link, Arthur S., et al. *The Papers of Woodrow Wilson.* Princeton, N.J.: Princeton University Press, 1966–. Vol. 40, *November 20–January 23, 1917*, 1982; vol. 41, *January 24–April 6, 1917*, 1983; vol. 42, *April 7–June 23, 1917*, 1983; vol. 45, *November 11, 1917–January 15, 1918*, 1984.

Lloyd George, David. *War Memoirs of David Lloyd George.* Boston: Little, Brown, 1933–. Vol. 4, *1917*, 1934; vol. 5, *1917–1918*, 1936; vol. 6, *1918*, 1937.

Ludendorff, Erich. *Ludendorff's Own Story: August 1914–November 1918*. Vol. 2. New York and London: Harper & Brothers, 1919.

———. *The General Staff and Its Problems: The History of the Relations between the High Command and the German Imperial Government as Revealed by Official Documents*. Trans. F. A. Holt. Vol. 2. New York: E. P. Dutton, 1920.

Lutz, Ralph H., ed. *Fall of the German Empire*. 2 vols. Stanford, Calif.: Stanford University Press, 1932.

March, Peyton Conway. *The Nation at War*. Garden City, N.Y.: Doubleday, Doran, 1932.

Marshall, George C. *Memoirs of My Services in the World War 1917–1918*. Foreword and notes by Brig. Gen. James L. Collins, Jr. Boston: Houghton Mifflin, 1976.

Order of Battle of the United States Land Forces in the World War. 5 vols. Washington, D.C.: U.S. Army Center of Military History, 1988. (Reprint originally published 1931–1949.)

Pershing, John J. *My Experiences in the World War*. 2 vols. New York: Frederick A. Stokes, 1931.

Scott, James Brown, ed. *Official Statements of War Aims and Peace Proposals, December 1916 to November 1918*. Washington, D.C.: Carnegie Endowment, 1921.

Simpson, Michael, ed. *Anglo-American Naval Relations, 1917–1919*. Aldershot, Eng.: Scolar Press for the Navy Records Society, 1991.

"Summaries of Intelligence First Army Expeditionary Forces." 2 parts. n.p., n.d. [Mimeographed copies in library, U.S. Army Center of Military History, Washington, D.C.]

U.S. Congress. Senate. Committee on Military Affairs. *Investigation of the War Department*. Hearings before the Committee on Military Affairs United States Senate. 65th Congress, 2d Session. 8 parts. Washington, D.C.: Government Printing Office, 1918. [Hearings held 12 December 1917–29 March 1918.]

U.S. War Department. *Histories of Two Hundred and Fifty-One Divisions of the German Army which Participated in the Great War, 1914–1918*. Washington, D.C.: Government Printing Office, 1919.

———. Notes on Recent Operations, July 1917. Washington, D.C.: Government Printing Office, 1917.

———. *War Department Annual Reports*. Washington, D.C.: Government Printing Office. *1917*. 3 vols. 1918; *1918*. 3 vols. 1919; *1919*. Vol. 1 in 4 parts. 1920.

SECONDARY WORKS

Agnew, James B., Clifton R. Franks, and William R. Griffiths. *The Great War*. Interim text, United States Military Academy, Department of History. West Point, N.Y.: 1977; rev. ed., 1980.

American Battle Monuments Commission. *American Armies and Battlefields in Europe: A History, Guide, and Reference Book*. Washington, D.C.: Government Printing Office, 1928.

Asprey, Robert B. *At Belleau Wood*. New York: G. P. Putnam's Sons, 1965.

———. *The German High Command at War: Hindenburg and Ludendorff Conduct World War I*. New York: William Morrow, 1991.

Ayres, Leonard P. *The War with Germany: A Statistical Summary*. Washington, D.C.: Government Printing Office, 1919.

Banks, Arthur. *A Military Atlas of the First World War*. New York: Taplinger, 1975.

Barnett, Corelli. *The Swordbearers: Supreme Command in the World War.* Bloomington: Indiana University Press, 1975. [First published in 1963 in Great Britain.]

Bean, Charles E. W. *ANZAC to Amiens: A Shorter History of the Australian Fighting Services in the First World War.* Canberra: Australian War Memorial, 1961.

Beaver, Daniel R. *Newton D. Baker and the American War Effort, 1917–1919.* Lincoln: University of Nebraska Press, 1966.

Bidwell, Shelford, and Dominick Graham. *Fire-Power: Army Weapons and Theories at War, 1904–1945.* London: George Allen & Unwin, 1982.

Blaxland, Gregory. *Amiens: 1918.* London: Frederick Muller, 1968.

Braim, Paul F. *The Test of Battle: The American Expeditionary Forces in the Meuse-Argonne Campaign.* Newark: University of Delaware Press, 1987.

Burk, Kathleen. *Britain, America, and the Sinews of War, 1914–1918.* Boston: George Allen & Unwin, 1984.

Chambers, John Whiteclay, II. *To Raise an Army: The Draft Comes to Modern America.* New York: Free Press, 1987.

Coffman, Edward M. *The Hilt of the Sword: The Career of Peyton C. March.* Madison, Milwaukee, and London: University of Wisconsin Press, 1966.

———. *The War to End All Wars: The American Military Experience in World War I.* New York: Oxford University Press, 1968.

Cooper, John Milton, Jr. *The Warrior and the Priest: Woodrow Wilson and Theodore Roosevelt.* Cambridge, Mass.: Harvard University Press, 1983.

Craig, Gordon A. *The Politics of the Prussian Army, 1640–1945.* London: Oxford University Press, 1955.

Cramer, C. H. *Newton D. Baker: A Biography.* Cleveland and New York: World Publishing, 1961.

Cruttwell, C. R. M. F. *A History of the Great War 1914–1918.* 2d ed. London: Granada Publishing, 1982.

Cuff, Robert D. *The War Industries Board: Business-Government Relations during World War I.* Baltimore, Md., and London: Johns Hopkins University Press, 1973.

DeWeerd, Harvey A. *President Wilson Fights His War: World War I and the American Intervention.* New York: Macmillan, 1958.

Dickinson, John. *The Building of an Army: A Detailed Account of Legislation, Administration and Opinion in the United States, 1915–1920.* New York: Century, 1922.

Edmonds, James E. *A Short History of World War I.* London: Oxford University Press, 1951.

Essame, Hubert. *The Battle for Europe, 1918.* New York: Charles Scribner's Sons, 1972.

Falls, Cyril. *The Great War.* New York: Capricorn Books, 1959.

———. *Marshal Foch.* London and Glasgow: Blackie & Son, 1939.

Ferrell, Robert H. *Woodrow Wilson and World War I, 1917–1921.* New York: Harper & Row, 1985.

Floto, Inge. *Colonel House in Paris: A Study of American Policy at the Paris Peace Conference, 1919.* Princeton, N.J.: Princeton University Press, 1973.

Fowler, Wilton B. *British-American Relations 1917–1918: The Role of Sir William Wiseman.* Princeton, N.J.: Princeton University Press, 1969.

Frothingham, Thomas G. *The American Reinforcement in the World War.* Garden City, N.Y.: Doubleday, Page, 1927.

Griffith, Paddy. *Forward into Battle: Fighting Tactics from Waterloo to Vietnam.* Strettington, Chichester, Sussex, Eng.: Antony Bird Publications, 1981.

Hardach, Gerd. *The First World War, 1914–1918.* Berkeley: University of California Press, 1977.

Herwig, Holger H. "The Dynamics of Necessity: German Military Policy during the First World War." In Allen R. Millett and Williamson Murray, eds., *Military Effectiveness*. Vol. 1: *The First World War*. Boston: Allen & Unwin, 1988, pp. 80–115.

Herwig, Holger H., and Neil M. Heyman. *Biographical Dictionary of World War I*. Westport, Conn.: Greenwood, 1982.

Herwig, Holger H., and David F. Trask. "The Failure of Imperial Germany's Undersea Offensive against World Shipping, February 1917–October 1918." *Historian* 33, 4 (August 1971):611–36.

Hewes, James E., Jr. *From Root to McNamara: Army Organization and Administration, 1900–1963*. Washington, D.C.: U.S. Army Center of Military History, 1975.

Hillgruber, Andreas. *Germany and the Two World Wars*. Trans. William Kirby. Cambridge, Mass.: Harvard University Press, 1981.

History of the Great War Based on Official Documents by Direction of the Historical Section of the Committee of Imperial Defence. Military Operations France and Belgium, 1918. Vols. 4–5. Ed. Brig. Gen. Sir James E. Edmonds. London: His Majesty's Stationery Office, 1947.

Holley, I. B., Jr. *General John M. Palmer, Citizen Soldiers, and the Army of a Democracy*. Westport, Conn.: Greenwood Press, 1982.

House, Jonathan M. *Towards Combined Arms Warfare: A Survey of Tactics, Doctrine, and Organization in the 20th Century*. Research Survey No. 2, U.S. Army Command and General Staff College, Combat Studies Institute: Fort Leavenworth, Kans., 1984.

Huston, James A. *The Sinews of War: Army Logistics, 1775–1953*. Washington, D.C.: Office of the Chief of Military History, United States Army, 1966.

James, Dorris Clayton. *The Years of MacArthur*. Vol. 1: *1880–1941*. Boston: Houghton Mifflin, 1964.

Johnson, Douglas Wilson. *Battlefields of the World War: Western and Southern Fronts: A Study in Military Geography*. New York: Oxford University Press, 1921.

Kennett, Lee. "The A.E.F. through French Eyes." *Military Review* 52 (November 1972):3–11.

———. *The First Air War 1914–1918*. New York: Free Press, 1991.

Kitchin, Martin. *The Silent Dictatorship: The Politics of the German High Command under Hindenburg and Ludendorff*. New York: Holmes & Meier, 1976.

Klachko, Mary, with David F. Trask. *Admiral William Shepherd Benson: First Chief of Naval Operations*. Annapolis, Md.: Naval Institute Press, 1987.

Koistinen, Paul A. C. *The Military-Industrial Complex: A Perspective*. New York: Praeger, 1980.

Kreidberg, Marvin A., and Merton G. Henry. *History of Military Mobilization in the United States Army, 1775–1945*. Department of the Army Pamphlet No. 20-12. Washington, D.C.: Government Printing Office, 1955.

Lewis, S. J. *Forgotten Legions: German Army Infantry Policy, 1918–1941*. New York: Praeger, 1985.

Liddell Hart, Basil H. *The Real War, 1914–1918*. Boston: Little, Brown, 1964.

———. *Reputations Ten Years After*. Boston: Little, Brown, 1928.

Lupfer, Timothy T. *The Dynamics of Doctrine: The Changes in German Tactical Doctrine during the First World War*. Leavenworth Paper No. 4. Fort Leavenworth, Kans.: U.S. Army Command and General Staff College, 1981.

Mahon, John K. *History of the Militia and the National Guard*. New York: Macmillan, 1983.

Marshall, S. L. A. *World War I*. New York: American Heritage, 1985.

Maurice, Frederick Barton. *The Last Four Months: How the War Was Won*. Boston: Little, Brown, 1919.

McClellan, Edwin N. *The United States Marine Corps in the World War*. Washington, D.C.: Historical Branch, G-3 Division, Headquarters, U.S. Marine Corps, 1968. [Facsimile edition of 1920 edition.]

McEntee, Girard Lindsley. *Military History of the World War: A Complete Account of the Campaigns on All Fronts*. New York: Charles Scribner's Sons, 1943.

Middlebrook, Martin. *The Kaiser's Battle: The First Day of the German Spring Offensive*. London: Allen Lane, 1978.

Millett, Allan R. "Cantigny, 28–31 May 1918." In Charles E. Heller and William A. Stofft, eds., *America's First Battles 1776–1965*. Lawrence: University Press of Kansas, 1986, pp. 149–85.

———. "Over Where? The AEF and the American Strategy for Victory, 1917–1918." In Kenneth J. Hagan and William R. Roberts, eds., *Against All Enemies: Interpretations of American Military History from Colonial Times to the Present*. Westport, Conn.: Greenwood, 1986, pp. 235–56.

———. *The General: Robert L. Bullard and Officership in the United States Army, 1881–1924*. Westport, Conn.: Greenwood, 1975.

———. *Semper Fidelis: The History of the United States Marine Corps*. New York: Macmillan, 1980.

Millett, Allan R., and Peter Maslowski. *For the Common Defense: A Military History of the United States of America*. New York: Free Press, 1984.

Millett, Allan R., and Williamson Murray, eds. *Military Effectiveness*. Vol. 1: *The First World War*. Boston: Allen & Unwin, 1988.

Moore, William. *Gas Attack! Chemical Warfare 1915–18 and Afterwards*. New York: Hippocrene Books, 1987.

Neame, Philip. *German Strategy in the Great War*. London: Edward Arnold, 1923.

Nenninger, Timothy K. "American Military Effectiveness during the First World War." In Allen R. Millett and Williamson Murray, eds., *Military Effectiveness*. Vol. 1: *The First World War*. Boston: Allen & Unwin, 1988, pp. 116–56.

———. "Tactical Dysfunction in the AEF, 1917–1918." [Unpublished paper.]

Palmer, Frederick. *Bliss, Peacemaker: The Life and Letters of General Tasker Howard Bliss*. New York: Dodd, Mead, 1934.

Paschall, Rod. *The Defeat of Imperial Germany 1917–1918*. Chapel Hill, N.C.: Algonquin Books of Chapel Hill, 1989.

Patterson, David S. "Woodrow Wilson and the Mediation Movement, 1914–17." *Historian* 33, 4 (1971):535–56.

Paxson, Frederic L. *America at War: 1917–1918*. Boston: Houghton Mifflin, 1939.

Pitt, Barrie. *1918: The Last Act*. New York: W. W. Norton, 1962.

Pogue, Forrest C. *George Marshall*. Vol. 1: *Education of a General, 1880–1939*. New York: Viking, 1963.

Rainey, James W. "Ambivalent Warfare: The Tactical Doctrine of the AEF in World War I." *Parameters* 13, 3 (1983):34–46.

Ritter, Gerhard. *The Sword and the Scepter: The Problem of Militarism in Germany*. Vol. 4: *The Reign of German Militarism and the Disaster of 1918*. Trans. Heinze Norden. Coral Gables, Fla.: University of Miami Press, 1973. [Originally published in Germany in 1968.]

Roskill, Stephen. *Hankey: Man of Secrets*. Vol. 1: *1877–1918*. Annapolis, Md.: Naval Institute Press, 1970.

Schaffer, Ronald. *The United States in World War I*. Santa Barbara: ABC-Clio, 1978. [A convenient bibliography.]

Schwabe, Klaus. *Woodrow Wilson, Revolutionary Germany, and Peacemaking, 1918–1919: Missionary Diplomacy and the Realities of Power*. Trans. Rita and Robert Kimber. Chapel Hill: University of North Carolina Press, 1985.

Smythe, Donald. *Pershing: General of the Armies*. Bloomington: Indiana University Press, 1986.

Terraine, John. *To Win a War, 1918: The Year of Victory*. London: Sidgwick & Jackson, 1978.

Toland, John. *No Man's Land: 1918: The Last Year of the Great War*. New York: Ballantine Books, 1980.

Trask, David F. "Woodrow Wilson and International Statecraft: A Modern Assessment." *Naval War College Review* 36 (March–April 1983):57–68.

———. *Captains and Cabinets: Anglo-American Naval Relations, 1917–1918*. Columbia: University of Missouri Press, 1972.

———. *General Tasker Howard Bliss and the "Sessions of the World," 1919*. Published as *Transactions of the American Philosophical Society*. New Series–vol. 56, pt. 8. Philadelphia: American Philosophical Society, 1966.

———. "Introduction." In *United States Army in the World War, 1917–1919*. Vol. 1: *Organization of the American Expeditionary Forces*. Washington, D.C.: U.S. Army Center of Military History, 1988, pp. xi–xxv. [Reprint of first volume in series originally published in 1948.]

———. *The United States in the Supreme War Council: American War Aims and Inter-Allied Strategy, 1917–1918*. Middletown, Conn.: Wesleyan University Press, 1961.

———. "William Shepherd Benson." In Robert William Love, Jr., ed., *The Chiefs of Naval Operations*. Annapolis, Md.: Naval Institute Press, 1980, pp. 3–21.

Travers, Tim. *The Killing Ground: The British Army, the Western Front, and the Emergence of Modern Warfare, 1900–1918*. London: Allen & Unwin, 1987.

———. "The Evolution of British Strategy and Tactics on the Western Front in 1918." *Journal of Military History* (April 1990) 54:173–200.

U.S. War Department. *Battle Participation of Organizations of American Expeditionary Forces in France, Belgium and Italy, 1917–1918*. Washington, D.C.: Government Printing Office, 1920.

U.S. War Department, Historical Branch, War Plans Division, General Staff. *Blanc Mont (Meuse-Argonne-Champagne)*. Monograph No. 9. Washington, D.C.: Government Printing Office, 1922.

———. "Major Operations of the United States Army in the World War." May 1929. [Preliminary draft manuscript in library, U.S. Army Center of Military History, Washington, D.C.]

———. *The Aisne and Montdidier-Noyon Operations*. Monograph No. 13. Washington, D.C.: Government Printing Office, 1922.

———. *Organization of the Services of Supply, American Expeditionary Forces*. Monograph No. 7. Washington, D.C.: Government Printing Office, 1921.

Vandiver, Frank E. *Black Jack: The Life and Times of John J. Pershing*. Vol. 2. College Station: Texas A&M University Press, 1977.

Walworth, Arthur. *America's Moment: 1918: American Diplomacy at the End of World War I*. New York: W. W. Norton, 1977.

Weigley, Russell F. *History of the United States Army*. New York: Macmillan, 1977.

Wilgus, William J. *Transporting the A.E.F. in Western Europe, 1917–1919*. New York: Columbia University Press, 1931.

Wilson, John B. "Mobility versus Firepower: The Post–World War I Infantry Division." *Parameters* 13, 3 (1983) 47–52.

Wilson, Trevor. *The Myriad Faces of War: Britain and the Great War, 1914–1918*. Cambridge, Eng.: Polity Press, 1986.

INDEX